ALL THAT GLITTERS

ALL THAT GLITTERS

COLEEN COOK

MOODY PRESS
CHICAGO

© 1992 by
COLEEN COOK

All Scripture quotations, unless noted otherwise, are from the *Holy Bible: New International Version*. Copyright © 1973, 1978, 1984, International Bible Society. Used by permission of Zondervan Bible Publishers.

The use of selected references from various versions of the Bible in this publication does not necessarily imply publisher endorsement of the versions in their entirety.

ISBN: 0-8024-0736-6

1 2 3 4 5 6 Printing/BC/Year 96 95 94 93 92

Printed in the United States of America

To my husband, John,
whose forbearance, continuous support, and servant's heart
made writing this book possible.

To my sons, Christopher and Kerry,
who have patiently tolerated a writer in their home.

And to my parents, Louis and Mary Cook,
for praying, encouraging and supporting,
and faithfully raising me to understand
that truth, not illusion, frees us.

CONTENTS

PREFACE

Many of us have experienced it. It's an hour after the big pro football game, and the home team has lost. Telephone lines to the local sports call-in show are jammed, brimming with irate callers eager to berate the coach for his mistakes. Most have never set foot on a pro football field or coached a game, but nevertheless they are "experts" who know exactly what went wrong and how the coach could have won. Although well-meaning, the truth is that most of the callers lack an insider's perspective necessary to effectively understand and second guess a professional coach's decisions.

I wrote this book for the same reason that football coaches must tire of being second guessed by fans. Frankly, I was weary of arm-chair TV critics—those well meaning pastors, laypeople, conservative watchdog organization leaders, ivory tower academics (who sometimes have degrees but no actual hands-on experience in commercial television), and newspaper critics, many of whom get paid to analyze a medium they do not understand or have never worked in. This book is my answer to those who claim an understanding and insight into television but have never actually wrestled with the technology and institution itself from the inside. It is a book written for those (many of them Christians!) who cannot see beyond the issue of liberal bias, which happens to be a much smaller portion of the total equation in TV than most people realize.

Yet it is also a book for those on the other side of the spectrum—those who trust implicitly in what they see because "seeing is believing." It is for those who never question or critique, but who only accept—often blindly and without thinking, whatever graces their picture tube. It is a book for those who give little or no thought to the grip television has on our culture and on our individual lives. It is for those who have never considered the ramifications and consequences of our dependence on this complicated technology. Few on either extreme understand the complexity of the factors that influence the final image Americans gaze upon for hours on end or how the images control and alter their perceptions of truth and life. This book is both a glimpse at the inside workings of a complex industry where there is much more than meets the eye and a look at the ramifications of our dependence on that industry.

Understanding television is much like looking at a tapestry, which appears colorful and slickly crafted from the finished side until we flip it over to the back side to see the myriad of tangled threads and loose ends that come together to create the final illusion on the cloth. It is not until we see the back side of the tapestry that we can understand a little more about what really forms the polished illusions that invade twentieth-century life in America so pervasively and influence it so thoroughly.

There is much more to understanding television than analyzing the political and ideological biases of news anchors and producers. Liberal bias is merely the tip of the iceberg. Although the people who operate the industry are sometimes guilty of manipulating the image, more often they are trapped and enslaved by the technology and institutional workings of the medium itself in ways that cannot be understood unless you have been a part of it.

Who am I to claim an insider's perspective? Perhaps I can better answer that question by pointing out who I am *not*. I am not

Jane Pauley or Diane Sawyer. Who am I? I am, as John the Baptist once claimed, just a "voice" crying in a vast twentieth-century technological wilderness. I am only one of thousands who worked the daily beats of local news reporting, who sat in the anchor's chair, and who experienced the television illusion from the inside out. I was one of many weavers of the TV tapestry—who wrestled to tangle and untangle, weave and reweave, the threads that made up the final picture. Just an ordinary person who had a relatively unspectacular, moderately successful career in TV broadcasting for a few years before trading the job of reporter for diapers, wiping runny noses, and the headaches of dealing with the influence of television on my own children.

Although some of what I have to say may seem critical of my industry and former colleagues at times, it is also my hope that the perspective I offer reflects in other ways some of the deepest frustrations and dilemmas of news reporters, producers, and anchors at both the highest and the lowest levels of television—frustrations that stem from being held responsible for all the abuses and shortcomings of a medium that is sometimes beyond human control. Who am I? Just an ordinary reporter who tried to make TV do what I needed it to do—reflect real life—and who discovered in the process that television does only what it is capable of doing, which is far less than most outsiders realize.

Come with me for a while and examine the back side of the television tapestry.

ACKNOWLEDGMENTS

I n addition to my family, I owe an enormous debt of gratitude to my good friends Teri Tunell and Jean Love, whose prayers, enthusiasm, encouragement, editorial insight, and many suggestions have contributed so much to seeing me through this project. Thanks to Glen and Karen Schreiber for their comments and suggestions in the final hours of editing. Thanks is also due to friends and fellow writers Dorothy Gaulde, Donna Goodrich, and Vic Kelly, and others from the Phoenix Christian Writer's Club, for their suggestions and help in understanding the business of Christian publishing. Special thanks is due as well to the Reverend Bob Reith of Media Fellowship for his encouragement to those of us in the broadcast industry over the years and for his help in the final months before publication.

My gratitude is also due to a number of people for their encouragement and direction about publishing: Florence Littauer, Eileen Mason, Ray Oehm, Al Janssen, Marvin Olasky, David Worley, and Dan McCracken—extra special thanks to Kin Millin for refusing to let me quit.

Special recognition must go to Pastor Frank Boswell and his wife, Jean, of Austin, Texas, for their helpful feedback and for sharing with me their vision of evangelizing the unchurched "television generation"—their views have changed my concept of church in the "TV age" forever.

Special appreciation to those brothers in Christ—Mark Grassman, Bob Lemon, Todd Boyham, and Robert Bishop, who helped me overcome "computer phobia" and "computer headaches"—I am indebted to your technical knowledge and your willingness to share it.

Recognition also is due to those who cared enough about what I was writing to contribute helpful research materials: Mom and Dad, Bill Kilgore, Craig Carpenter, Maggie Cornelius Barduson, Lisa Urias, Martha Davidson, Dr. Bennie Faul, Linda Wohleber, Frank and Pat Consalvo, and George Soltau.

Special thanks to friends Rick and Susan Osial for taking care of Chris and Kerry in the final days of preparing this manuscript.

And, finally, to editorial director Jim Bell, adult trade editor Anne Scherich, and the people of Moody Press for their enthusiasm for, commitment to, and belief in this project.

1

BEHIND
THE SCENES

We're three minutes to air!"

The director's warning cue in our earphones startled both of us. Jim's fingers fumbled for the right button on the Minicam® that would bring my troubled face into focus. "The microwave signal to the station is still dropping in and out," he groaned in a half-shout, half-whisper. "The network is going to be furious!"

His panic was contagious. I could feel the fear building in the pit of my stomach. As hard as I tried to concentrate, I simply couldn't bring my scattered thoughts under control.

"Two minutes to air!"

Our director's second warning jarred my thoughts once more. "Just two minutes away from fiasco—coast to coast," I lamented. This was not exactly the way I had planned my first live network report. The impression I might be leaving on millions of viewers made me wince. In a few moments, I would interrupt a popular soap opera to bring viewers the news of America's first woman appointee to the United States Supreme Court. I felt less than prepared for this impromptu debut, and looking that way would make our news brief even more of an intrusion.

Another unexpected warning from our director came blaring through my earpiece. "We have no direct audio line to Washington, Coleen. All we can give you is network sound straight off of your own field monitor." Another bomb exploded in my stomach. His announcement meant that the sound I would have to depend on to hear ABC news anchor Ted Koppel would be delayed as it traveled down line from Washington to our station in Phoenix, then across the airwaves and into the television monitor next to me. The time gap would create a distracting echo in my earpiece, making words and voices harder to distinguish. When Ted Koppel asked me a question, it would actually take several seconds for his query to reach me, leaving an embarrassing on-air gap of several seconds. Another handicap to work under!

I sighed and shut my eyes for a moment, trying to block out the frantic activity around me. The courtroom I stood in at the state capitol complex was normally more than adequate for onlookers, but today it could barely hold the reporters and photographers now occupying every available space. President Ronald Reagan's unexpected announcement of Sandra Day O'Connor's nomination to the U.S. Supreme Court had sent both local and national reporters scurrying. Although an ABC correspondent and crew were en route from Los Angeles, they couldn't make it in time for the hastily called press conference. So the job of telling ABC viewers about this history-making event on national television had fallen to me.

The crush of bodies and the glare of a half dozen high intensity camera lights made the Phoenix courtroom where we waited as hot and uncomfortable as the sweltering summer heat in the desert outside. The microphone I held grew sticky in my perspiring palm. My fingers closed around it in a death grip as I raised it to position a few inches from my mouth. Behind me and beside me, a sea of reporters from every imaginable news media stood or sat, with pens poised and cameras ready. Television crews stood prepared to beam the expected announcement to the nation in seconds, before newspaper reporters could even get to the telephone.

We all waited in the tension of the moment for a once obscure Arizona appeals court judge to walk into the courtroom and begin making history.

"Sixty seconds to air, Coleen!"

Sixty seconds! What could I tell Ted Koppel and millions of viewers about a woman I knew little about myself? My train of thought derailed once again as I realized what I had on. "Why in the world did I wear this black and white plaid jacket today?" I moaned to my photographer. Jim nodded back in sympathetic agreement. "You're going to look like a giant test pattern."

"Thirty seconds to air, Coleen!"

Thirty seconds! I had less than a minute to prepare. I tried to stop thinking about the faulty microwave signal and bring my mind under control. There was no time for research—and it was so difficult to remember! Sandra O'Connor had hardly been the focus of Arizona television prior to this nomination—judges rarely are. I could only console myself with the thought that no matter how little I knew, at that moment Ted Koppel probably knew less than I did.

"Stand by, Coleen."

It was my last warning from our director. I glanced at the television air monitor. Koppel was now at the center of the screen. "This is an ABC news bulletin," a deep-voiced announcer proclaimed. "Now in Washington, here's Ted Koppel." The camera zoomed in. "Good day," Koppel began. "President Reagan, in a surprise announcement made this morning in Washington, has nominated a woman to fill the current vacancy on the United States Supreme Court. His nominee is Sandra Day O'Connor, a judge on the Arizona Court of Appeals. Judge O'Connor is about to make an appearance at a press conference in Phoenix." The reverberation in my earpiece made it difficult for me to understand Koppel's words. "Standing by for us at that press conference is Coleen Cook, a reporter with our ABC affiliate in Phoenix. Coleen, what's happening where you are at?"

I was on. My mind a total blank for a moment, I opened my parched lips to answer Koppel's question, feeling nothing short of sheer terror. Suddenly, the courtroom stirred as Judge O'Connor and her family entered, walking a few steps behind a tall stranger in a gray suit. In a split second, I ditched my planned remarks and answered, "Judge O'Connor has just entered the room, Ted. She's about to make her opening statement." I breathed a momentary sigh of relief as our Minicam® made a shaky zoom away from me and to the podium.

"Good morning." It was the stranger in the gray suit speaking into the cluster of microphones. He introduced himself, but the sound of his voice bounced in my earpiece like an echo off the Swiss Alps. I failed to catch his name, but it wouldn't matter, or so I thought. He introduced Judge O'Connor as she moved to the podium. Just as she began to speak, I heard an electronic crackle in my ear. A glance at the television monitor confirmed my worst fear. The unstable microwave signal that had worried us in the moments before the broadcast had just died midstream. The screen was black. Sandra O'Connor was making history without us.

ABC switched quickly back to the studio in Washington. "We seem to be having some technical difficulty with our affiliate in Phoenix," Koppel calmly explained to the audience. I could see Jim mouthing obscenities behind the camera. I began to pray— silently and desperately.

As abruptly as it failed, our signal bounced back onto the air again. Judge O'Connor finished her opening remarks, which were followed by a barrage of popping flashbulbs and a flurry of pointed questions from reporters. Our signal went down for the second time but quickly popped on the air again, just as I asked the judge a question. Her answer was followed by another crackle of static as our screen plunged again into black. The network switched briefly to Washington, where Ted Koppel apologized anew for the technical chaos. The temperamental microwave signal made one last comeback, just as Judge O'Connor, her family, and the tall man in the gray suit made their way through the crowd of reporters and left the courtroom.

The camera zoomed back center screen to me. "Coleen," Koppel asked politely, "who was the stranger in the gray suit who introduced the judge?" I felt the color drain from my cheeks as I realized he had asked me something in front of a nationwide audience that I couldn't answer. I had missed the stranger's name! "I'm sorry I can't tell you that, Ted." I brushed by his query as quickly as possible. "However, I can tell you a little about Sandra O'Connor." I began to tick off facts about the judge that I had mentally assembled in the moments before the broadcast.

Koppel must have sensed his question had caught me off guard. He listened politely, then thanked us for standing by in Phoenix and pitched to Sam Donaldson at the White House, who promptly identified the man in the gray suit as the press aide to then vice president George Bush. My baptism by fire on live national television had ended as quickly as it had begun. For better or worse, I had been a part of history-making news on that July morning in 1981.

After returning to the station, a playback of the taped broadcast confirmed my worst fears. Although I had done the best I could, the constant dropping in and out of the microwave signal had rendered the broadcast a technical disaster. I had simultaneously experienced the incredible power and the frustrating limits of the TV medium. I had enjoyed the privilege of telling millions of people about an important moment in history, but at the same time my attempt to use the power I held in my hands was neutralized by the very technology that makes TV possible. Technical problems had overshadowed much of what we had tried to convey.

In spite of the disheartening problems that ravaged our broadcast of the O'Connor nomination, the small but steady trickle of mail I received shortly after reporting that national news brief reminded me anew of the power television has to evoke something mysterious in people. Although I appeared for only a few brief moments, I actually got mail from viewers—fan mail! A greeting from a cousin in Ohio I barely knew and a note from long lost high school friends now living in California. There was a letter from a Buena Park, California, teenager who requested a photograph of me and a note with a hollow ring of loneliness from a handicapped gentleman in Fort Meyers, Florida, who mentioned seeing me on the O'Connor news brief. He asked wistfully for a picture, along with an apology that he was confined to a wheelchair and was "unable to pursue my own career in this field." What compelled these people to go to the trouble to hunt for our station address and write to someone they had seen for only a few moments? What was it, I wondered, that made a total stranger respond in such a way to another stranger he saw on television?

My years in broadcasting have taught me that television is a powerful tool for communicating. Its influence and its effect on our society is difficult to ignore. Local and national broadcasters hold the keys to information many Americans are now conditioned to depend on. If the pen is mightier than the sword, then television surely rivals the A-bomb in impact. Year after year, survey after survey shows that TV is regarded by a large percentage of Americans to be the primary, pervasive, most reliable source of news, information, and entertainment in the country today. The latest surveys show TV news leading its competitors as the most used and most trusted vehicle of public information.[1]

> *If many Americans are in love with the way TV informs us, far more are addicted to the way it entertains us.*

From time to time, press credibility in general takes a nosedive in popularity, but even when the antimedia mood runs strong, television news is always rated the most reliable medium among Americans who are polled. The vast majority of Americans in the last decade say that TV is the primary source of all they know about the world. They rate it more than twice as believable as a newspaper. Half of those surveyed in recent years declare it to be the only source of information they ever use.[2]

Av Westin, former exeuctive producer of ABC's "20/20" news magazine, admits: "The power of television news astonishes even those of us who work for it."[3] Former Secretary of State Alexander Haig conceded: "There is seldom a day when [government officials] are not affected or influenced by what is broadcast by Dan Rather, Tom Brokaw, Peter Jennings, Ted Koppel and the rest of the broadcast journalist friars."[4] Those who govern know the power of television and are both fearful of it and eager to use it to their advantage.

After years of working in broadcasting and interacting with people about the medium, such survey results and comments never surprise me. They confirm the feedback I have received from viewers myself. In spite of occasional bursts of public outrage, I am convinced that the majority of Americans carry on a love affair with the tube. TV is so convenient. We appreciate the way the networks and local news operations deliver quick—even entertaining—information that takes minimal effort to understand. Using TV to be informed is something like going to McDonald's and getting a burger and fries—and maybe a toy in our Happy Meal® that makes us feel good.

We know that television can reduce distance at the flick of a switch, shrinking the miles between Washington and Moscow in a moment and reducing the world to a global village. It gives us a ringside seat at important events. It takes us places and shows us things we would otherwise never be able to see. Many viewers assume, in fact, that television has unlimited potential to take us anywhere and show us anything it wishes. They believe TV has made us the best informed public in history. With the continuing explosion of new and greater technologies, the possibilities for use of the television medium are endless—or so we are told. Thanks to TV, we now have everything we need to know at our fingertips. Or do we?

If many Americans are in love with the way TV informs us, far more are addicted to the way it entertains us. For millions of Americans, television is a daily game of Trivial Pursuit®—hour after hour. One survey suggests that Americans get more pleasure from watching television than from food, hobbies, sports, marriage, sex, money, and, sadly enough, religion.[5]

We are entranced with what we think is television's ability to inform and entertain us at the same time. We now feel sophisticated and knowledgeable on a wealth of topics. The storage banks in our minds are brimming with the intimate details of the private lives of movie stars and rock music personalities. We can regurgitate the details of every major sports event. Television has neatly filed this knowledge in our mental computers to be called up at the flick of a mental button. The prefabricated images of television dance in our minds like visions of sugarplums the night before Christmas. Those images motivate us—compelling us to try the myriad of consumer products that beckon to us from the screen.

Television, observes a former advertising executive, motivates us to do what we might otherwise not do, to think what we otherwise might not think, and to buy what we might otherwise never have purchased.[6] It holds our attention hostage for hours, influences our political views, and predisposes our most important choices. It induces us to accept or to participate in a lifestyle considered by many to be completely unacceptable a mere fifty years ago. Yet most people watch television without thinking about the power it wields in their lives.

We have been told that television has unlimited potential as an educator, and many parents assume it has unlimited potential as a reliable baby-sitter. Consequently, television has produced a whole new generation of sophisticated children. This explosion of knowledge is good for kids, isn't it? TV educates them—and besides, it keeps them occupied. Few parents ever stop to wonder what it is about TV that keeps many children so quiet and engrossed.

Since television appears to be a powerful and effective way to feed Americans the day's events, to sell them products, to help them escape the pressures of life, and to baby-sit and educate their children, doesn't it stand to reason that it is the best possible way for Christians to communicate the gospel? Can't we compel people to make a decision for Christ via the tube, much the same way advertisers compel us to buy their products? What could compare with this powerful tool for evangelism? It's enough to make us wonder why Jesus didn't come when He could have taken advantage of television to spread the good news.

The majority of Americans are convinced that television is "where it's at." Our love for and faith in the reliability of the tube is demonstrated by the fact that the average American household now spends more than seven hours a day tuned in, with the average adult consuming more than four hours of TV a day.[7] Research shows that women watch more TV than men and that blacks and some other minorities watch more than nonminorities. Research also suggests that professing Christians spend about as much time watching television as society in general and that Christians tune to the same soap operas, game shows, comedies, and dramas as the rest of society and in almost identical proportions.[8]

Although some Christians have been subjected to repeated warnings from the church pulpit about TV's unwholesome influence in their lives, many continue to watch long hours anyway, keeping the TV set on as a constant companion in their homes. Some professing Christians are far more reluctant to miss "60 Minutes" or their favorite sitcom or game show than they are to skip Bible study or church. Like the general public, many Christians are hungry for the diversion from the dull or stressful realities of life that television offers. So they turn to the tube, investing hours a week in what is now considered to be the main source of truth in our culture.

Some claim that TV has made us the best informed society in history. Are they right? Is the stream of mechanical illusion and chatter that flows from the screen really truth that can be trusted? If not, why not?

In just fifty years, America has undergone a noticeable shift in values and morals—a significant turnabout of acceptable lifestyle in both thinking and behavior. Ideas once considered radical and immoral are now largely mainstream. Surveys show that many professing Christians reason like society in general on questions of divorce, abortion, materialism, premarital sex, and other social and moral issues. In a speech to writers one Christian publisher warned that even within Christian circles the biblical thinker is disappearing. Secular ideas have so permeated the views of the average churchgoer that he is likely to hold much the same worldview as his unchurched neighbor.

Why are the radical ideas of the sixties and seventies now representative of mainstream America? Is the answer related to the fact that television has poured the same images, ideas, symbols, role models, and emotion-evoking imagery into a whole generation of people, Christians and non-Christians alike?

Is television a good, bad, or neutral influence, or all three at once? Is it just a harmless little box in the corner of the living room, or is it, as some claim, an instrument of mass behavior modification—an influence that erodes dividing lines between those who profess belief in biblical Christianity and those who don't? Is there a correlation between the parade of morally negative visions it offers and the growing social problems that modern society faces?

We cannot answer those questions until we have some understanding of how television works. If you depend on and are fascinated by TV, this book is intended to give you an insider's perspective on television you perhaps have never considered. Christians—who are concerned about truth—need to understand the nature of the TV medium and how that nature affects its ability to tell the truth.

As public television news anchor Robert MacNeil once noted, television is a medium we know so well but understand so little.[9] We are familiar with television but complete strangers to the actual process of how TV works. We only know that the box provides us with an endless stream of images and events that, at times, seems almost overwhelming.

Someone has said that television doesn't just tell us what to think, it tells us what to think about. TV news claims to provide us with all we need to know, and on occasion inundates us with more events than we really need to see, but there are other times, as a group of California residents discovered several years ago, when TV news doesn't show and tell us nearly enough.

NOTES

1. The last of the annual Roper polls conducted by the Television Information Office in 1989 showed TV to be the primary source of news for the public. In 1987, the poll showed that television enjoyed a better than two-to-one lead over newspapers as the most believable source in America for news. Fifty-five percent of the public said they would believe a TV report over a newspaper report. However, that vote of confidence declined slightly in 1989, from 55 to 49 percent who said TV was the most believable source of information. In spite of the decline, television still led newspapers by a nearly two-to-one margin in 1989, in terms of being considered the most credible news source.

   The 1987 Roper survey also showed that 50 percent of Americans now cite TV as their only source of news, and almost two-thirds (66 percent) of those polled list television as their primary news source, compared to 36 percent for newspapers. In 1989, TV still enjoyed its almost two-thirds margin of popularity, whereas newspapers enjoyed an increase in popularity to 42 percent ("America's Watching: Public Attitudes Toward Television," *TIO/Roper Report*, 1987, pp. 4-5, and "America's Watching: 30th Anniversary 1959-1989," *TIO/Roper Report*, 1989, pp. 14-15).

   In a 1991 poll in Phoenix, Arizona, television news not only enjoyed twice the credibility of newspapers in terms of being considered the most trustworthy and believable but outranked local city government officials, the governor, and the state legislature (Don Harris, "TV News Leads 'Republic,' Politicians in Trust Survey," *The Arizona Republic*, April 3, 1991, p. B-8).

2. "Public Gives TV News High Rating," *Broadcasting*, May 13, 1985, p. 58.

3. Av Westin, *Newswatch: How Television Decides the News* (New York: Simon & Schuster, 1982), p. 11.

4. Alexander Haig, Jr., "TV Can Derail Diplomacy," *TV Guide*, March 9, 1985, p. 5.

5. "More Enjoy TV Than Sex, Says Ad Agency Study," *TV Guide*, July 12, 1986, p. A-1.

6. Jerry Mander, *Four Arguments for the Elimination of Television* (New York: William Morrow, 1978), p. 13.

7. *The Nielsen Report*, 1989, p. 6; and "Media Comparisons," *Television Bureau of Advertising Research Report*, 1990, pp. 7-9.

8. Beth Spring, "A Study Finds Little Evidence that Religious TV Hurts Local Churches," *Christianity Today*, May 18, 1984, p. 71.

9. Robert MacNeil, quoted by editor Les Brown, in a subscription letter endorsing *Channels* magazine.

2

WHAT IF HOSEA GAVE A PRESS CONFERENCE AND NOBODY CAME?

t had all the earmarks of a nationally significant news story, but it never became one. The story began in the spring of 1982 in an ordinary-looking steel storage container that would turn into a Pandora's box of horrible secrets. Workers at the Martin Container Company in Wilmington, California, had just repossessed the twenty-foot-long container from behind the posh Woodland Hills suburban home of Malvin Weisberg. Weisberg, the former owner of a pathology laboratory in the Los Angeles area, had leased the container for what he said was "personal use." But the check he used to pay the leasing fee had bounced, and after repeated attempts to collect the money it was owed the Martin Container Company confiscated the box and took it back to their storage yard for unloading.

The first thing they noticed, according to forklift operator Ron Gillet, was the "strong smell" when they opened the container. It was filled from top to bottom with boxes. As workers began removing them, a box was dropped. It broke apart, spilling its contents onto the ground. "I stared at a large object, but I couldn't tell what it was," said Hank Stolk, another employee. "I called my boss over to take a look. All of a sudden we realized, with great horror, that it was the decapitated body of a baby."

More boxes were opened, more bodies and body parts were found. The sight and the smell were overwhelming. Container company officials, horrified over what they had uncovered, quickly notified authorities.

The Los Angeles County health officials who investigated the incident eventually counted more than sixteen thousand bodies of unborn babies. Almost two hundred of the fetuses were found to be older than twenty weeks—making them completely developed except for size. A fetus of this age is at least a foot long and can weigh more than a pound. Some of the fetuses were decapitated; most were mutilated in some way. Disturbed over accounts of the grizzly find, Los Angeles County Supervisors demanded an autopsy and further investigation.

---

*The focus of the resulting barrage
from reporters became not the morality
of what the pictures testified to but
the legality of showing the pictures.*

To some, it looked like the biggest single mass murder story in California history. But not everyone saw it that way, to the surprise of those who found the bodies. "They're just fetuses," said one container company employee in disbelief, "but they sure looked like little babies to me." How seriously the incident was viewed became a question of moral perspective. "The average person will be left with a nauseating feeling in the pit of his stomach," commented one California state senator. He might have been right —except that the average Los Angeles resident would never know the entire story, and most Americans would barely see or hear anything about the incident.

An investigation and autopsy of the largest bodies found in the container produced some of the most disturbing pictures of abortions ever taken. A group of doctors and concerned public officials later released some of the pictures at a press conference in Los Angeles, to back up their demand that the bodies be released for public burial. The photos were graphic and sobering—close-ups of dead babies with well-developed bodies and clearly distinguishable facial features.

Such brutally frank portraits of abortion evoked humanitarian concern in those who called the press conference, but the reporters who came to cover it saw the photos differently. They reacted with belligerence, firing a barrage of verbal gunfire at conference participants. "It was the most hostile press conference I've ever attended," remembered Jeannette Dreisbach, the wife of Dr. Philip Dreisbach, who participated in the autopsy. "We felt like we were really hitting a raw nerve with the press." Jeannette particularly recalled a reporter from the ABC network-owned-and-operated TV station in Los Angeles. "A woman from the Feminist Women's Health Center was with him—standing beside his camera and feeding him questions. He had apparently been tipped by someone in the coroner's office that pictures of dead people can't legally be shown to the public." In spite of the fact that the law doesn't recognize a fetus as a person, displaying these graphic photos at a public press conference was illegal and unethical, the reporter insisted.

The focus of the resulting barrage from reporters became not the morality of what the pictures testified to but the legality of showing the pictures. Incensed by the hostility he was encountering over the graphic photos, David Roberti, a California state senator debating the hostile reporters, shouted back in frustration, "They took pictures at Auchwitz, didn't they?"

"The hostile reporter kept grilling Roberti, while the other stations taped the exchange," Mrs. Dreisbach recalled. "The hostility didn't end with the press conference. The angry reporter from ABC waited for us outside the front door of the Los Angeles Press Club, yelling, 'I'm really going to get those people!' We were emotionally spent—some of the participants had never experienced anything like this before. We finally left through the back door of the Press Club kitchen. We just didn't have the strength to face that reporter and his camera again."[1]

I remember seeing the raw, unedited tape of a similar press conference at the station where I worked as a reporter. Right to Life had called the media together to protest an abortion attempt on a baby only three weeks away from birth. The abortion had been botched—the baby was born live, and word of the incident had leaked. When Right to Life advocates tried to publicly protest the travesty, they too encountered a skeptical room full of reporters. I remember wincing as I glanced at the playback in the editing booth next to me. Equally hard to watch was the reaction of the reporter who had covered the press conference. He was laughing as he watched the replay.

I wish I could tell you from personal experience that such unfriendly scenarios are isolated cases of abuse, but I can't, at least where the abortion issue is concerned. Anyone who has been on the cutting edge of an issue that challenges the current wave of sexual freedom has similar horror stories to tell about encounters with the media. It's like driving the wrong way on a one-way street. The display of bad attitude and the abuse of power against those considered to be coming from the "wrong" direction springs from the deeply ingrained biases of the journalists involved.

The focus of most of the local media coverage that followed the Los Angeles press conference centered on the side issue of whether or not county and state officials had legally released the pictures. I am told that the photos of clearly recognizable infants, powerful statements in and of themselves, were never shown on local television in the Los Angeles area. But whereas the Los Angeles media shunned the pictures and shifted the focus away from the obvious moral considerations they raised, most of the national media ignored the story altogether, in spite of the fact that it had national repercussions. The question of whether or not to bury more than sixteen thousand bodies or to incinerate them like garbage touched off a bitter court battle that was waged all the way to the United States Supreme Court. Three years later, the bodies were buried publicly in the Los Angeles area after a Supreme Court ruling ended the dispute.[2]

The story broke at a time when abortion was a hotly debated national issue and had been the focus of controversy during the presidential election a year and a half before. Although the incident was publicly condemned by the White House and mentioned briefly in the back sections of a few newspapers, the story lacked the single necessary ingredient to make it common knowledge—national television coverage. The networks simply weren't interested. The medium that prides itself on making its viewers "eyewitnesses" of events closed its powerful glass eye and looked the other way as the bizarre and shocking story fell through the cracks of national public awareness.

When I read the words of the prophet Hosea (700 B.C.), I wonder if he didn't have similar problems with the "media" of his day:

> Hear the word of the Lord, O people of Israel;
>> for the Lord has a controversy with the inhabitants of the land.
>
> There is no faithfulness or kindness,
>> and no knowledge of God in the land;
>> there is swearing, lying, killing, stealing, and committing adultery;
>> they break all bounds and murder follows murder. . . .
>
> Yet let no one contend,
>> and let none accuse,
>> for with you is my contention, O priest. . . .
>
> My people are destroyed for a lack of knowledge,
>> because you have rejected knowledge.
>
> (Hosea 4:1-2, 4, 6; RSV*)

The priests of Hosea's day had the responsibility of telling the people of Israel the truth. The "priests" of the twentieth-century media have the responsibility of deciding what you and I are going to read, hear, and see.

The story of the Los Angeles babies was very visual, but television, a picture-oriented medium, ignored the incriminating pictures. I once asked a news director I worked for why pictures of

* *Revised Standard Version.*

aborted babies were never shown on the air. His annoyed response was, "People don't want to see them!" But is the criterion for news only what people *want* to see?

It wasn't the criterion two years later, in 1984, when another story involving highly disturbing, distasteful pictures of children and adults came along. The story was famine in Africa—not necessarily a new subject. What was new were some unusually vivid, heartrending pictures taken by an African photographer for a European news service. The power and the presentation of the pictures was unusually compelling: huge piles of dead children and shots of others waiting to die with glazed eyes, extended bellies, and arms and legs like fragile sticks. One network decided to air the graphic footage, and others in the United States and Europe quickly followed suit. The public who watched in horror responded en masse with an outpouring of assistance to an assortment of relief organizations. An Irish rock singer organized something called Live Aid. The rest is history—history that hinged on the decision of a small handful of TV producers.

The ultimate conclusion of the true liberal is that to be truly objective and nonpartisan a journalist can't have any personal ideas about what constitutes right and wrong.

Network anchor David Brinkley once admitted, "News is what I say it is—it's something worth knowing by *my* standards!"[3] Not all stories involve the kind of judgment calls that invokes personal bias, but in some cases what reporters do with a story comes down to what they believe about what they are being asked to report and about life itself. Research on the attitudes of press members reveals that a high percentage of America's leading journalists describe themselves and their colleagues as ideological liberals, especially on social and moral questions. The majority are overwhelming supporters of sexual freedom in general, with 90 percent in favor of abortion. The majority of leading media decision makers emerge as natural opponents of anyone questioning the concept of complete sexual freedom.[4]

Such research paints a composite picture of the people I worked with in my years of news reporting. When we consider the responses of those surveyed on the issue of abortion, it dispels any question of why the story about the babies found in the Los Angeles storage container never made it to network news and why the local media attacked the press conference participants so vindictively. Such behavior was an incriminating barometer of personal bias.

Researchers have found another dominating characteristic of media decision makers: few of those who make key editorial decisions are religious. Out of several hundred interviewed, exactly half said they had no religious affiliation at all, and an overwhelming majority reported that they almost never attend any type of worship.[5]

This conclusion was also true of the people I personally encountered in the news business. Most of those I knew, like their network counterparts, weren't religious in any meaningful way. The few of us who were quickly learned from our peers that we ought to keep it to ourselves. I discovered early on as a reporter that part of the prevailing mentality of the TV business is the idea that religious convictions, especially if they are biblically based ones, don't belong in the newsroom because they hamper "objectivity." There was an unwritten rule that if a reporter was "religious" he shouldn't let it interfere with the job of being "objective." Why were religious people always regarded as subjective? I used to wonder. Since when does agnosticism qualify one as neutral on an issue?

A revealing statement by America's most respected news anchor sheds some light on that question. Walter Cronkite publicly stated that journalists are "certainly liberal, and possibly left of center as well. I think most . . . by definition have to be liberal."[6] What did he mean by such a statement? Forget about the bundle of political connotations that come with the word *liberal* for a moment and examine a definition of a liberal once offered by Cronkite. It sheds light on the nature and the problem of liberal bias. Cronkite stated in a magazine interview a number of years ago that he was a "true liberal." A true liberal, he explained, is "someone not bound by doctrine or committed to a point of view in advance."[7]

Cronkite's definition is a good one. It is also an accurate explanation of how many reporters view the idea of objectivity. On the surface, his definition seems both desirable and commendable, until "true liberalism" is carried to its logical extreme. The ultimate conclusion of the true liberal is that to be truly objective and nonpartisan a journalist can't have any personal ideas about what constitutes right and wrong. To believe in an idea of absolute right and wrong is to embrace some kind of doctrine—to "commit to a point of view in advance," which, Cronkite points out, must be avoided.

Many newspeople equate this view of liberalism with openmindedness but fail to see the pitfall in their line of reasoning. To them, the only objective journalist is the one who holds to no fixed, unchanging standards of belief. His only standard for what is true is that nothing is necessarily true. The flaw in this type of thinking is that there can never be an escape from absolutes. Declaring that there is no absolute right or wrong is in itself an absolute. In trying to worm out from under one type of dogma they have created a new one.

This brand of open-mindedness becomes a pivotal point of judgment against people and issues the journalist opposes. Moral absolutes become personally threatening to the "true liberal," and so absolutists are dubbed "narrow-minded" and "dogmatic." What began under the guise of journalistic tolerance and objectivity degenerates into intolerance and hostility. The journalist has now developed a different kind of bias—a prejudice against any person or group who enters the public arena "bound by doctrine and committed to a point of view in advance"—unless that point of view happens to match his own.

It is this kind of reasoning that prompts hostility toward prolife activists on the part of reporters without the least regard as to whether or not such hostility reflects bias toward a particular point of view. In the mind of the reporter, he or she is the objective one. Right?

It is not surprising that media elites who either consciously or unconsciously hold this definition of objectivity and truth are skeptical of or disinterested in religion. Christianity in particular, with its fixed points of moral reference, evokes hostility. Reporters who lack a fixed idea of absolute truth are on a collision course with a dogmatic Jesus who insisted He was "the way, the truth and the life" (John 14:6).

Does that mean that the popular conception among some evangelicals that the majority of media people are part of an organized, industry-wide, smoke-filled back room conspiracy to "get" God and godly people is accurate? Not at all. It is true that some journalists have deliberately abused some Christians, but most of the time such behavior isn't premeditated action so much as it is unconscious reaction. Most newspeople I have known are more interested in getting away from God than getting even with Him. They unconsciously keep God at a distance in their lives, and they unconsciously assume that it is part of their job to keep God at arm's length from the public for whom they interpret news. Reporters who have never come to grips with sin in their own lives are poorly equipped to interpret newsworthy events that result, as some do, from sin in the lives of other people. It is tough to be fair with the pro-life movement if you have had an abortion or think you might need one someday.

No doubt the secular attitudes of news decision makers are an important part of the reason the crises of society that parade across our nightly news screens are reported without the interference of a spiritual perspective. Combine permissiveness on moral issues with the immense power of the media—especially television—to convince and alter opinion, and the result can be disturbing.

In 1991, the issue of unnerving pictures on television news emerged again, this time in the Persian Gulf War. The voices of American electronic and print journalists were raised in a collective scream over "censorship" and the "sanitizing" of war coverage by U.S. government and military officials. A few days before the conflict began, network news executives and correspondents voiced their intention to cover what they called "the horrors of war," regardless of the manipulative effect of that coverage on public morale. One network declared that it would push vigorously to find ways to get around military control of information through pool reporting, regardless of Pentagon restrictions. "We're taking our own measures to cover the war," declared CBS news executive Don DeCesare, "whether they want us to or not."[8] Correspondent Bob Simon and a CBS news crew were exploring such options when they disappeared less than two weeks later and were taken prisoner by Iraq.

In a subsequent broadcast of ABC's "Prime Time Live" during the Persian Gulf War, correspondents Judd Rose and Sam Donaldson expressed criticism of efforts the military might take to shroud graphic or unpleasant battle video that might be forthcoming: Said Rose: "The 'top-gun' view of war that we've been allowed to see so far is very seductive. But if and when the body bags come back, will we be allowed to see that too? It may be painful, but it may be necessary to judge whether the price is worth paying."

Donaldson, responding to Rose, declared: "Our role is to report what we find and see to the best of our ability. If people don't like it, I'm sorry, but they really need to know what's happening." Concluded Rose: "We really are the conveyers of truth in a very critical time and people need to know that truth."[9]

Stirring words, gentlemen. I understand your frustration with military censorship. You have a hard and dangerous job to do. I know from my own experience that the military can be difficult to deal with at times. I share your concern for truthful reporting. But for people like Dr. Philip Dreisbach, his wife, Jeannette, and others who have experienced firsthand the journalistic schizophrenia of television where disturbing pictures and uncomfortable truths are concerned, unsettling questions about the medium's long-term commitment to showing truth still linger. While the battle over media coverage was being waged in the Saudi Arabian desert in the nineties, back in California some continued to ask where television's faithfulness to unvarnished truth was residing in the eighties.

Does that mean that conservative Christians are right to lay all the blame for TV's ills at the feet of its human decision makers? Is it right for Christians to argue that the real problem with television is that what we see is completely controlled by those whose thinking is ungodly and slanted to the left or who are out to steer viewers toward a particular way of thinking? Is it accurate to say that the problems of television could be corrected if we could just inject a conservative, Christian point of view? Not really. On the basis of my own experience in TV news, I am convinced that the problem and the solution are not as simple as critics claim. There are other equally potent considerations that motivate newspeople and affect their judgment.

NOTES

1. This account was compiled from the following sources: Daniel W. Pawley, "The Abortion Mess in Los Angeles," *Christianity Today*, September 17, 1982, pp. 46-48; Judith Michaelson, "500 Fetuses Found in Storage," *The Los Angeles Times*, February 6, 1982, part. 2, p. 6; Mark Gladstone, "Evidence Sought in Death of 500 Fetuses," *The Los Angeles Times*, February 7, 1982, part 2, pp. 1-4; a brochure from The Center for the Documentation of the American Holocaust in Palm Springs, California; my own telephone interviews with Dr. Philip Dreisbach and Jeannette Dreisbach, May 21 and May 27, 1985.
2. Karen Scalf Linamen, "Pro-Life Groups Host Memorial Service for 16,500 Aborted Infants," *Focus on the Family*, July 1985, p. 11.
3. David Brinkley, quoted by Edith Efron, "Why Speech on Television Is Not Really Free," *TV Guide*, April 11, 1964, p. 7.
4. S. Robert Lichter and Stanley Rothman, "Media and Business Elites," *Public Opinion*, October/November 1981, p. 45.
5. Ibid., p. 42.
6. Dinesh D'Souza, "TV News: The Politics of Social Climbing," *Human Events*, August 16, 1986, p. 12.
7. Walter Cronkite, quoted in "Cronkite Spears Agnew," *Variety*, November 4, 1970, p. 28.
8. Don DeCesare, quoted by Randall M. Sukow and Rich Brown in "The Storm and the Eye," *Broadcasting*, January 14, 1991, pp. 52-53.
9. "Prime Time Live," ABC Network, January 24, 1991.

3

SEEING IS BELIEVING

I n recounting his four years of dealing with the Washington media, Jody Powell, press secretary for President Jimmy Carter, readily acknowledged that ideological bias was a factor in Carter's press problems: White House reporters couldn't understand a president who prayed. But a still stronger influence in journalism prevailed, Powell insisted: power lust. "Members of the press," he wrote, "wrestle with the most basic and pervasive of all human emotions: greed and ambition."[1] I would have to agree. Most of those I worked with in the news business were motivated more by personal ambition than some pet agenda of belief.

Using media power to get ahead was certainly a temptation I wrestled with. Such ambitions are greatly enhanced by the twentieth-century tools of electronic communication. A career in TV news in particular can be a marvelous vehicle for self-exaltation because of the notoriety that on-camera personalities develop. Even in the smaller, local news markets, I could feel it, especially during election coverage. The crowds of enthusiastic, applauding supporters of a candidate, the bands playing, the flashbulbs popping, combined with my almost instant access to talk with and be close to a would-be U.S. senator who was the focus of so much attention—being part of it all could be an intoxicating experience. Venturing into the smoke-filled rooms of political decision making that were off-limits to the average person was part of associating with the powerful. Such associations gained you status in return. The aura that came with special favor subtly began to make you feel that you were a little bit above the rest of the public. And, in terms of privilege, you were. So at times, ideology and ambition combine, but the personal drive to get ahead in a highly competitive industry can sometimes be the more potent motivator.

The process of scrutinizing public business on the news serves the positive and necessary function of creating and sustaining a balance of power in society, but the inherent side effect is that it gives the exposer too much power in return. In my experience, it is the rare investigative reporter who searches for corruption and scandal out of mere concern for public welfare. Scandals catch public attention, and tremendous professional rewards flow from lowering politicians and public figures a notch or two. It is the bias of power lust in action.

But in their haste to criticize journalists for peddling ideology or succumbing to power lust, some detractors give journalists more credit than they truly deserve. By doing so, they overlook another widely prevalent, less sinister influence on accuracy and fairness: ignorance. There is a built-in measure of uncertainty inherent in the news business. Reporters are turned loose in a society awash with complicated and misleading information. We rush through it like rats in a maze, searching for the correct story line. Much of the information comes at us fast and furious, raw and unanalyzed, and the commercial pressure to report it first w..ks against accuracy. We gather our facts helter-skelter, catch-as-catch-can, hit-or-miss. CBS anchor Dan Rather once observed that news reporting was "not a precise science," but "on its best days, a very crude art."[2] That's putting it politely. The dynamic operating behind inaccuracy and unfairness is sometimes nothing more than sheer ignorance.

Ignorance was a major factor in the coverage of the Three Mile Island nuclear power accident. Journalists were plunged into a situation that few had the technical expertise to even begin to understand for themselves, let alone interpret for millions of other Americans. I can vividly remember those tense evenings in 1979 as television reporters across the country stood with microphones in our hands and looks of authority on our faces, spewing out a combination of fact, rumor, innuendo, and technical information we could barely comprehend. Television news operations were positioned, armed and ready, their vast arsenal of technical and electronic weapons set to beam the truth—but unfortunately no one knew for sure exactly what the truth was.

But though some viewers have learned to doubt the objectivity or proficiency of editors, producers, and reporters, few viewers think to doubt the medium of television itself.

The bias of ignorance influences the way religious events are reported. Since most journalists aren't religious, many don't know the difference between Armageddon and an armadillo. Evangelical journalist Wesley Pippert points out that bad religious reporting is often nothing more than ignorance at work: "A large segment of good journalists simply turn off moral information. It's as if they are tone deaf in this area. They don't understand Christian doctrine and they don't really understand the Judeo-Christian ethic. Since they don't understand it, they find difficulty in interpreting it fairly. They lack a cultivated religious and moral sense."[3] It becomes easier to avoid religious angles or stories rather than risk a misinterpretation that is almost certain to bring a storm of criticism.

Before becoming a reporter myself, I used to wonder how news organizations got all the information they needed and how they could be absolutely sure that that information was correct.

After I became a reporter, I discovered that the answer to those questions is that they sometimes can't and they sometimes aren't. What Americans see and hear on TV news each day is as much the result of the information we cannot get—the interview we could not arrange or the unreturned phone call before the deadline—as it is the information we have access to. In our trying to avoid error by leaving out what we do not know or understand enough to interpret correctly, ignorance becomes a type of censorship.

The problems of power lust and ignorance feed on one another and intertwine. Power corrupts journalism because it discourages honesty about the journalist's ignorance on a subject. When a news organization or its members have created the illusion of being invincible, it is hard to shatter that illusion by admitting ignorance about information the public looks to you for. When you admit ignorance, you must relinquish some power and thereby risk letting your competition gain the edge. The tendency is for reporters to use the power afforded by the First Amendment not just to do the job of reporting but on some occasions to mask incompetency and poor judgment as well as personal bias, pride, and ambition. So the human biases of ideology, power lust, and ignorance all contribute to distortion in television news.

But though some viewers have learned to doubt the objectivity or proficiency of editors, producers, and reporters, few viewers think to doubt the medium of television itself. Why does television lay claim to being the most credible purveyor of realism and accuracy on the American media spectrum, enjoying significantly more credibility and allegiance than its print competitors? I think that a major reason behind TV's immense believability is that it shows us moving pictures that resemble real life—and we believe what our eyes tell us. Television's credibility hinges on how much reliability we assign to what it shows us.

The late Malcolm Muggeridge, a well-known TV news commentator in Great Britain, and a Christian, pointed out a crucial but often overlooked difference between the way people look at television and the way they read magazines or newspapers. Most people are at least vaguely aware that what they read in a newspaper or hear read to them on radio is someone else's interpretation of an event or issue, Muggeridge observed. Written words are assumed to be subjective. But when people watch TV they unconsciously assume the neutrality of the picture. They assume that most of the imagery they are seeing is objective—nobody's interpretation—because they trust what their eyes tell them.[4]

Television can be dangerous, Muggeridge declared, because it projects images that are assumed to be unbiased and are taken to be the same as witnessing reality. Our minds unconsciously process most of the imagery TV gives us in the same way we would if we were actually observing an event. That is, after all, what TV news promises—to make us "eyewitnesses" of events.

Since TV promoters have led us to believe that television can show us whatever we need to know, we think we are being informed by merely watching. So when the viewer sees something on television, he is more likely to accept it as credible, drawing important and far-reaching conclusions about what has been shown because he assumes, almost without question, that he has seen all he needs to.

Perhaps another reason people are more convinced by what they see on the TV screen is that it is far easier to see than to think. We are more influenced by what we see than by what we hear because ingesting imagery is easier than thinking through the information conveyed by the spoken or written word. Merely seeing and absorbing what is seen caters to our human nature and masquerades as an easy, effortless way to be informed.

But are we wise to accept the imagery TV offers as unbiased? Can we assume the imagery that TV offers is just as good as "being there"? Can we depend on and make judgments based on the pictures television reflects to us? The question of reliability is of paramount importance. If we are Christians, what is true about the world we live in is crucial. Christians believe in a God who is in the truth business. He came to earth as a human being to reveal the truth to other human beings. Christ claimed to be "the way and the truth and the life" (John 14:6). Christians especially should be concerned about whether powerfully delivered TV images are a reliable reflection of the truth if they are to allow those image to formulate their thinking.

TV images are far more than what somebody's philosophy, ambitions, or ignorance mold them into. There are larger, less personal forces at work that shape the TV product. TV imagery is subject not only to somebody else's interpretation but to the interpretation of the technology that created those images to begin with.

The "biases" of television are not merely a function of the weaver's perspective but are problems within the very warp and woof of the TV tapestry itself. Far from being neutral, the very threads that are woven together to create the TV image contain inherent biases of their own. The technology we put so much faith in may mislead us more than we realize and affect us more deeply than we are aware. It is these "hidden biases" of television, which frequently escape the notice of viewers, that we will explore in this book.

There were countless times when I discovered that I couldn't show and tell my viewers what I needed to because of a wide variety of circumstances beyond my control. How could that be? How does television—as both a news and entertainment medium—mislead or underinform us in ways that even its creators can't contain? That is a difficult question to answer unless you have struggled, as I have, with television's inadequacies firsthand. Come with me and take a second, inside look at this medium of communication. What we find on the other side may surprise you.

NOTES

1. Jody Powell, *The Other Side of the Story* (New York: William Morrow, 1984), p. 16.
2. Dan Rather, quoted by Stephen Lesher in *Media Unbound: The Impact of Television by Journalism on the Public* (Boston: Houghton Mifflin, 1982), p. 11.
3. Wesley Pippert, quoted in "If God Held a Press Conference," *Christianity Today*, May 21, 1982, p. 12.
4. Malcolm Muggeridge, *Christ and the Media* (Grand Rapids: Eerdmans, 1977), p. 106.

4

THE ELECTRONIC DICTATOR

n 1960, a series of now-classic debates between presidential candidates John F. Kennedy and Richard M. Nixon were broadcast to millions of Americans via radio and television. When researchers polled radio listeners and TV viewers to find out which candidate they thought had won the contest, an interesting pattern developed. The majority of radio listeners insisted that candidate Nixon had won easily, saying that Mr. Nixon's carefully worded arguments were stronger and more sensible. Television viewers came away from the screen with a different account. They were entranced by the young, handsome, charismatic Massachusetts senator, maintaining that Kennedy was a hands-down winner. The sharp disagreement that emerged over who won illustrates an important point about the difference between the way radio and television communicate information, a difference I learned early in my TV news career: *people are far more influenced by what their eyes tell them than by what their ears tell them*. It is the image on the screen that grips the mind and emotions, especially if that image is inherently compelling.

I found that the videotaped pictures I used to window-dress my stories often spoke more powerfully to my audience than the information I tried to give them in my narration. If the video portion of my story was weak, my reports fell flat and the point of my story was missed. Similarly, when I was anchoring news on the set I discovered to my dismay that my personal appearance was sometimes a distraction. It was apparent from the letters I received that many viewers were far more interested in what I looked like—my personal screen image—than in the content of the news I was reading to them.

Unfortunately what is newsworthy cannot always be easily photographed, projected on a TV screen, and instantly understood by a viewer. The major flaw in depending on TV for news lies in not understanding that.

Pictures are what makes television powerful and give it a competitive edge over all other media. Television correspondents in the Persian Gulf War who adamantly protested government restrictions on TV coverage were well aware of their dependance on pictures to aggressively outdistance their radio and print rivals. Most of the time, the camera, not the reporter, is the dominant storyteller in TV news and TV entertainment. A story without good pictures is a problem for TV, which is why only about 3 percent of network news stories are presented without some type of accompanying visual.[1] Pictures are the focal point of anything TV tries to communicate.

One of the most erroneous ideas ever thrust upon the American public by television critics, educators, viewers, preachers, and broadcast executives is the notion that television has an unlimited potential to communicate and educate. Those who embrace that idea may sincerely believe they are right, but their analysis is false. What is true is that television has immense potential to communicate some types of messages powerfully—and it does—but it cannot communicate all things powerfully. It is only powerful to the degree that it can convert important ideas into something that can be seen.

When this visuality is not available, television's credibility and impact is lost. Naked information alone, without the accompanying clothing of strong visuals, is of limited use to a TV producer unless the information itself is so compelling that it can stand alone. There are events, such as the assassination of a president or the audio description by reporters in Baghdad of the 1991 air attack on Iraq, that are strong enough to hold public attention without good video, but those are the exception to the rule. Television most effectively communicates when good pictures are available.

Unfortunately, what is newsworthy cannot always be easily photographed, projected on a TV screen, and instantly understood by a viewer. The major flaw in depending on TV for news lies in not understanding that. There are many important stories in the world which, for one reason or another, cannot be captured meaningfully through a camera lens. Television is not equipped to respond to those stories. It can respond effectively only to events that generate good pictures. Moreover, information must be editorially tailored to fit the narrow, rigid requirements of video production. TV reporters are forced to focus on a relatively narrow aspect of an issue or story and must turn every issue into something visual.

That means that when a TV reporter and cameraman cover a story, in many instances they aren't nearly as pressured to focus on what suits their ideological biases as they are compelled to zero in on what meets the rigid visual criterion for televised communication. They must be on the lookout for whatever is interesting to look at, colorful, exciting, action packed, dramatic, entertaining, or sensational. Producing such pictures is the plumbline of success or failure in TV news.

I saw this illustrated time and again in my years of reporting. While I was working in Cleveland, Ohio, several years ago, the city was caught in a political struggle between the mayor and the banking community and became the first major American city to go into financial default. Credit ratings tumbled and financial repercussions reverberated throughout the community. The people of Cleveland wanted to understand what was happening, but television, the medium that most of them turned to for the answers, had a difficult time delivering that information. After all, how do you photograph a city going into default on a bank loan? How do you picture bankruptcy?

The lack of something tangible for the camera to focus on affected the way television presented the story to Cleveland residents. TV reporters limped along in their coverage, able only to regurgitate some bite-sized blips of what the newspapers had to say. Though the story had far-reaching implications for the entire community, from beginning to end it was a newspaper story, and that was reflected in the limited way television reported it. There was simply too much complex information that could not be pictured in a meaningful way.

The story suffered from technological understatement. The end result? The majority of Cleveland residents who leaned on television news for understanding came away from the screen confused and underinformed. The unavailability of pictures was a powerful bias that had a profound effect on the length, slant, and angle of every attempt at coverage we made. Very little analysis or background information could be offered because there was so little to show.

On the eve of Cleveland's financial default, the station I worked for ran a story I covered on the city's impending financial crash. The report was a scant thirty seconds long and was padded with static pictures of city council members sitting around a table discussing ways to avert the disaster. The most important story of the day was dismissed, out of necessity, in a thirty-second summary tailored to fit the available videotape.

But later in the same newscast the station ran a feature story several minutes in length. It was about a chicken trained to play ticktacktoe with people. As incredible as that might seem in terms of news judgment, the chicken got more coverage that night because a chicken is more visual than a bankruptcy. A couple of minutes of a bird pecking its way across a ticktacktoe board in fierce competition with one of our news anchors (who, incidentally, lost all three rounds to the chicken) was more visibly interesting and easier to photograph than the city's greatest financial crisis. The chicken got more air time because it played better in the theater of TV news than the city's financial default.

There are pitfalls in depending on a visual medium for an understanding of a political crisis. The pictures demanded by an action-oriented medium will prevail every time. ABC anchor Peter Jennings saw this principle in action during his tenure as a correspondent in Lebanon in the seventies. He recalls the downside of visual dependence in trying to cover the civil war then going on in Beirut: "A lot of the correspondents would say at the time [that] the only way to get on the air was to lead with 'bang bang' [footage of fighting and bombing that was dramatic]. We went through the entire civil war [with] just one long series of pictures of violence. It didn't mean anything [to the viewer]. Therefore, nobody understood [what was going on in] Lebanon."[2]

Few viewers seem aware that TV's greatest strength, its ability to visualize, has a downside—its inability to communicate the important but invisible.

Years later, most Americans still do not understand conflict in the Middle East because they have largely depended on an image-oriented medium to explain it to them. Although it may be argued that TV reporting is now more sophisticated that it was in 1975, TV coverage of the 1991 war against Iraq was still predominantly video "bang bang," as Jennings put it, only this time with more technological immediacy. Television coverage of the war against Iraq, particularly on CNN, was preoccupied with unnerving sounds of live air raid sirens, images of flying missiles, and adrenaline-pumped correspondents fumbling with their gas masks. Television's fixation with Scud attacks and surreal gas mask drills was entirely predictable from my perspective and had little to do with their actual importance. Many televised attacks turned out to be false alarms. Their televised presence had everything to do with TV's incapacity to show its audience any other compelling images of war. It was no accident that CNN and ABC, the two networks who, early on, relied the heaviest on emotionally compelling images, garnered the highest number of viewers.

Christians who complain about the religious void on TV need to realize that since much of religious experience is inward and invisible, religious experience is difficult for TV to handle. Some Protestants complain to me that Catholics receive more news coverage. That is probably true, but one reason is that the Pope, in all of his colorful splendor and ceremony, is such an easy camera target.

Larry Speakes, former White House press secretary for Ronald Reagan, was well aware of the paramount importance of pictures to news coverage. In his book *Speaking Out*, he confessed to learning to think like a TV producer: "When the President was pushing education, the visual was of him sitting at a little desk and talking to a group of students, or with the football team and some cheerleaders, or in a science lab. . . . We knew very quickly that the rule was no pictures, no television piece, no matter how important our news was."[3]

Speakes unabashedly tailored White house events to cater to this technological bias because he understood that in television the camera is a tyrant, shaping editorial decisions in line with what the lens is capable of accomplishing. He learned, as I did, that TV news responds, not so much to the forces in society that really affect our lives as to whatever generates good videotape.

Few viewers seem aware that TV's greatest strength, its ability to visualize, has a downside—its inability to communicate the important but invisible. Not until viewers understand that can they grasp the magnitude of TV's vulnerability as a medium of communication. Few grasp the significance of a technology that dictates what they shall know and see. Fewer still realize how the tendency to cater only to the visual not only alters public awareness but sometimes leaves this powerful medium wide open for manipulation.

NOTES

1. David L. Altheide, *Media Power* (Beverly Hills, Calif.: Sage, 1985), p. 118.
2. Peter Jennings, quoted by Rushworth M. Kidder, "Videoculture 3: Do 'Media-genic' Candidates Make Good Leaders?" *The Christian Science Monitor*, June 12, 1985, p. 19. Reprinted by permission from *The Christian Science Monitor* © 1985 The Christian Science Publishing Society. All rights reserved.
3. Larry Speakes with Robert Pack, *Speaking Out: The Reagan Presidency from Inside the White House* (New York: Scribner, 1988); in "Beat the Press," *TV Guide*, May 14, 1988, p. 10.

5

TELEREALITY

Television's preoccupation with visual imagery spawns a subtle side effect that author Jan Novak labels "telereality." Events that can be televised take on added significance in the minds of viewers over those that cannot. Something researchers call the "publicity effect" takes place. A person becomes suddenly notable—his importance rooted in the simple fact that he has been on television. Events become "telereal"—bigger than life.

American TV viewers are now so conditioned to telereality that many are unmoved by news that is invisible to the eye of electronic journalism. Ethiopian starvation several years ago was a case in point. Novak observed in an article for *Newsweek* magazine: "To enter Western consciousness these days, a person or event must be, above all, telereal. The famine in Ethiopia had been written about in newspapers for years, yet the stories were calmly read and put out of mind. Then, when a British television crew . . . managed to render the massive suffering and starvation real—on television—the West suddenly exploded with disbelief, guilt and good will."[1]

It is one thing for television news to show us pictures of what happened, but quite another for it to show us pictures of why or how. Even after the cameras had illuminated the Ethiopian situation, we saw and heard much about the suffering the Ethiopian people were undergoing but understood little about the historical circumstances behind it. Television could graphically portray the pained faces of the starving, but the members of the Marxist regime that engineered the drought and subsequent famine were inaccessible to TV photographers and, consequently, faded into anonymity—away from the Western camera lens that might have made them telereal and thus significant to the rest of the world.

The self-aggrandizing efforts of some rock music stars and networks who profited from organizing a benefit concert were telereal. What was not telereal were the quiet efforts of hardworking Christian relief workers, most of whom were laboring out of range of the camera lens long before Live Aid organizer Bob Geldorf or rock star Mick Jagger took center stage.

> *Telereality distorts war. The ugliness of the conflict that flows into our living rooms via the TV screen repulses us, overshadowing the important but intangible reasons for fighting such wars.*

The danger of telereality is that visibility determines what is true for the audience. Ethiopian famine is "real" for us because we have "seen" it with our eyes and must respond to the emotions evoked by the imagery, but starvation in the Sudan may be just as severe—but not telereal—and so cannot command the same sense of urgency.

Several years ago I made a brief appearance as an announcer in "The Hope Factor," a nationally televised appeal for famine relief in Ethiopia. As is frequently the case, the program was full of graphic video of gaunt-looking children. Afterward, I had dinner with Ted Yamamori, president of Food for the Hungry, the Christian world relief organization that had produced the television special. I questioned Ted about the pictures, pointing out that some criticize relief organizations for showing such footage because it is considered to be manipulative. "It bothers me a lot that we have to make these films," he replied. "We make the films because people respond to them. Frankly, I think that Christians in particular should contribute to relief efforts not because they see graphic pictures but because Jesus commanded us to feed the hungry. To me, Christ's command should be motivation enough, but it's not. We make the films because people are suffering and the films bring results."

Why is it that the words of Jesus alone and verbal awareness of the need are insufficient to move Christians to action? Could our conditioned mind-set be part of the reason that many American Christians will give dollars to build impressive looking Christian real estate empires, which are the visible measures of Christian "success," yet are slow to send dollars to a horribly needy part of the world that is not sufficiently telereal to us?

Telereality distorts war. The ugliness of the conflict that flows into our living rooms via the TV screen repulses us, overshadowing the important but intangible reasons for fighting such wars, forcing them to pale in significance compared to the imagery. That this happens was well understood by the U.S. military in the Persian Gulf conflict. I suspect it was this concern that prompted officials to restrict TV coverage. War is only attractively telereal when it is a product of Hollywood or when its imagery can be confined to tapes of surgical bomb raids that bear closer resemblance to a Nintendo® game than to most battle scenes. Otherwise, war will seldom fare well on the screen because television will always understate the invisible reasons for the conflict.

The Vietnam War suffered from such technological distortion, argues former news correspondent David Halberstam. We saw the action, the violence, mostly from our side where the cameras could gain access, and what we saw repulsed and frightened us. TV brought us the horrors of war but could not convey the meaning behind the images.

Conversely, the strength and control of the enemy were understated because of the unavailability of TV visuals. The networks could not show how skillfully the Vietcong replenished themselves, says Halberstam, because they lacked the film to depict it and other important aspects concerning the enemy. Yet those elements were major factors in the outcome of the war.[2]

It remains to be seen if America has the courage to fight necessary wars in the future that may fare poorly on TV because the reasons behind them are not sufficiently telereal.

Accessibility is always a major factor in what becomes telereal. Television news was criticized several years ago for ignoring conflicts in Afghanistan and Cambodia, but as one frustrated network producer pointed out, "How are you going to charge your [camera] batteries when you're in the middle of the jungle?"[3] The same question was raised by photographers in the Saudi Arabian desert where TV crews covering the Iraqi war battled with melted video cables and cameras full of sand. I can sympathize to a degree. My crews and I experienced similar technological horrors while trying to cover news in the sweltering summer heat of the Arizona desert.

Coverage can be greatly affected by something as simple as a camera breakdown. Events of great importance can happen, but if the camera is not present or able to record them, they pale in significance or fade into oblivion. Can you imagine what a difference in impact it might have made had cameras not been on hand to record the explosion of the space shuttle in 1986? Although a story of that magnitude would still have been important, the impact on the public might have been decidedly different had Americans not been subjected night after night to replays of the explosion and the paralyzing emotional fallout from it.

Jan Novak points out the political dangers of being conditioned to salivate only to what can be seen through a camera lens. The Western world, with all its problems and warts, he writes, evokes emotional reaction and criticism in the eyes of the world, whereas the faults of totalitarian regimes recede from consciousness unless a sudden flash of something seeable illuminates them. Injustice in South Africa is vividly telereal to the West, but serious human indignities and atrocities in the Communist bloc or the Middle East remained hidden from Western sight for a long time and were, for years, considerably less conscience provoking or fashionable to care about.[4] It is a distorted view of the world, argues Novak, to allow TV visibility to dictate significance.

When the availability of pictures dictates coverage, editorial decision making becomes slanted toward convenience, because generating good videotape is a laborious, demanding job. Producers often lean toward covering stories that can be easily photographed in the least amount of time, trouble, and expense. That tends to make TV news highly scheduled and bureaucratic. Decisions are made in the direction of events that are almost sure to pan out as opposed to those that might in essence be more newsworthy but are less predictable in terms of visual outcome. This tendency creates an inherent bias toward what we call media events—those visible spectacles that are easily planned for and quickly and easily photographed.

> *When Americans become too conditioned to telereality they are in a position to be emotionally manipulated by whomever or whatever controls the TV camera.*

Because pictures are crucial, events sometimes must be reenacted or at least orchestrated in an effort to capture something usable on videotape. That is an unfortunate but necessary by-product of TV news. No matter how legitimate the story, sometimes what viewers see on video is contrived to a certain degree. The practice is not the result of a deliberate attempt on the part of the producers or the subjects to misinform so much as it is a necessary attempt to satisfy the needs of the camera. The rise of TV news brought with it the growth of contrived protest created for the sake of making causes telereal.

Sometimes necessity leads to extremes. I recall one incident in my career when I showed up late to cover a planned protest against nuclear power after being sent to a breaking news story first. When my crew and I finally arrived at the protest site, the demonstrators were sitting on the ground and in their cars, impatiently tapping their feet and checking their watches. "Where have you been?" the organizer yelled at us. "We were supposed to start forty-five minutes ago!"

Suppressing an urge to jump into the news van and drive away, I motioned to our cameraman to begin taping. Almost immediately, the group jumped to their feet, placards raised, and began pacing back and forth for the camera's benefit. They staged their protest no longer than it took us to gather enough tape for the evening news, stopping only moments after the camera quit taping and vanishing before we could even load our equipment back into the news van.

Having to cover such events was troubling to me. But we did so in that instance because it was Saturday, a traditionally slow news day in television, and because nuclear power is a newsworthy but difficult-to-visualize subject. The demonstrators staged the protest to make their objections to nuclear power telereal. In the end, we used each other out of the necessity to satisfy the needs of a visual medium.

When Americans become too conditioned to telereality they are in a position to be emotionally manipulated by whomever or whatever controls the TV camera. Protesters eventually learned that they only had to stage their made-for-TV display long enough to meet the needs of TV crews. Not only did elements of fantasy and theatricality begin to creep into real issues of public concern, but television news was now wide open for exploitation. I suspect that the Kent State shootings were at least partly the result of manipulation by radical individuals who understood that deliberately inciting violence would generate publicity. While working for a major network, I was told by a veteran cameraman involved in covering the Kent State incident that the night before the shootings his news bureau was tipped by telephone to be present because something significant was going to happen. If that was true, it would demonstrate the length to which some will go to make their cause telereal.

It is unsettling to realize that most of what tomorrow's generation will know and understand about today may hinge almost entirely on how TV treats it. History that has not been prerecorded will be difficult to make telereal. Historian Daniel Boorstin expressed the fear a number of years ago that without video or film footage the mere facts of history would lose significance to literal, image-oriented people in the TV age. Lamented Boorstin: "By filling his present moment with experiences engrossing and overwhelming, television [has] dulled the American's sense of his past."[5]

We know that when producers want to favor a view, pictures can be manipulated. But at other times, when technological factors begin to assert their influence, the camera lies in spite of the best efforts of any producer to prevent it. British TV journalist Malcolm Muggeridge once said of TV images, "Not only can the camera lie, it always lies."[6] What did he mean by such a statement? Is what TV shows an unhampered reflection of actual happenings or a mechanically created illusion? Stay tuned.

NOTES

1. Jan Novak, "'Telereality' in the Soviet Bloc," *Newsweek*, May 27, 1985, p. 16.
2. David Halberstam, "TV and Vietnam—Looking Back: Medals—and Demerits— for Performance Under Fire," *TV Guide*, April 20, 1985, p. 34.
3. Rod Townley, "The Wars TV Doesn't Show You—and Why," *TV Guide*, August 18, 1984, p. 3.
4. Novak, "Telereality," p. 16.
5. Daniel Boorstin, quoted by Daniel Schorr, *Clearing the Air* (Boston.: Houghton Mifflin, 1977), pp. 289-90.
6. Malcolm Muggeridge, *Christ and the Media* (Grand Rapids: Eerdmans, 1977), p. 106.

6

HOW AND WHY THE CAMERA LIES

What the late British TV journalist Malcolm Muggeridge meant when he said that the camera always lies is that nothing goes through the television production process and comes out exactly the same way. There are necessary and important changes that occur in the process of photography (especially moving picture photography) and editing. Those changes inherently transform the final impressions left behind by pictures.

Perhaps some of you have discovered the truth of this, as I have, after taking a vacation trip. My husband and I have spent hours pouring over travel brochures in an effort to pick out the most desirable place to visit, only to discover after arriving that the alluring photos we based our expectations on weren't completely representative. Upon arriving in the Bahamas for our honeymoon, we discovered that the glossy pictures of crystal blue waters, spotless white sand, and lush green vegetation did not accurately depict the dirty, worn conditions of some of the heavily used beaches or the damp, mildewed hotel interiors that are the inevitable result of high humidity on a tropical island. Such subtle details simply aren't communicated in photographs. We were oversold by the photos.

Although it can be argued that in this case the deception was due in part to what the editors of the brochures chose to show, it is also true that there is a limit to how much can be conveyed though a photograph. Having been on both sides of the lens, I have discovered that substantial amounts of nuance and detail can be lost in the excursion from real life to videotape. As one author points out, we fail to think about, or we underestimate, what touch, taste, smell, or just mood and intuition contribute to our perception.[1] Although those nuances are subtle, they make a difference—and all are lost in the journey through the lens. As one critic put it, it is the total "aura" of something that withers away in the mechanically reproduced image.[2]

> *So what the viewer sees is not the actual event but an edited recreation of the event.*

Some accuse reporters of interpreting events exclusively from their own limited perspective, but it seldom occurs to most critics that cameras too have their own limited way of viewing things. All kinds of distortions are built into the technology of motion picture taking. I personally found pictures themselves to be much more interpretive and less flexible to deal with at times than human producers. Robert MacNeil, the anchor of public television's "Mac-Neil-Lehrer News Hour," once remarked: "Like the human digestive system, *television alters what it consumes*—comedy, sports, news, drama, education, religion."[3]

What MacNeil means is that TV news footage is subject to all kinds of rigid demands in the production process. Much of what television shows us as a final product has been changed in some way from its original state because of technological factors. Television audiences don't stop to think, for example, that when a photographer begins to take pictures of an event, not everything that happens is recorded. Instead, only bits and pieces of the event are recorded from different angles. The different scenes are later joined in the editing process to look as though they occurred in sequence. The moment a camera begins its work, images are frozen in time and space and are lifted out of their original circumstances to be played back in a highly compressed sequence at a later time and in a different place. The original context of all televised events is lost to the viewer.

So what the viewer sees is not the actual event but an edited recreation of the event. Viewing a news event through the eye of a camera and drawing a conclusion is like trying to decide what kind of city you live in based only on the view from the peephole in your front door. The camera lens can point only in one direction at a time, display only what is within the camera's range at that time, and capture only a limited portion of whatever it focuses on. The impression left is as much a function of what the camera cannot show as what it can.

After passing through the lens, real experience is transformed into a flat, celluloid image that is greatly compressed, affected by distance, and limited to one dimension. Every picture is confined to the limits of the camera's own perception. I have yet to see a picture post card or movie of the Grand Canyon that can fully capture its beauty and grandeur or the feeling that comes when you stand on the edge and peer into its vast expanse. To truly appreciate the Grand Canyon, you must experience it in person, with the full range of your senses.

The inherent lack of context in photography can distort a viewer's final impression. When I first began reporting TV news in the Phoenix area, Arizona was in a cycle of winter flooding that transformed typically dry washes into raging torrents. Water roared down the Salt River bed and into the metropolitan Phoenix area at two hundred thousand cubic feet per second. Roads built through the normally dry river bed would wash away, and bridges not constructed to endure such a flow would crumble like Tinker-toys® in the wake of the water's awesome force.

Those spectacles made great TV news footage, and each time they occurred television crews flocked to the banks of the Salt River to photograph the raging torrent. The pictures were then beamed via satellite to network outlets in New York and Los Angeles for the national news. Sometimes after the pictures would make their network appearance, my mother—or a friend or relative from someplace else—would call, anxious to see if I was washing away with the entire city. And indeed, if the pictures were indicative of the condition of the entire Phoenix area, my callers had reason for concern.

But in reality, most of Phoenix and its surrounding suburbs were unaffected by the floods. That was the context of the story. But those surrounding circumstances, even when pointed out verbally, were lost in the tightly photographed images of roaring water. The camera's range was too limited to show the river flow in relationship to what was happening in the rest of Phoenix. Although no reporter had made a deliberate attempt to deceive the viewer, a type of technological deception took place by way of the image.

Information via the camera becomes relative. When visual events are lifted out of their original framework, it is difficult to know whether what you see is the exception to the rule or the norm, since television deals with both in the same general way. The TV viewer is left with raw impressions based not only on pictures lifted out of their original setting but often on pictures that had been further rearranged for maximum cosmetic appeal.

Faulty impressions of a vacation spot or a flood are relatively harmless examples of how TV's editing affects viewer perception. However, when context affects judgment about governments and national or international events, or when matters of public policy and world destiny are affected, the question of distorted TV imagery takes on a more disquieting tone. Think back for a moment to the televised images you remember from the Iranian hostage crisis in 1980. Remember those chanting demonstrators outside the American embassy in Teheran, packed in front of the camera like canned sardines, waving their fists at the lens, and chanting "Death to America!"? The impression Americans were left with after watching those reports was that Teheran was a city in complete turmoil.

But one American journalist told a different story. When he traveled to Teheran to cover the crisis, apprehensively expecting to be greeted by mass uprising, he discovered upon his arrival that such signs of visible animosity towards America were for the most part confined to short, carefully orchestrated demonstrations performed by a handful of zealots for the benefit of American television networks. Newsman George Lewis told NBC colleague Garrick Utley: "The cameras convey a picture of a nation in the grip of madness, and yet just a few blocks away from the embassy gates people are going about their lives in a normal fashion. Mothers are taking their babies to the park. Businesses are opened. Teheran is pretty much working as normal."[4]

If we had been able to view the angry crowd of demonstrators within the context of the whole city, would our perception of the hostage crisis and of Iran have differed? Were the chanting demonstrators truly representative of the feelings of most Iranians? Were the demonstrations a dependable gauge of the political state of the country? What about the disposition of those in power, but out of range of the camera's eye? Those are important questions the camera alone cannot answer. In the Iranian hostage situation the networks were using a staged demonstration in an attempt to portray the reality of a situation not easily accessible or visible. The pictures left a distorted impression, but not to have used them would have left news producers with a blank screen.

Both the demonstrations and the American hostage situation were made-for-television events. Yet it is also true that there was a legitimate political crisis in Iran. How accurately did the videotape of the demonstrators communicate the real situation? That is a question that needs to be asked by viewers each time a similar visual drama unfolds anywhere in the world. Similar images of anti-American demonstrations in Jordan filled TV screens during the Gulf War. Such images are difficult to interpret on face value alone.

Physical conditions such as the amount of available light, how much space a photographer has to maneuver in a room, or how competent the photographer is can exert a major influence on the quality of the image. The camera's zoom lens either diminishes or magnifies whatever or whomever it focuses on. What is large and imposing often shrinks under the eye of the lens, whereas what is small or ordinary is magnified and grows in stature and significance.

The majority of TV camera shots are close-ups, because too much detail is lost at a far away range to give objects visual significance. Consequently, what we see in a typical visual sequence is a string of highly magnified close-up shots. Ordinary people and objects become instantly more significant under the camera's magnified gaze. The psychological effect is subtle, but powerful. Riots, demonstrations, and other events look more important after their transformation by the camera lens. On the TV screen, game show hosts, actors, politicians all loom larger than life. Presidents appear heroic and almost superhuman in office until they transgress under the glaring eye of the TV camera. Highly amplified character flaws sometimes overpower a carefully cultivated public relations image, which quickly melts away in the heat of mass exposure.

> *The editing process is something like*
> *verbally exaggerating stories for*
> *maximum effect—a practice some*
> *of us enjoy from time to time.*

Editing also adds major elements of distortion to moving pictures, but the changes are barely noticeable to the untrained eye. In editing, recorded images are chopped up, rearranged, sped up, slowed down, shortened, interrupted, and blended with parts of other images—and then reassembled into a simulation of reality that gives the appearance of a logical sequence of action. Editing removes our senses still another step from authenticity.[5]

Though sometimes a story is edited in a certain way deliberately to make a point, far more frequently the specific editing that occurs is dictated by technological demands. Consider, for example, an account in a Christian magazine about antiabortion legislation coverage in Colorado. The state's proabortion governor publicly debated an antiabortion activist, and the debate was covered by local TV news operations. The governor's remarks were politely applauded by the audience, whereas the statements of the spokesperson opposing abortion received a standing ovation. Antiabortion activists were justifiably upset when a Denver TV station showed the governor speaking, with shots of the audience's standing ovation immediately following. A faulty final impression was the result, and the station was accused of deliberate distortion.[6]

I don't blame antiabortion activists for being angry, and the effect could have been deliberate, but in many deadline-pressured situations, often the tape editor is genuinely unaware of the natural sequence of events and how they should come together. Based only on the fragmented raw video shots that editors work from, it was probably impossible for the editor to know who the audience was applauding, because most raw videotaped shots are seen by editors out of their original context. To an editor hastily searching through raw video for the pictures he needs to meet an on-air deadline, it will not be obvious who was applauding whom. One type of shot is edited to follow the next because certain types of pictures are needed at that particular moment to create an attractively choreographed video sequence, not necessarily because an editor is intent on slanting story content.

I am guessing that, in this situation, an editor had a shot of a speaker at a podium (the governor in this case) and he needed to follow it with a shot of the audience. The most attractive, action-packed picture was the standing ovation. What looked like deliberate misinterpretation could merely have been an error stemming from ignorance of the actual sequence of events. Such sequential errors are common and in the heat of the deadline almost unpreventable in TV news.

In many ways, the camera has revolutionized our lives for the better. Now, with the advent of film and video, important fragments of the past can be relived again and again via celluloid and tape. We have learned to trust the camera for glimpses of history we would otherwise never be a part of.

But we should not be so fascinated by the color images that pour from the set each day that we are unaware that such pictures are not always reliable standards of judgment. We need to develop the conscious awareness of a television insider and remember that the television illusion is often like an image in a fun house mirror—a distorted, disproportionate reflection that can, in the end, mislead regardless of the producer's intention.

Now that many Americans have home video cameras to capture their own personal events on tape, they are finding out how unattractive and boring unedited video can be and are beginning to appreciate the need for polishing. The editing process is something like verbally exaggerating stories for maximum effect—a practice some of us enjoy from time to time. It accomplishes the same result visually.

Editing heightens drama, action, and interest; minimizes the camera's shortcomings; gets rid of unusable, unattractive, lengthy, or boring video sequences; and renders the finished product clean and smooth in appearance. Editing adds interest, which, we will discover, is another indispensible component of the television illusion.

NOTES

1. Malcolm Muggeridge, *Christ and the Media* (Grand Rapids: Eerdmans, 1997), p. 106.
2. Walter Benjamin, quoted by Jerry Mander, *Four Arguments for the Elimination of Television* (New York: William Morrow, 1978), pp. 279-85.
3. Robert MacNeil, quoted by Billy Graham, "TV Evangelism: Billy Graham Sees Dangers Ahead," *TV Guide*, March 5, 1983, p. 5.
4. George Lewis in an NBC-TV Special Report, "Crisis in Iran: One Year After the Shah, Day 75," January 16, 1980, 11:30 P.M., quoted by David Altheide, *Media Power* (Beverly Hills, Calif.: Sage, 1985), p. 84.
5. See Mander, *Four Arguments*, p. 248, on this process.
6. Sharon Donohue, "David Beats Goliath in Abortion Clash," *Moody Monthly*, February, 1985, p. 93.

7

THE GREATEST SIN
IN TELEVISION

C hristian speaker and author Patsy Clairmont tells of sending
her son Jason off to school one morning, only to hear the
doorbell ring moments later. When she opened the front
door, there stood her little boy. "Jason," exclaimed Patsy,
"what are you doing here? You're supposed to be on the bus!"

"I don't want to go to school," came the reply.

"Why?" demanded Patsy.

Jason shrugged, "It's too long, and it's too boring."

"Jason," Patsy countered, "you've just described life—now
get back on the bus!"

Real news events, like school and real life, are often too tedious and too boring to fit well into the confines of the TV format.
Television claims to show events just as they happen, but if it really
did, the majority of Americans would not watch for very long. Like
Jason and school, we reject what we see if it bears too strong a
resemblance to real life. We turn to television more often to escape
the boredom of real existence than to experience it. If we don't find
the escape we are searching for, we turn to something else.

News events are often too tedious, lengthy, and unexciting to be accurately portrayed by a medium that must be constantly stimulating to hold its audience. In television news, comments PBS anchor Robert MacNeil, "You have to broadcast for two kinds of people. You have to broadcast for the interested and the attentive, and the uninterested and inattentive, inevitably, or you wouldn't get the numbers [the audience]. [So] you put on lots of visual gimmickry . . . so that there's more chewing gum for the eyeballs for the inattentive and uninterested."[1]

> *Many viewers who are heavily conditioned to televised dramas, which have a definite beginning and a quick resolution, found themselves unconsciously viewing coverage of the Persian Gulf War as though it were a fictional miniseries.*

With so many things competing for our attention, the only way television can assure itself of an audience is to pelt our senses continually with action-packed images interesting enough to draw us away from the other aspects of life that claim our time. In both news and entertainment, sense bombardment is the chief means it has of getting and keeping viewers.

Much of television is a continuous stream of fast-paced imagery. The TV production process effectively isolates the dramatic from the mundane, ties it up into a neat little package, and delivers it in engaging fashion. The result in TV journalism is news for people who hate news. The outcome is stimulating to look at, but not necessarily a completely accurate recreation of events.

Like oil and water, interest and importance do not blend easily. Injecting interest into a story slants the material and sometimes comes at the expense of information. When a producer programs for the marginally interested, the emphasis shifts toward amusement and action and away from mere information. In each successive presidential campaign, we hear more and more complaints about the lack of issues discussed on television news. That is not surprising, because, unfortunately, the issues are often visually boring and undramatic. Issues fail to capture the public's attention in the same way that a good round of political name-calling does. However, every moment added to political coverage for the sake of visual excitement, drama, cosmetic appeal, or entertainment value takes time from something that may be more important but carries less diversion value.

Part of the problem, points out communications professor Neil Postman, is that television is simply too "user friendly"—it's just "too easy to turn off," so it must be made enticing.[2] The measuring stick of public information in America today, declares Postman, is not whether something is true but whether it is interesting. Postman, author of the provocative book *Amusing Ourselves to Death*, insists that since television must be interesting in order to hold audience, both events and personalities channeled through television "appear inevitably to be packaged as a form of entertainment."[3]

Important issues and events, matters of public business, even war itself, inevitably deteriorate into matters of show business on TV. We saw this happen during Operation Desert Storm. Many viewers who are heavily conditioned to televised dramas, which have a definite beginning and a quick resolution, found themselves unconsciously viewing coverage of the Persian Gulf War as though it were a fictional miniseries. The confusion is understandable. Complete with theme music and flashy, colorful, computer-generated graphics and titles, the "Showdown in the Gulf," as CNN called it, might just have easily been called "Shogun in the Gulf." One newspaper columnist put this way:

> The Persian Gulf is a stage, and all the world an audience . . .
> just relax in that easy chair, open a beer, a bag of chips maybe, and
> tune into "WAR IN THE GULF." . . . Television has made war
> seem almost surrealistic . . . especially when CNN's "WAR IN THE
> GULF" logo in bold red with pounding war drums flashes on the
> screen. Especially when television cuts easily from Iraqi Scud mis-
> sile attacks to Alpo dog food commercials.[4]

Some feared that if the fighting failed to resolve itself as quickly as the plot of a miniseries, Americans would eventually grow bored and demand a happy ending.

The box has been simultaneously spewing out both news and entertainment packaged in much the same way for so many years now that distinctions between the two have simply blurred in the American mind. Av Westin, former executive producer of ABC's "20/20" news magazine, believes that viewers are now conditioned to hold the same expectations for both news and entertainment. He notes: "Americans have been video-educated" by sitcoms and cop shows "to expect emotional payoffs every twelve minutes. . . . The payoff-every-12-minutes format is so dominant that the news divisions have been forced—not unwillingly, in many cases—to adopt it."[5] Eighty-three percent of those asked in a study on viewer attitudes said they expected television to inform them, whereas almost as many—82 percent, expected it to entertain them. Viewers expect both at the same time.[6]

Although the end product of TV often
does reflect a humanistic view, for
a variety of complex reasons such an
analysis of the TV industry is simplistic,
shallow, naive, and misleading.

Don Hewitt, the executive producer of CBS's highly successful TV news magazine "60 Minutes," summarizes the dilemma of making news on the same screen that spews out situation comedy and drama: "There's a fine line between reality and show biz, and the trick is to walk up to that line, touch it with your toe, and make sure you do not cross it, if you do a show like I do."[7]

But often the magnetic pull of ratings and revenues on the other side of the line becomes a powerful undertow, drowning accuracy in entertainment value. The fact that "60 Minutes" consistently ranks among the most watched TV programs, along with the most popular sitcoms and dramas, should tell us something.

The danger in TV's bias toward interest and entertainment is that it conditions viewers to believe and expect that vital information can always be stimulating. We unconsciously approach the set with the attitude that if what we see doesn't hold our attention, it must not be worth knowing. Many claim TV has made us the best informed generation in history, but how can this be if we are attentive only to what amuses and titillates us? Like little Jason, we are less terrified of ignorance than we are of boredom. We can't be truly informed because, like drug addicts, we can't rid ourselves of the insatiable desire to feel pleasure in the process.

Interest is a fickle standard for newsworthiness. When interest takes precedence over importance, initially uninteresting events are often ignored until their public significance suddenly escalates, leaving networks and news operations scrambling to catch up on their coverage. While I worked as a reporter at a local network station several years ago, our news staff was subjected to a presentation from a news consulting service designed to heighten our awareness of what people were really interested in seeing on the news. It was called "Carrie Ann" and was a videotaped profile of an allegedly typical female viewer. The way to hold Carrie Ann's attention, according to this presentation, was to focus on consumer stories about the price of beef in the local supermarket. Forget reporting about international affairs, we were advised, because "Carrie Ann doesn't care about what is happening in Iran."

But Iran cared what was happening to Carrie Ann. It was 1979, and dark skinned, angry looking Iranian students were demonstrating against the Shah almost daily outside our station in an effort to attract network attention. Our cameras ignored them day after day, until several months later, when fifty Americans were suddenly seized as hostages at the American embassy in Iran. Within hours, hundreds of thousands of "Carrie Anns" were shocked, angry, and confused, demanding to know what had prompted such an action. Iran was suddenly more interesting than the local price of beef. The taped presentation we were urged to emulate was spirited into oblivion by an embarrassed news management that now scrambled to explain to a demanding public what had led to the events in Iran.

The quest for what will hold a fickle public's interest and translate into cumulative audience and subsequent revenues is a bias that underlies and controls most of the TV industry. Audience rejection is far too costly a price to pay in a medium totally dependent on an audience for its economic survival. A newspaper makes a profit simply by selling a paper, but television must hold its audience to turn a profit. In my experience, the pressure to hype for the sake of interest was, at times, a far greater bias than any pressure to conform a story to someone's moral agenda.

One preacher and author has asserted that the first objective of the networks is not to make money but to spread antimoral humanism.[8] Although the end product of TV often does reflect a humanistic view, for a variety of complex reasons such an analysis of the TV industry is simplistic, shallow, naive, and misleading. It vastly underestimates the need of a TV producer to generate interest for the sake of profit. As one former CBS executive point-blank admitted to sociologist Todd Gitlin: "I'm not interested in culture. I'm not interested in pro-social values. I have only one interest. That's whether people watch the program. That's my definition of good, that's my definition of bad."[9] It is a pervasive view that one TV screenwriter dubs "Capitalist Realism."[10]

Television in America is big business. The primary goal of all television is to sell a product. Owning a TV station, in the words of one broadcaster, is like having a license to print money. Admits "60 Minutes" executive producer Don Hewitt: "Nobody's ever asked me a question about television to which the answer was not money."[11]

Holding public attention translates into millions of dollars in advertising revenue. A single thirty-second commercial spot in a network news show can cost between fifty and sixty thousand dollars; a thirty-second commercial in a popular sitcom can run as high as one hundred to three hundred thousand dollars apiece.[12] The loss of a single ratings point in prime time can cost a network millions. Although many TV producers may hold liberal views, especially where sexual morality is concerned, news and entertainment producers are not just pushing a liberal moral agenda; they have simply discovered that debauchery sells better than virtue. It is not the philosophy of humanism they worship, it is the great god Nielsen. Ideology may enter in to a degree, but when it does, in many cases it is tightly intertwined with the profit motive.

Television is an awkward love triangle between information, entertainment, and profit. Sometimes I think that TV producers are better theologians than they get credit for, at least in terms of understanding the depravity of man. The Bible tells us that in our natural fallen condition we are predisposed not to want good, but evil. Unfortunately, in either news or entertainment, sex, violence, and controversy are highly effective, intriguing types of sense bombardment that have proved to be effective formulas for generating audience.

Former White House Press Secretary Jody Powell insisted: "The major bias in journalism, it seems to me, the one most likely to promote deception and dishonesty, has its roots in economics. The fact is, news has to sell, or those who report it and edit it will find themselves searching for a new job. And that creates a bias to make news reports interesting."[13] According to Powell, the problems arise when the requirements of being interesting and being accurate part company.

In the news business, competition for viewers breeds a bias toward sensationalism. I discovered early in my reporting career that the meek in TV journalism are definitely not the ones who inherit the earth, or the next rung of the corporate ladder. Reporters who play the "make-it-interesting" game with the greatest zeal are those who are the most handsomely rewarded. As a Christian, I found myself torn between being accurate in reporting and trying to please my employer. On one occasion, I invested considerable time and effort on a local political story only to find it to be worthless in terms of being newsworthy. "The story's not that interesting," I warned my executive producer. Desperate for something to fill a spot on our six o'clock show, he fired back: "Then you *make* it interesting!"

When I worked as a TV reporter, we were told in a set of written guidelines from a major TV news consultant that everything we produced should attempt to "bait, lure, grab, tempt, invite, entice, arouse, beckon, seduce, attract, promise, enchant, capture, intrigue, tantalize, and fascinate." It was our job, the consultants said, to tease our viewers into watching. An in-house memo we received concluded: "Teases don't deliver, they just promise to." Broken promises in television news are acceptable as long as the desired result is achieved—the audience is beguiled into watching.

Network news operations accused of trying to undermine the government are often simply trying to broadcast what sells.

It is proverbial that the greatest sin in TV is to be boring. And if the greatest sin is to be boring, then the greatest temptation is to be entertaining and interesting, even at the expense of fact, context, slant, and accuracy.

One way to keep people watching is to show something guaranteed to strike a responsive chord in the viewer. Often dissonant chords work better than harmonious ones. We are born with a certain amount of normal fearful curiosity—an innate desire to investigate the negative, potentially dangerous, or frightening. A psychiatrist who has studied the subject writes: "The mass media have discovered, through intuition and research, that negative messages are highly interesting to large audiences, and they are providing increasing amounts."[14] Viewers may complain about gory news footage of accidents or intrusive shots of mishaps, but most people are glued to their sets, gazing in rapt curiosity while such stories are shown.

Crisis is another audience builder. As one network news executive noted, a bonding process takes place between news anchors and the audience in times of crisis. Perhaps at no time in the history of television news was that more apparent than in 1991 during the war in the Gulf.

Similarly, it is the unusual event that woos the camera. We are curious about the exception, not the rule—the car that didn't make it home safely, not the thousands that did. TV news bends toward controversy, because it is conflict, not tranquillity, that holds us spellbound. And so the parade of news stories across our TV screens is often a string of sense-bombarding calamities and conflicts, occasionally sweetened with features to break up the negativism.

The tendency of reporters to chip away at an incumbent president is a manifestation of the need to focus on controversy. Verbal criticism of people and policies is laden with natural drama. Network news operations accused of trying to undermine the government are often simply trying to broadcast what sells, but by endlessly pursuing controversy for the sake of interest, they publicly amplify the nation's ills to the point of distortion.

Unfortunately, the constant stream of negative imagery leaves a pessimistic residue and affects our ability to care. As TV critic Tom Shales notes: "Persistent exposure to televised calamities . . . may have given us all asbestos sensitivities."[15] Television, concludes Robert MacNeil, has wound the events of our day into a spiral of urgency and sensationalism. "Every year the dial is turned another gauge on what is acceptable in terms of visual shock."[16] MacNeil warns that the bias of interest brings out the worst practices in some journalists—winding the world's events up to the extreme of tension, danger, and violence. Many viewers are now so conditioned to this approach that unless information charges like a bolt of electricity they no longer hear the message or care about what they see.

Keeping news and entertainment tightly packaged and quick moving—a series of high points strung together in rapid video sequence—is another way to hold audience interest. Like a master illusionist, the sleight-of-hand tricks of TV production can so preoccupy our thought processes that we barely notice the unreasonably short amount of time the information is delivered in or the lack of real content. Everything in television, both news and entertainment, is gathered and presented at a greatly accelerated pace— but like a car driven too fast for conditions, vehicles of information moving at too high a speed can kill accuracy, awareness, and understanding.

NOTES

1. Robert McNeil, quoted by Rushworth M. Kidder, "Videoculture 3: Do 'Mediagenic' Candidates Make Good Leaders?" *The Christian Science Monitor*, June 12, 1985, p. 19. Reprinted by permission from *The Christian Science Monitor* © 1985 The Christian Science Publishing Society. All rights reserved.

2. Neil Postman, *Amusing Ourselves to Death* (New York: Penguin, 1985), p. 121.

3. Neil Postman, quoted by Kidder, "Videoculture," p. 19.

4. Peter Durantine, "TV Coverage, Too Much, Too Fast," *The York Daily Record*, January 27, 1991, p. 1-G.

5. Av Westin, quoted by Don Kowet, "Documentaries Witness a Revival," *Insight*, October 30, 1989, pp. 47-48.

6. "Behind the Viewing," *Broadcasting*, November 12, 1984, p. 76.

7. Don Hewitt, quoted in "Hewitt Defends CBS's News Programming," *Broadcasting*, February 18, 1985, p. 76.

8. Tim LaHaye, *The Battle for the Family* (Old Tappan, N.J.: Revell, 1982), p. 110.

9. Arnold Becker, quoted by Lloyd Billingsley, "TV: Where the Girls Are Good Looking and the Good Guys Always Win," *Christianity Today*, October 4, 1985, p. 39. Copyright © 1985 by *Christianity Today*. Used by permission.

10. Ibid.

11. Don Hewitt, quoted by Tom Shales, "'60 Minutes' Pot of Gold Lures Networks," *The Arizona Republic*, May 26, 1985, p. F-6.

12. A. C. Nielsen and the Television Advertising Bureau, 1990.

13. Jody Powell, *The Other Side of the Story* (New York: William Morrow, 1984), p. 15.

14. Jack B. Haskins, "The Morbid Seducers," *Channels of Communication*, January/February, 1986, p. 79.

15. Tom Shales, "Coverage of the Hostage Crisis Accustoms Viewers to Tragedy," *The Arizona Republic*, July 5, 1985, p. E-5.

16. Robert MacNeil, quoted by Kidder, *Videoculture*, p. 19.

8

GOLIATH'S FOOT IN DAVID'S SHOE

Television is a mental roller coaster that moves its audience at a speed faster than real life. It whisks us from one crisis or amusement to another in breathless succession, with little or no transition. One reason TV news stories are fast paced is to hold the viewer's interest. However, a less obvious but important reason is because it is a complicated, time-consuming task to assemble even the briefest news story. It is partly out of sheer necessity that reporters crush the world's problems into tiny time frames. Longer stories would require significantly more time, effort, and expense to produce, and meeting deadlines would be harder.

Time limits exert tremendous editorial control and are really another type of censorship. When I produced, I was forced to be more attentive to the clock than to content. We had to sort through details and accept only what can be fused into a few statements. Such constraints are suffocating. ABC's Jeff Greenfield complains that time constraints are one of the most troubling biases of TV news: "There's never enough time to tell the whole story; never enough time to prepare; never enough air time to explain the subtleties. Network news may be presented in living color, but often the substance comes out black and white because it would take too long to note all the shades of grey."[1]

Sometimes stories are lengthened or other stories added to a news program not because of their inherent significance but because it is a slow news day and there is time to fill. Conversely, on days loaded with major events, dozens of other newsworthy events must be ignored or abbreviated because of the sheer lack of time in the program. Most stories average from thirty seconds to a minute and a half in length. To think that a realistic impression of any situation could be adequately presented in such a short interval isn't just bad mathematics, it's the ultimate fantasy.

Program constraints are equally stifling. Both the networks and local stations promise a comprehensive look at our world, but the real world simply will not fit into a half hour. Each day, a handful of events are chosen from among hundreds of potential stories and a dozen or so are shoehorned into about twenty-two minutes. A significant amount of money and effort is invested in TV news production, yet the end result sometimes translates into relatively little in terms of actual substance. Although TV news delivers the imagery that newspapers often cannot, most viewers who regard it so highly are unaware that the actual volume of written information from a nightly newscast could not fill the front page of a daily newspaper.

Yet research suggests that viewers show a preference for newscasts containing more stories that are shorter than for newscasts containing fewer stories that have greater depth. Shorter stories in greater numbers leave the viewer with the illusion of more information. Viewers unconsciously trade quality for quantity.

Most people perceive TV's highly condensed news stories to be much longer than they actually are. It is not how long it is, a former boss once told me, but how long it seems to the viewer that counts. Most viewers come away thinking they have "seen it all" when in fact they have seen very little—and they have barely noticed.

Televised information is not only delivered quickly, it is gathered quickly. Concludes ABC-TV commentator and syndicated columnist George Will: "Journalism, at all times, but especially television journalism, is done on the fly, and there's often just not enough time."[2] Not enough time to carefully select viewpoints, sift information, or consider all angles.

Reporting, from my own experience, was a mad rush from city hall to the state legislature, never stopping long enough to fully think through the workings of either. I sometimes found it impossible to weed through the volumes of circumstances surrounding important events and at the same time meet unrealistically short deadlines. It is a problem that plagues the industry at all levels. NBC anchor Tom Brokaw admits: "We rush from event to event, simply because we are able, too seldom pausing to reflect on what we have just witnessed."[3] The last may be first in the spiritual realm, but in the pressure cooker world of modern media deadlines, the reverse is true.

TV news reporters work under a heavier deadline burden than print reporters, because they must not only gather information but engage in the cumbersome job of video production.

Unfortunately, information reported too quickly is often insufficiently analyzed or researched. Sometimes a story simply has not had time to develop and evolve to the point of accuracy. This bias toward immediacy was embarrassingly obvious in early TV coverage in the Persian Gulf war. Live coverage of reporters spouting off-the-cuff information about missile attacks spawned a global rumor mill instead of an informed public. The frenzied, surreal coverage of Tel Aviv bombings during the first forty-eight hours of the Middle East war were a case in point. Much of the information released in those initial delirious moments later proved inaccurate. But in the rush to be first, reporters were pressured on the air by the capacity for immediacy long before they were sure what they were talking about.

Hasty information gathering, compelled by pressure to beat the competitor, greatly increases the margin of error in news gathering and places immense pressure on people being interviewed. All are the by-products of a system driven by deadlines artificially imposed by commercial competition. Being first and fast sometimes takes precedence over being right.

As we saw in the war with Iraq, much of what TV now shows is undelayed, for technology now allows us to beam back pictures instantly of whatever is visual and accessible. But this latest influx of high technology has its own downside. "The technology drives the machine," complains ABC news anchor Ted Koppel. "We're getting to the point where reaction time has to be instantaneous. . . . Leaders are given no time [by the news media] to consider anything. . . . Some nights, I wish the satellite wouldn't work. I'm not sure that simply to do it first, slickly, instantly, even competently, is the way to do it thoughtfully."[4]

TV news reporters work under a heavier deadline burden than print reporters, because they must not only gather information but engage in the cumbersome job of video production. I was often forced to spend more time handling technological details than in researching the story. Foreign network correspondents wrestling with global satellite capacity grumble that they are losing control to the machine. Complains ABC news correspondent Charles Glass: "Out of a 24-hour day . . . you have perhaps only three hours in the field to gather information. The rest of your time is spent in getting it out—dealing with the crew, making sure the tape is OK, editing, seeing that the satellite works. . . . You're dealing with the communications apparatus, and sacrificing time on the story."[5]

Story length and speed of delivery conspire to create another bias in television, the bias against complexity in an increasingly complex world. When news events are redesigned to fit time limits and oversimplified to fit the format, content changes. It is something like making cookies with cookie cutters. Information comes as a disorganized, shapeless lump of dough, and the producer rolls it out, molds it, and cuts it into a well-defined shape. But a good bit of the dough is left outside the cutter. Side issues or complex details that won't fit within the confines of the format get left out. As TV critic Howard Rosenberg puts it, even the world's best journalists can't fit Goliath's foot into David's shoe.[6]

As a reporter I found myself facing the impossible task of compressing events that took hours, or even days, into a minute or two, and at the same time making sure that everything I said was fair, accurate, and completely in context. I found it easier for a camel to go through the eye of a needle than to spend five hours listening to complicated legislative debate and then try to adequately summarize what was said in simple language and in a minute and a half. Contrary to the old adage that there are two sides to every story, I found that there are often many different and confusing sides to every story. Viewpoints multiply like baby rabbits, and most issues abound with tangents to become lost in. Because of gray areas, there can actually be a bias against checking story facts too closely because the more closely facts are examined the more complicated the story becomes, and thus the more difficult to report intelligibly.

> *The dilemma is that when information is presented as simpler than it truly is, it is inevitably deceptive.*

Another reason TV struggles with complexity is that newscasters could throw volumes of facts and figures at the audience every night and still not communicate. Complex information verbally delivered at an accelerated pace whizzes by so quickly that few can make meaningful sense out of it. The snippets of rhetoric whip past viewers before they can focus their thoughts. Consequently, information that cannot be explained clearly and grasped instantly upon hearing fares poorly on TV. The viewer's mind cannot stop to ponder the intricate but instead must shift into neutral and coast with the speed of the newscast. So everything must be simplified into easily consumed capsules and delivered in half hour segments that are palatable to the public's appetite.

Still another reason TV news has difficulty when it tries to communicate complex or abstract information is that its audience is too easily distracted. As a TV news producer, I was well aware that information cannot be structured to require any real concentration because it is delivered primarily in the home, where barking dogs, dishes, dinner, laundry, and conversation compete for a viewer's attention. We knew our stories had to be presented simply enough to achieve immediate understanding upon being seen and heard.

The problem of conveying complexity is aggravated by the need to communicate visually, because visual imagery cannot convey complex detail. Neil Postman says that using television to communicate complex information is like trying to use smoke signals to carry on a discussion of philosophy. It is a case of form excluding content.[7] Imagery of the type that must be on television can impart only simple, face value ideas. Television excels at projecting scenes but is less adept at projecting the ideas that must accompany those scenes. Far from being an unlimited window on the world, as many claim, television more closely resembles a giant filter that screens out the obscure, the abstract, and the multidimensional.

The dilemma is that when information is presented as simpler than it truly is, it is inevitably deceptive. Truth in packaging is a problem in TV news, observes a *TV Guide* critic, because "[TV news] . . . is a [kind of] visual and verbal shorthand of easy-to-understand labels and generalities that can—and often do—mislead viewers."[8] The more detailed and less visual a story is, the greater the potential for distortion. Sports and television, for example, are a marriage made in heaven, because shots of brightly clad players chasing each other across a field is the whole story. However, when abstract considerations thread their way through newsworthy issues, the camera can be more of a liability than an asset. Intangible details are lost when ideas become images. In a story about peace negotiations, for example, televised pictures of an American president smiling and shaking hands in the White House rose garden with a Soviet premier convey little or nothing of substance about the complex spectrum of U.S.-Soviet relations.

Economics presents another problem for producers. How do you explain inflation with a picture or photograph of an expanded money supply? TV news is often criticized for shallow economic coverage, but out of necessity the brush of televised imagery paints such theoretical concepts with broad and confusing strokes. Inflation via the camera translates into nothing more than a woman squeezing oranges in the supermarket and pictures of higher price tags. The confusion is not intentional, but inevitable.

Christians who criticize TV for avoiding religion seldom stop to consider the staggering number of groups that crowd the American religious scene. Can anyone seriously suggest that TV news could do a meaningful job of covering such diversity in a medium so impotent in conveying complexity? Complex issues with moral overtones are also cans of worms that can't be easily opened and then quickly closed within the quick-paced television blueprint.

Oversimplified TV stories do not always reflect what is newsworthy, important, and necessary for the survival of a free and informed society, and yet complex, abstract events play poorly in the theater of television. United States Senator John McCain, a Vietnam veteran and former POW, was once asked what was the most important lesson the United States government had learned from the Vietnam War. The Senator's reply: "That we'd better be able to come up with a foreign policy we can explain in two sentences to the man in the street, if we expect any broad base of public support for it."[9]

McCain's answer highlights the danger of presenting complicated problems in simplified media formats. If a little knowledge is a dangerous thing, then TV news dispenses danger every day. The policies of cities, states, and nations are molded daily in some way by the pressures exerted by a few minutes of quickly gathered, highly compressed, and greatly oversimplified information. Intricate national issues are reduced on television to a battle of minced words. Public figures are compelled to offer quick answers that have the right look and feel to them. Such dialogue creates the illusion that problems can be resolved by quick and easy formulas and sometimes leaves viewers with false, unbalanced, or unrealistic impressions of the world.

Elaborate and sophisticated events appear simpler on TV than they are in reality. Something as incredibly intricate as putting astronauts into space was taken for granted by viewers for many years until, in one horrible moment, the gap between TV-created illusion and the real dangers of space flight were bridged in a split second. As the country watched in stunned silence and horror, the shuttle and its crew disintegrated before the cameras, shocking the nation into realizing that launching people into space is not that simple, but only looks that way on television.

If no one watches, nothing is communicated, but if events are artificially shortened to hold viewers, little substance is communicated.

Almost two-thirds of the public admits to receiving most of its news from television.[10] Yet research by two University of Maryland professors reveals that those who leaned on TV news the most appear to be among the least well-informed.[11] Viewers assume incorrectly that meaningful information can be contained and conveyed as easily within a minute of video as on a printed page, just as complex information can be stored on a tiny computer microchip. But television news has more in common with fast food. It is delivered quickly and swallowed easily, but it is often nutritionally inadequate. In our pop culture, where products are "instant" or "light," we are conditioned to news in the same vein. We crave fast food and fast news. Regardless of the reality of the situation, we want uncomplicated, no hassle, instant understanding of complex, difficult-to-understand issues that are sometimes crucial to our survival.

Such greatly oversimplified TV bulletins carry tremendous power to persuade and change minds in a matter of seconds. Many accept whatever impression the box delivers and charge ahead in their judgments, overconfident of their ability to understand, quick to criticize and to jump to conclusions, and sometimes hasty to take political retribution at the polls.

Over time, something happens to people who spend hour after hour watching accelerated versions of real life events. After a while human beings begin to perceive the artificially speeded up version they see as being more "real" and desirable than the real pace. We become conditioned to wanting our problems to be resolved as quickly and easily as those we see on TV. We prefer quick and easy solutions to careful deliberation.

Some researchers believe that television's rapid fire pace has drastically eroded the attention span of viewers. If the discussion is lengthy and detailed enough to do justice to the subject, news producers run the risk of alienating the audience. It's a kind of catch-22. If no one watches, nothing is communicated, but if events are artificially shortened to hold viewers, little substance is communicated.

Another by-product of TV's stringent time limits is that they foster stereotypes because attempts to make fine distinctions are crushed. The brief summarizations often leave sweeping and over-generalized impressions. All politicians are dishonest, all women are feminists, all Christians are fanatical fundamentalists—cliché and formula are the inevitable result in a medium with no room for detail.

Some claim that TV stimulates their thinking, but information and impressions come so quickly that often viewers are not really thinking but simply absorbing imagery and reacting emotionally to it. TV's rapid-fire pacing can generate a type of mental meltdown with viewers. Story facts begin to blur together, leaving information uncomprehended and audiences confused. Although detailed information is harder to absorb and retain via television, viewers are still left with strong emotional impressions from the visual imagery, which can deeply influence thinking. A viewer leaves the screen with negative or positive emotions regarding an issue but lacking any tangible, factually based reason for feeling such a way.

The pictures that TV delivers into our living rooms and our minds do alter our judgments, and, as we will find if we look more closely, the final impressions they leave tend to move our emotions more readily than they inform our intellect.

NOTES

1. Jeff Greenfield, "Stop the Nightline Express; This Journalist Wants to Get Off," *TV Guide*, April 4, 1987, p. 47.
2. George Will, quoted by John Weisman, "What TV Isn't Telling Us About Those Soviet Spokesmen," *TV Guide*, April 26, 1986, p. 5.
3. "Brokaw Defends Network Mandate," *Broadcasting*, March 30, 1987, p. 174.
4. Ted Koppel, quoted by Howard Rosenberg, "Reining in a Tiger," *The Arizona Republic*, June 9, 1986, p. B-10.
5. Charles Glass, quoted by Joanmarie Kalter, "Foreign Correspondent Burnout: They're Working Harder and Enjoying It Less," *TV Guide*, May 9, 1987, p. 18.
6. Howard Rosenberg, "Network News Informs Less and Less as Technology," *Onward*, September 30, 1986, p. 26.
7. Neil Postman, *Amusing Ourselves to Death* (New York: Penguin, 1985), p. 7.
8. Weisman, "What TV Isn't Telling Us," p. 3.
9. "The MacNeil/Lehrer News Hour," PBS, April 30, 1985.
10. "America's Watching," *Television Information Office/Roper Report*, 1989, p. 14.
11. John Weisman, "Do Local Anchors Know Their Current Events?" *TV Guide*, November 22, 1986, p. 6.

9

TV EMOTION: STIMULATION OR INFORMATION?

What is it that television is really foremost at communicating? Talk show host and former news correspondent Geraldo Rivera, a master at emotionally manipulating his audiences, once answered that question by pointing out that "recording sound and fury is what television does best."[1]

What the camera shows is often more stimulating to our emotions than to our intellect because TV is simply a better image planter than a fact planter. "The camera is a deficient news-gathering instrument," charges syndicated columnist George Will. "It is used most naturally and potently not to transmit information but to convey scenes, some of great emotional impact."[2] Scenes, he reminds us, can be more passionate than informative.

Sometimes the end result is not a bucket of information but a bundle of feelings. "When you add the dimension of picture and sound," agrees ABC news anchor Peter Jennings, "what comes out of the box is essentially affecting the emotion to a greater extent than it is affecting the intellect. We deal with fact, but sometimes fact is simply overpowered by the emotional equation in that story—even if it's the smallest [part of the] equation."[3]

We have been led to believe that the camera's ability to transmit what is colorful, sensational, exciting, and emotionally stimulating is one of its great journalistic strengths, but viewers seldom seem to notice how those ingredients can manipulate viewer impressions and block objective communication. Pictures transmit powerfully, but ambiguously. It is hard to predict what chord a picture will strike in each person who sees it.

As a reporter, I tried to be articulate and careful in the phrasing of my stories, knowing I could exercise some degree of control over the impact of my spoken or written words, but especially in the heat of a deadline I could never be quite certain about how a certain mix of sound and pictures would finally be interpreted by members of my audience. I discovered that each viewer assigns a slightly different meaning to the visual symbols he sees, based on his particular life experience. An attention-getting image can make a powerful statement all by itself, overpowering any narrative attempts to qualify it. The accompanying dialogue is sometimes lost in a wash of provocative imagery. All sorts of electronic impressions can be left by photos that a producer never intended to convey.

> *The reach-out-and-touch-someone philosophy that now permeates television news has a limited capacity for objectivity.*

I saw this happen in coverage of the 1984 presidential election, when a *Wall Street Journal* article raised a furor over whether or not Ronald Reagan was too old to run again. ABC news did a story about the controversy over Reagan's age. According to news anchor Peter Jennings, the producers were extremely careful to point out in the narration of the story that age doesn't always determine quickness of mind and that many people have risen to greatness later in life. But in the course of the videotaped story, the producers showed a quick shot of the President dozing off in public. "My mail came in by the bagful," Jennings remembers. "'How dare you attack our President!' That one moment of visual emotion— visual impact—overwhelms the words we say. . . . I say to myself, 'But hold it, folks, didn't you hear everything we *told* you?' And the answer was clearly, 'no.' That bothers me," admits Jennings, "that bothers me a lot."[4]

Eliciting emotional response is sometimes an innocent by-product of electronic journalism, but in my experience it has also become the deliberate aim of much of TV news. How my photographer and I used to hate being assigned to cover the funerals of crime victims or to be sent knocking on doors of their grieving relatives! We were compelled to go by ambitious news management, not for information but for the purpose of bringing back something "gripping" on tape.

The industry is well aware of the camera's potential to pack a passionate wallop. The deliberate attempt to arouse feeling evolved in the sixties and seventies after television news operations, acting on the results of research, the advice of news consultants, and the nudgings of intuition, discovered that emotion, not reason, worked best on TV. The station or network that programmed news from that angle won the ratings race.

This bent toward emotion can be demonstrated scientifically. Research demonstrates that viewing stimulates primarily the right side of the brain, which specializes in fantasy and emotional responses, rather than the left hemisphere, where thinking and analysis are performed. By measuring viewer brain waves, periods of right-brain activity were found to outnumber left-brain activity by a ratio of two-to-one.[5]

The temptation to exploit this tendency is very great. "The kind of thing we're are looking for [in stories] is something that evokes an emotional response," a former CBS news executive admits. "A lot of stories have inherent drama, but others have to be done in such a way that will bring out an emotional response." He concludes that stories need to "reach out and touch people."[6] To which George Will asks: "Is this the evening news or some kind of an encounter session?"[7]

The reach-out-and-touch-someone philosophy that now permeates television news has a limited capacity for objectivity. The sight of a mother sobbing in grief on a news program over the loss of her son in some war-torn spot in the world will move us emotionally and strongly influence our thinking. Her grief is legitimate and what the camera is conveying is factual in one sense, but in another sense it is not. It does not tell us much that is objective or informative about the military conflict her son was involved in. It simply makes us react. Yet what we have seen will stir emotions that can influence our thinking on an important question of international policy. Again, the emphasis in communication has shifted to what can be seen—the grief of a soldier's mother—and away from the abstract, yet important, considerations that surround any armed conflict.

In 1991, at the outset of the war against Iraq, U.S. military officials were concerned about the emotional wallop that video of bloody combat, death, and destruction shown out of context could pack, and they fought to limit such photos. TV news executives and reporters, concerned about censorship, furiously insisted that they would show the "horrors of war" regardless of whether or not such images reduced the viewing public to a collective emotional basket case. American military concerns about emotional manipulation via TV pictures were predictable, especially after Vietnam. One of the dangers of war in the television age is that the question of public support for waging a war could be reduced ultimately to a battle of images.

The danger of emotional bias was also evident in the eighties each time an American was taken hostage in the Middle East and the networks showed pictures of distraught hostage families. Television became a forum for displaying what George Will calls "the pornography of grief."[8]

News broadcasts became outlets for distraught families to vent their feelings in the heat of the crisis. Such spectacles had a disastrous effect on America's ability to make long-term policy regarding international terrorism. Anyone trying to maintain some degree of objectivity squirmed with discomfort after listening to one heartrending clip of sound after another. No attempts by government officials to verbally point out the abstract considerations that surrounded the situation could compete with the vicarious agony the emotionally moving pictures of victims or their families brought to viewers.

"[On television] the lives of the hostages take precedence over the broader interests of the American people," lamented former Secretary of State Alexander Haig during the 1985 Middle East hostage crisis. "TV tends to reverse priorities in such situations."[9] "Television tends to transform what is an essentially political issue into a personal drama," agreed former National Security Advisor Zbigniew Brzezinski. "It prevents the government from dealing with the situation as a political problem and forces it to think of it as a personal problem."[10] Former Secretary of State Henry Kissinger warned in the eighties that if the American government bargains to save the lives of hostages, it will endanger the lives of all future hostages, because terrorism's goals will have then have been achieved.[11] But such careful reasoning can be obscured by emotion-laden imagery.

*A broken law cannot cry
in front of a camera.*

It is true, of course, that television pictures can move people positively and can evoke sympathy that is beneficial. The sense of emotion and togetherness generated by the sight of the tall ships at the bicentennial celebration or the sight of hundreds of waving yellow ribbons to welcome home hostages and soldiers can evoke unity among Americans that is touching and refreshing. Pictures of a grieving mom holding her three-year-old son who has been the victim of a drunk driver will move many to join in the fight to get drunks off the road. But we need to recognize that TV-induced emotion has the capacity to be manipulative and dangerous.

Take the coverage given by TV news magazine "20/20" in the fall of 1985 to a man accused of mercy killing his wife in Florida.

In March of 1984, seventy-five year-old Roswell Gilbert shot his seventy-three-year-old wife, Emily, who suffered from osteoporosis and Alzheimer's disease. Focusing the emotion-provoking power of the camera on that event inevitably created sympathy for Gilbert, a sweet-looking old man who bore little physical resemblance to the stereotyped villains of TV crime dramas. Gilbert cried on camera, and a stream of sympathetic neighbors testified about how faithfully Gilbert cared for his wife.

Although air time was afforded to Gilbert's prosecutors, the deck was clearly stacked in the direction of passion, and millions of viewers were rallied to empathy for a man who gunned down his wife, regardless of the motive. A broken law cannot cry in front of a camera. Television cannot look beyond outward emotion to determine invisible motives or abstract considerations. One TV critic questions the propriety of TV's transporting the public into playing judge and jury in such highly complex legal situations. "On television," he concludes, "the question of Gilbert's innocence becomes a spectator sport."[12]

Many viewers simply take the emotion-laden imagery of such stories at face value and react. They fail to analyze beyond what they have seen. What else is important in the situation that the camera could not show? Do the pictures portray all the considerations in this story? Are my impressions being guided by my feelings about pictures, which may not tell the whole story? These are questions viewers need to ask but too often do not.

Because of the inherent tendency of the camera to elevate feeling over fact, television news suffers from an inherent problem of imbalance. Pictures often tip the scales too far to the side of passion and away from reason, tipped not just by ideology, liberal bias, Communist conspiracy, or any of the other accusations often hurled at television journalists, but by the nature of TV imagery itself and the willingness of the public to buy what the camera has to sell of the world's emotionally compelling goods. If the images are strong, they will stay in the minds of viewers for a long time. The information accompanying the image may not be remembered, but the residue of feeling the image evokes will linger. Concludes George

Will: "It remains unclear how television, a slave to the camera, can best serve a society in which the public generally has a high ratio of passion to information."[13]

NOTES

1. Geraldo Rivera, "Why TV News Needs More Passion," *TV Guide*, September 27, 1986, p. 28.
2. George Will, "Television: The Camera Is Deficient As a News-Gathering Tool," *The Arizona Republic*, November 1, 1982, p. A-7. © 1982, Washington Post Writers Group. Reprinted with permission.
3. Peter Jennings, quoted by Rushworth M. Kidder, "Videoculture 3: Do 'Media-genic' Candidates Make Good Leaders?" *The Christian Science Monitor*, June 12, 1985, p. 19. Reprinted by permission from *The Christian Science Monitor* © 1985 The Christian Science Publishing Society. All rights reserved.
4. Ibid.
5. James Mann, "What Is TV Doing to America?" *U.S. News and World Report*, August 2, 1982, p. 28.
6. Will, "Camera," p. A-7.
7. Ibid.
8. George Will, quoted by Edwin Diamond, "The Coverage Itself—Why It Turned into 'Terrorvision,'" *TV Guide*, September 21, 1985, p. 7.
9. Alexander Haig, quoted by Neil Hickey, "The Impact on Negotiations—What the Experts Say," *TV Guide*, September 21, 1985, pp. 20-22.
10. Zbigniew Brzezinski, ibid.
11. Henry Kissinger, ibid., p. 21.
12. John Corry, "For Better or Worse," *The Arizona Republic*, August 8, 1987, p. F-7.
13. Will, "Camera," p. A-7.

10

THE FINE ART OF "TELEGENICITY"

Television by nature is a cosmetically conscious, personality-oriented craft. The camera tends to cater to visually attractive events and physically appealing, articulate, charismatic people. I discovered that those who had the natural or cultivated ability to project their personality positively on camera by use of emotion, sex appeal, eloquence, or humor were the ones who most effectively made use of the power that TV exposure affords. Those who could not found themselves at a profound disadvantage, regardless of how factual their position might be.

On television, what is "true" to the viewer becomes not as much a question of what is being said but how it is being said and who is saying it. If the person being interviewed lacks a pleasant or authoritative voice, the impression he leaves is that he is less intelligent, less capable, less friendly, less sexually attractive than others who might oppose him—all qualities highly important to viewers in an image-oriented society. If the person looks good and speaks well, viewers will be impressed with him because they are drawn to the speaker himself rather than to his logic. Because of this built-in bias, successful TV communication hangs on a person's ability to come up with a quick, right-sounding answer and project a credible on-camera image. The camera demands that its subjects be good performers.

But is such performance a reliable standard of judgment? I learned from my own experience after interviewing thousands of people on a myriad of topics that a person's ability to please the camera cosmetically was an unreliable indicator of how smart or right he was. I saw a number of important issues go down the drain in the public eye simply because the wrong performer got before the camera to defend them.

TV viewers unconsciously assume that the presence of a camera does not affect human behavior, but I can assure you that it does.

In the television age, style often triumphs over substance. "Telegenicity," a phrase coined by a writer for the *Wall Street Journal*, refers to the quality of looking and sounding good on TV.[1] It is now a major manipulator of public opinion. The inclination to be influenced by attractive personalities is not the invention of TV, but I am convinced that television has heightened our natural tendency to react in this way.

Sensational or outrageous statements laced with hyperbole and exaggeration are, unfortunately, desirable on-camera commodities when information is fused with cosmetic style. As a reporter, I knew that to interview someone who made statements that were articulately phrased, outrageous, emotionally charged, and stirring was not only a surefire audience pleaser but also a dependable way to keep my bosses happy as well.

We used to call people who exploited their on-camera prowess "media hogs" because they were so adept at playing TV's bias toward the dramatic and hogging the spotlight because of it. Whether they were credible or accurate was sometimes secondary to their availability to the camera and their capacity to be pleasing to watch.

TV viewers unconsciously assume that the presence of a camera does not affect human behavior, but I can assure you that it does. I observed in my interviewees that most people do not act exactly the same way or say things the same way that they would if they were not being photographed. Yet I am certain that most viewers assume that on-camera subjects behave as though the camera were the proverbial "fly on the wall." But to presume that someone can walk around "doing his thing" unaffected by and oblivious to a photographer with a cumbersome video camera, a sound man with a boom and glaring TV lights, and a producer, coupled with the awareness that thousands or millions will see him, is ridiculous when you stop to think about it. As Malcolm Muggeridge noted: "To suppose that life could really be lived followed about everywhere by a camera . . . really [does] represent the ultimate fantasy, not just of television, but of life itself."[2]

Yet we see it often, on "60 Minutes," for example, in personality profiles—the camera following someone in his day-to-day routine, journeying down halls and streets with the person. The accuracy of such real-life documentaries rests on the underlying supposition that the subjects are behaving the same way as they would if the camera weren't present in all of its obtrusiveness.

Some are afflicted more than others by the self-consciousness that the presence of the camera fosters. Some folks flourish in front of an audience, grandstanding for the lens, whereas others freeze and shy away, unable to perform under the pressure. I remember one person in particular who had a considerable knack for show, turning tears on and off in an academy award performance as soon as the camera's red indicator light came on. Some celebrated criminals, I observed, could create undeserved sympathy for themselves at the drop of a hat because they had the innate ability to manipulate the camera's need for compelling visuals.

Immense amounts of money, time, and effort in TV news production go toward cosmetic effect. Sometimes the informational aspect of TV journalism is robbed financially for the sake of what is eye pleasing and illusionary. One station I worked for had an inadequate number of people employed to research and document story facts but spent several thousand dollars to give our leading female anchor a face-lift, after viewers complained about dark circles under her eyes.

The TV consultants I worked under were more concerned about our vocal patterns and verbal delivery than the accuracy of what we were reading. We were coached and criticized on pacing and physical animation. It was not a question of how to be better reporters but how to look better. As one TV news consultant told us in an internal station memo: "If [the delivery] is dynamic, it is probably effective; and if it's dynamic, it is more likely to be perceived as credible."

It is the illusion of credibility, not credibility itself, that is the industry's concern, because illusion is what television projects best and what audiences demand. It would be easy to blame the TV news industry for emphasizing such superficialities, but in fact the business is only following a clear mandate from its audience. The vast majority of news viewers evaluate news anchors, consciously or unconsciously, on cosmetic attractiveness. Many viewers are obsessed with it. In all the years I worked in television news, I got more comments from viewers on the way I wore my hair, on the color of lipstick I chose, the sound of my voice, and my choice of clothing than on the content of any story I ever covered or reported. One letter I received was particularly revealing about the priorities established by the visual medium. It read:

Open letter to Coleen Cook:

I am a daily watcher of [your] channel. . . . I hate to write this to you Miss Cook but really it's about time someone did.

When you go on the air that head shaking to emphasize your words at different times just does not fit your style at all.

Also, when you take a deep breath your microphone picks it up and really makes a loud noise, like wind rushing by. You are constantly raising and lowering your eyelids when you give out the news. This is a very hard sight to watch on TV.

Your hair could stand a different styling, and that phony smile you give at the end of your broadcast is gross.

I know what I have written might make you angry, but its for your own good, and for viewers rating.

Sure hope you can alter these things I have written. If you do, I sure will write back to you and let you know.

It was signed "Just a viewer." No, she never did get around to writing me back.

If television had existed in Lincoln's day, would his assassin have been his on-camera image and not John Wilkes Booth?

Even more alarming than the cosmetic selection of news anchors is the cosmetic selection of national and international leaders. Is it a coincidence that the Soviet Union put Mikhail Gorbachev into power, a telegenic leader who typified how sophisticated the Soviets had become in dealing with the TV-dominated Western media? Perhaps one of the best and most serious examples of the cosmetic power of television in the eighties was the Philippine revolution, where the presence of American television was the primary factor in bringing down the ruler of an entire nation. One media critic concluded: "The visuals did [Ferdinand] Marcos in."[3]

As an attractive young woman struggling against a homely, old, despotic tyrant, Corazon Aquino met all the cosmetic requirements for a heroine. Unbeknownst to much of the watching world, an American public relations firm actually took part in orchestrating the speeches, crowds, and events for color TV. The Aquino color-coded campaign of brilliant yellow, which made dazzling television news footage, was no coincidence, but the brainchild of an American designer of scenic effects who advised the Aquino coalition on how to perform for the cameras.[4]

Perhaps we can argue correctly that in spite of the staged quality of the Aquino victory the hard evidence indicates that the best person won. Yet the incident should make us rethink the power of TV cosmetics. As another critic warns, where Cory Aquino's victory was concerned, "For once, virtue had visuals, and we rejoice at that. But what about the many cases in the world where virtue is not photogenic?"[5] The world can only hope for more "telegenic" performers who also miraculously happen to be genuinely capable of governing if leaders are to survive the distorted scrutiny of the electronic age.

Colonel Oliver North's extraordinary ability to project his personality into American living rooms was an example of how deeply affected viewers are by style. Regardless of whether he was right or wrong in the Iran-Contra affair, his ability to handle himself before the cameras tended to obscure the facts surrounding the situation.

Supreme Court nominee Robert Bork faced exactly the opposite problem. Bork's judicially cold, somewhat aggressive on-camera style worked against him in his battle to overcome the rumors and accusations surrounding his nomination. In an age where charisma overrides competence, Robert Bork's biggest liability might have been that he taught law, not drama, at Yale University. Bork could not win via television, regardless of the facts, and Oliver North could not lose.

The effects of a television presence on Congress are now clear to those close to the legislative body. Some senators complain that members who are powerful and effective behind the scenes look uncomfortable and ineffective in front of the camera's red light, whereas other lawmakers who are long on personal style and short on substance perform superbly, leading unsuspecting viewers to think that they are the real powers on Capitol Hill. One veteran lawmaker points out that it is now in the interest of members of the Senate to say things that are colorful, flamboyant, and make nice, quick bites on the evening news.[6]

Other lawmakers complain that many are now enticed to leave important work being hammered out in committees to orate in the chamber. Floor arguments are now more frequent, more members populate the floor for show, more want to make brief speeches, and more tend to use outrageous visual effects to get their points across.[7]

Columnist George Will has observed that "we are developing a nation of citizens who depend on rhetorical performance to base our most important decisions on."[8] The same dynamic is at work in the American presidency. More than ever before in the history of our country, a person's ability to ascend to power and retain it depends on how he looks and sounds. As Neil Postman puts it: "You can't have a three hundred pound man run for president of the United States. The Constitution doesn't forbid it; television forbids it."[9] One critic notes that had television existed in earlier centuries, the public would have learned that George Washington had unattractive, wooden false teeth; that Lincoln had a high, reedy-sounding voice; and that Thomas Jefferson spoke with a slight speech impediment.[10] If television had existed in Lincoln's day, would his assassin have been his on-camera image and not John Wilkes Booth?

Television's bias toward the cosmetic has been demonstrated from the time of John Kennedy, the first great television president, to Richard Nixon, who made the mistake of trying to question the power of media to create images, to Lyndon Johnson, who never seemed quite able to warm up to television, to Ronald Reagan, a president who really understood TV and had the ability to beat it at its own game. Reagan, perhaps more than any president of late, understood that politics is no longer a contest of ideology but a battle of images and publicity clichés. I say this not to ridicule Mr. Reagan but simply to point out that he did what is now absolutely necessary for political survival in the electronic age.

Evidence suggests that the role of American political parties has dwindled significantly because of TV news.[11] Americans who used to rely on parties for information are now manipulated by the wizards of political image making. Media illusion now usurps party platforms, issues, and ideology. "My greatest concern about national political campaigns," worries Peter Jennings, "is that we will elect people in the future who are extremely adept at organizing their arguments and their campaigns for TV, but who are vastly less [well] informed on the issues."[12]

When the framers of the Bill of Rights wrote that document, they assumed that the public could be entrusted with the vote as long as it had access to unrestricted information. I doubt that they ever envisioned the possibility that communications technology itself might restrict the flow of information through distortion because of TV's penchant for elevating style over substance.

Av Westin makes the point well:

> Someone has written this story about the first days of the United States: James Madison is seated, working on a draft of the First Amendment. He has just put his quill to paper and scratched out the words "Congress shall make no law . . . abridging the freedom of speech or of the press." The door to his study opens and an aide walks in. "Sir!" he begins. "I have had this vision. Someday there will be a glass box which will sit in our living quarters, and on it will appear moving images: People will be seen and heard, laughing, crying, speaking, playing music, cheering. On this box we will watch our government leaders as they conduct the affairs of state!" Madison looks up at his aide, thinks for a moment, and then tears up the paper on which he had written the text of the First Amendment. "If you are right," Madison says, "then this document is not what I had in mind."[13]

A little over two hundred years later, in 1981, authors John Tebbel and Sara Miles Watts would point out that the White House briefing room had been remodeled to accommodate television correspondents in the front row, with the rest of the press relegated to back seats. Cameras had been repositioned so that the president could carry on a direct dialogue with the TV audience for whom the press conferences were now primarily designed.

Three years after those changes were made, still another Hollywood touch was added during the Reagan administration for cosmetic effect during the nationally televised press conferences held in the East Room of the White House. The doors behind the presidential podium, guarded by a marine in colorful full-dress uniform, now swung open in full view of the camera to reveal a long, broad, and dramatic-looking corridor leading into the executive offices. After the last press question, the president could move toward the swinging doors and the cameras watch him retreat slowly down the corridor until he disappeared into the executive offices. The scene was strongly reminiscent of the old-time cowboy movie hero riding slowly off into the sunset. Fade-out.[14]

NOTES

1. Martha Bayles, "As the Senate Turns," *The Wall Street Journal*, May 16, 1986, p. 10.
2. Malcolm Muggeridge, *Christ and the Media* (Grand Rapids: Eerdmans, 1977), p. 51.
3. Thomas Griffith, quoted by Gary Wills, "TV Can Make a Difference," *TV Guide*, July 26, 1986, p. 3.
4. Ibid., pp. 3-4.
5. Ibid., p. 4.
6. "Rough Week for TV in the Senate," *Broadcasting*, February 10, 1986, p. 32.
7. Norman Ornstein, "Yes, Television Has Made Congress Better," *TV Guide*, July 25, 1987, p. 6.
8. "ABC News," October 22, 1984.
9. Neil Postman, quoted by Alvin P. Sanoff, "TV Has Culture by the Throat," *U.S. News and World Report*, December 23, 1985, p. 59. Copyright, 1985, *U.S. News & World Report*.
10. Robert Kubey, *Channels of Communication*, September/October 1985, p. 69.
11. David L. Altheide, *Media Power* (Beverly Hills, Calif.: Sage, 1985), p. 65.
12. Peter Jennings, quoted by Rushworth M. Kidder, "Videoculture 3: Do 'Mediagenic' Candidates Make Good Leaders?" *The Christian Science Monitor*, June 12, 1985, p. 19. Reprinted by permission from *The Christian Science Monitor* © 1985 The Christian Science Publishing Society. All rights reserved.
13. Av Westin, *Newswatch: How Television Decides the News* (New York: Simon & Schuster, 1982), p. 11.
14. John Tebbel and Sara Miles Watts, "Starring the President," *Channels of Communication*, January/February, 1986, p. 79.

11

THE "MINDLESS" MEDIUM

once heard a clinical nutritionist point out the essential difference between a real egg and an egg substitute. They look alike, smell and taste alike, and perform in much the same way when used in cooking, but for all that, science cannot yet reproduce a real egg with the same nutritional value simply by rebuilding a chemical chain. In the same way, television cannot reproduce reality by building a chain of processed images that resemble the actual event.

Before actually working in TV news, it never occurred to me that there was any intrinsic difference between the way TV communicated messages and the way other media did. But once I was within the industry I discovered that much of what television delivers as "eyewitness" material is as processed as the food on our grocery store shelves. Jerry Mander, a former advertising executive and author of *Four Arguments for the Elimination of Television*, points out that we are the first generation in history to substitute what Mander calls "secondary, mediated experiences" seen via the tube for direct ones and, for the most part, to assume without thinking, that both are equal.[1] Television, argues Mander, encourages us to mentally substitute an indirect experience for a direct one.[2] Yet like real eggs and egg substitutes, there are striking differences between the two.

Mander argues that TV succeeds on the same principle used by many well-known religious cults—by controlling our environment and confining our experience.[3] Since the frame of reference needed to evaluate information is inherently lost on the tube, new arbitrary "realities" are substituted for old ones. Consequently, the new "mediated" environment causes us to doubt the validity of personal experience. We need "experts" to tell us what our own experience was once adequate to tell us.[4] If we are heavily dependent on TV for information, Mander insists, we are in danger of becoming the "hermit in the cave who knows only what the TV offers."[5]

Author and pastor Kevin Perrotta cautions: "The danger [of television] is that while holding the correct set of beliefs about God and his Word we [are] allowing something quite different to shape our minds."

I have so far focused primarily on television news because it is my own field of specialization and because it was part of my purpose to illumine TV's weaknesses in the very area in which it enjoys its highest degree of public trust. But now I would like to broaden my examination of television's weaknesses to include entertainment programming, for if television news is illusionary then TV entertainment is even more so.

I say that because because the illusions and distortions present in television news operate even more strongly in televised fiction. Entertainment programs often give the illusion of reality, but since greater liberties can be taken in production and viewers are less critical of content accuracy, the distortion level is even higher. When television attempts to deal with real issues in a dramatic fictional format, as in the so-called docudramas about social issues, even greater conflicts emerge between real life and the final impressions left by television.

Consider, for example, what messages and impressions are delivered via soaps and sitcoms. Do viewers consciously distinguish between the artificial impressions left in their subconscious minds by television fiction and what is true in real life? When TV attempts to deal with real issues and real people in a dramatic fictional format, as in the so-called docudramas, what conflicts emerge between real life and the final impression left by the imagery? How are views affected?

Although most viewers claim to understand that televised fiction is not real, there is strong evidence that the viewing public accepts much of televised fiction as "real" at a heart level, regardless of claiming to know that it's not. There are disturbing indications that what we watch may motivate us in ways that we are barely aware of and desperately need to gain understanding of.

"The bias of a medium sits heavy, felt but unseen, over a culture," observes Neil Postman.[6] The residue, or the mood, left behind by a powerful communications medium like television can and does have a subtle but pervasive effect on our society. Television exerts an extraordinary degree of mental influence whether or not that influence is grounded in fact. Why viewers are so influenced by what they see may be more apparent after taking a closer look at how television actually delivers its messages into our minds.

If you use television at all, it is influencing you in some way. If you claim to be a Christian, then you are professing a desire and an intention to be conformed to Christ in your thinking and lifestyle. Can you indulge indiscriminately in television and resist being conformed to the world it presents? Author and pastor Kevin Perrotta cautions: "The danger [of television] is that while holding the correct set of beliefs about God and his Word we [are] allowing something quite different to shape our minds."[7]

Coming up with conclusive research to document the impact of television is difficult, because TV is so pervasive. Since almost everyone has a TV set, scientists find it difficult to isolate a control group for scientific comparison or to control other factors that could skew their findings. However, studies that have been done to document how TV works on the mind are intriguing, disturbing, and worthy of attention.

A major reason behind television's influence, according to Jerry Mander, is that TV doesn't just give us ideas, it determines how we will visibly recognize those ideas. He points out that too few grasp the significance of a machine that can determine how we will see something in our minds, especially when much of what it shows is artificial or altered to begin with.[8] Consider that along with the thought that we mentally process much of what we see on TV as though it were real, and the importance of television imagery becomes even more apparent.

Mander cautions that viewers need to begin by being more conscious of how they actually watch. He points out that we often sit before the set quiet and relaxed in a darkened room, with our eyes still and focused in one spot. We stare into a flickering florescent light, sometimes for hours on end, sometimes while distractions around us are reduced to a minimum.[9] Mander points out that this practice is strikingly similar to being hypnotized and is a major reason behind television's power to instill ideas.[10]

Mander contends that in both TV viewing and hypnotism, the mind is vulnerable and open to suggestion. Only moments after we begin to watch, he says, we begin to feel ourselves mesmerized. The messages roll into our minds, with little or no effort made on our part to think through them or resist them. Other mental health professionals confirm that there are definite parallels between a mild trance and the process of gazing into a flickering TV screen for hours. Some are critical of the use of hypnotic techniques in TV advertising: "There is no question that hypnotic techniques are being used in certain commercials [today], whether knowingly or not," warns psychiatrist Elliot Wineburg.[11]

Wineburg, himself a former ad copywriter, uses hypnosis in his psychiatric practice. He cites rapid scene changes, repetitive phrases, pulsating music, and the recurring flashing of logos among the many techniques that affect viewers hypnotically. Wineburg also notes that one out of four adults is highly susceptible to hypnosis, which may offer some insight as to why some people are more affected by what they see on television than others.[12]

A second reason for television's potency, Mander says, is that watching television is a form of sense deprivation. We think of TV as something bringing the world to us, he says, but we seldom consider how it separates us from directly experiencing events, places, and people.

Real knowledge of the world, Mander reminds us, comes from the kind of direct, personal observation that involves not just seeing and hearing, but also tasting, touching, and smelling. We never stop to consider that TV renders those other senses useless. Even our senses of sight and sound are used only in an artificial, secondary kind of way. Our so-called "sixth sense" of feeling, or intuition, is greatly curtailed.[13] As we watch in our darkened, quieted rooms, making use of only two of our faculties in a limited way, we are being sense deprived even though the effect is subtly masked by our enjoyment.[146] And sense deprivation, as any prisoner of war can attest, opens the mind to suggestion. Mander cautions: "When you are watching TV, you are experiencing mental images. As distinguished from most sense-deprivation experiments, these mental images are not yours. They are someone else's. Because the rest of your capacities have been subdued, and the rest of the world dimmed, these images are likely to have an extraordinary degree of influence."[15]

The former ad executive points out that television is an invasion of our private mental processes far more extreme than a pushy door-to-door salesperson or high-pressure telephone solicitation. We react in anger to such sales pitches, but we sit passively while TV suggestion walks over us and into our minds.[16]

A third reason for TV's power, according to Mander, is that it communicates subliminally, which means that much of what we see is absorbed below the threshold of conscious comprehension. Visual imagery impacts us deeply at a subconscious level, and the impressions left by it are too subtle to be consciously discerned.

Years ago, there was an uproar in America over the potential use of subliminal advertising, the practice of flashing messages on the TV screen faster than a viewer can consciously recognize them. The promise of subliminal advertising was that messages would enter the subconscious mind of the viewer without his realizing that he had seen anything. They would bypass his reasoning process and exert extraordinary mental influence[17] by inducing him to buy or do things without knowing why.[18]

Although there is no evidence that such extreme subliminal techniques are now being used, critics point out that advertisers are trying the next best thing: flashing images before the viewer so quickly that the mind sees but barely has a chance to register them.[19] Research confirms that watching a sequence of quick changing imagery produces an automatic increase in brain wave activity, which in turn boosts the viewer's ability to remember the images. The result of such "high-tech, hard-to-resist commercials," critics say, is that "not-quite-seeing" becomes "believing."[20] Some advertisers are even enlisting the aid of psychologists and neurophysiologists to make sure their commercials have the desired effect at a subconscious level.[21]

Mander points out that all television, to some degree, is subliminal. Most TV imagery moves at a speed faster than the human eye normally processes imagery, which means that the message comes faster than we can reason with it. Consequently, says Mander, TV stops the critical mind. The tendency is to simply lie back and mentally surrender to whatever comes. Since TV sets its own visual pace, the only way to stem the flow is to turn off the set. To watch is to accept the electronic imagery at whatever speed it comes.[22]

Mander contends that TV is a way of force-feeding information far more potent and disarming than mere words on a page. Television imagery "pours" into us much like water pours from a pitcher into a glass, even against our will.[23] Those images continue to glow inside our heads, remaining like an aftertaste and returning to our awareness hours later.[24]

What are the practical implications of television's subliminal power? Several years ago, when ABC introduced the first lesbian character into a now defunct TV series called "Heartbeat," Gail Strickland, the actress who played the part, admitted: "I hope to create *subliminal* tolerance [for a lesbian character], which will come from the writing and my portrayal."[25]

The game plan for conditioning audience acceptance of a lesbian relationship between Strickland's character and her live-in lover through imagery was to first portray the couple in pleasant, normal, supportive scenes of affection and caring, before later progressing to a more intimate relationship on the screen.[26] Although the series never got off the ground, its producers were apparently tuned into the potential of imagery to alter thinking at a subconscious level.

> *Schoolteachers tell me the most effective way to teach is to use . . . directly involve as many students as possible in first-hand interaction with the material. . . . But TV's rapid pace encourages us to be spectators only.*

One reason TV messages communicate subliminally may be because TV watching physically reduces eye movement. Jerry Mander points out that hundreds of studies show a connection between eye movement and thinking. The act of seeking information with the eye, as in reading, forces the seeker into a state of mental alertness. When the eyes are not moving, but staring in zombie-like fashion, the process of thinking actually diminishes.[27] This can be measured electronically. Scientists have found that when a person is viewing television the mind produces the kind of brain waves normally associated with daydreaming or falling asleep. Researchers also found that viewing suppresses the kind of brain wave activity normally produced in thinking.[28]

A team of Australian researchers found that though TV appears to educate, it actually inhibits real learning. Their conclusion? Television is a type of "sleep teaching" that involves subconscious absorption of imagery while the viewer is in a mild daydream state.[29]

Dr. Eric Peper, the researcher who conducted some of the studies mentioned, underscores an important point about how we process what we see: "The horror of television . . . is that the information goes in, but we don't react to it. It goes right into our memory pool and perhaps we react to it later but we don't know what we're reacting to. When you watch television you are training yourself not to react and so later on, you're doing things without knowing why you're doing them or where they came from."[30]

Mander concludes that if we are blind to the power and the illusionary nature of televised imagery, we will be defenseless against its effects. Assuming that our rational process will protect us from indoctrination, we fail to realize our own carelessness about distinguishing between what is real and what is imaginary. Artificial imagery and reality have merged. When we lose control over artificial imagery, he insists, we have lost control of our minds.[31]

To me, all of this is an indication that the widely parroted claim that TV is "educational" should be questioned. Education in the truest sense is the process of thinking through ideas and arriving at conclusions based on active thought. Schoolteachers tell me the most effective way to teach is to use as much as possible techniques that directly involve as many students as possible in first-hand interaction with the material, as, for example, in question-and-answer sessions between teacher and students.

But TV's rapid pace encourages us to be spectators only. It is one-way communication in which the viewer is actually discouraged from reacting to information. Television deprives the viewer of the advantages and the responsibilities of feedback while at the same time influencing him subliminally.[32] Considering the psychology involved, perhaps TV is a better indoctrinator than educator.

Kevin Perrotta warns that television "has a curious access to our minds, an ability to bypass to some degree our rational evaluation of material as fictional or distorted. When we watch TV, we do more than look at the world through other people's eyes, we submit to them the process by which we orient ourselves to the world."[33] I would add that we submit, not just to someone else's view, but to a view offered by the constraints of a machine as well.

Over a century ago philosopher Søren Kierkegaard wrote: "Suppose someone invented an instrument, a convenient little talking tube, which could be heard over the whole land. I wonder if the police would forbid it, fearing that the whole country would become mentally deranged if it were used."[34] A hundred years later, the little talking tube of Kierkegaard's imagination is now one of the family's best friends. There is evidence that viewers are more influenced by its messages than they think. If so, what emerges from the noisy companion in the corner of the living room may be a matter of much deeper concern than most realize.

NOTES

1. Jerry Mander, *Four Arguments for the Elimination of Television* (New York: William Morrow, 1978), p. 249.
2. Ibid., p. 24.
3. Ibid., p. 107.
4. Ibid., p. 69.
5. Ibid., p. 266.
6. Neil Postman, *Amusing Ourselves to Death* (New York: Penguin, 1985), p. 18.
7. Kevin Perrotta, "Television's Mind-boggling Danger," *Christianity Today*, May 7, 1982, p. 21. Adapted from *Taming the TV Habit*, by Kevin Perrotta (Ann Arbor, Mich.: Servant, 1982). Copyright © 1982 by Kevin Perrotta. Used by permission.
8. Mander, *Four Arguments*, pp. 240-45.
9. Ibid., pp. 164-65.
10. Ibid., pp. 195-201.
11. David Freedman, "Why You Watch Some Commercials—Whether You Mean to or Not," *TV Guide*, February 20, 1988, p. 7.
12. Ibid.

13. Mander, *Four Arguments*, p. 79.
14. Ibid., pp. 168-69.
15. Ibid.
16. Ibid., p. 16.
17. Freedman, "Why You Watch," p. 5.
18. Mander, *Four Arguments*, p. 194.
19. Freedman, "Why You Watch," p. 5.
20. Ibid.
21. Freedman, "Why You Watch," p. 5.
22. Mander, *Four Arguments*, p. 200.
23. Ibid., pp. 203-4.
24. Ibid., p. 159.
25. Gail Strickland, quoted by Fred Rothenberg, "ABC Boasts First Lesbian Character in Series, Looks Forward to Steamy Bedroom Scenes," *New York Post*, April 5, 1988, reprinted in *The American Family Association Journal*, July 1988, p. 5.
26. Ibid.
27. Mander, *Four Arguments*, p. 201.
28. James Mann, "What Is TV Doing to America?" *U.S. News and World Report*, August 2, 1982, p. 28.
29. Mander, *Four Arguments*, p. 205-9.
30. Ibid., p. 211.
31. Ibid., pp. 259-69.
32. Ibid., p. 210.
33. Kevin Perrotta, quoted by Karen Scalf Linamen, "What Is Your Family Watching?" *Focus on the Family*, March 1985, p. 3.
34. Søren Kierkegaard, quoted by Charles Colson in an address to the Christian Booksellers Association Convention, July 21, 1983.

12

THE MODERN DAY
MYTHMAKER

nswering the telephones in a TV station, as reporters who work nights or weekends are occasionally required to do, can be an education. It never ceased to amaze me how many people who call TV stations seem to have their mental train parked somewhere in the imagination station. People would call the NBC owned and operated station in Cleveland I worked for and ask to speak to everyone from Johnny Carson to Tom Brokaw. They sometimes became quite indignant when I tried to explain that NBC in Cleveland was not the same as NBC in New York or Hollywood.

Their perceptions of life according to TV were apparently not much better than a woman who wrote a "letter to the editor" in my local newspaper recently. This young woman expressed dissatisfaction with the current political climate in America. Her particular concerns were not as intriguing to me as the sources of information she offered to prove her point. She did not quote *Time, Newsweek,* or even NBC, ABC, or CBS news. The basis she offered for her social conclusions were several illustrations from a Hollywood movie and a reference to the half-time show from last year's Super Bowl game. She apparently failed to notice that her view of political reality was at least in part anchored somewhere in fantasyland. The leftover images of TV were the basis for her real world perceptions.

Our mental images, observes Jerry Mander, are either the product of our direct experience, our own imagination, or the visual media. Can we readily separate one from another? It takes effort to do so. He notes that once television feeds us an image, it's ours for life. Mander urges us to think for just a moment how this is true even where real-life characters are concerned. Moses takes on the face of Charleton Heston. Rhett Butler looks like Clark Gable. Woodward and Bernstein are Redford and Hoffman in our memories.[1] Our memories brim with "mediated" imagery. What do we use these images for?

Someone who has searched actively for an answer to that question is George Gerbner, dean of the Annenberg School of Communication and perhaps the foremost authority in America on the social impact of television. Based on extensive research in the eighties, Gerbner contends that TV viewers receive a grossly distorted picture of the real world that most tend to take more seriously than reality itself. Gerbner concluded after studying a wide cross section of the population that there is a definite correlation between distorted perceptions of reality and the number of hours spent viewing television each day. He and a team of researchers compared the ways television depicts life situations with more realistic, factually grounded views and then quizzed thousands of viewers about them. His conclusion: the more a person watched TV, the more his perceptions of life tended to reflect the televised view instead of the real, factually grounded view. Gerbner defined a "heavy viewer" of TV as those who watch four hours a day or more, which he says accounts for at least 30 percent of the American population.

After analyzing the views of real life offered by some 1,600 prime time programs involving some 15,000 characters, Gerbner and his staff documented both the television view of life and the factually grounded view. Both views were represented in a multiple-choice questionnaire given to a large cross section of Americans. The following findings, published in *Newsweek* magazine during the eighties,[2] were intriguing, to say the least.

In regard to men and women, male prime time characters in the world of television outnumber females by a margin of three to one. With only a few exceptions, women in TV-land were portrayed as "weak, passive satellites to powerful, effective men." Most of the important characters portrayed by television were white, male, middle class, unmarried, and in the prime of life, whereas TV women were cast either as lovers or mothers. Less than 20 percent of female TV characters worked outside the home, compared with 50 percent in real life. Yet those who watched the most television stated in Gerbner's survey that only a few women held jobs in America. Those who watched the most TV agreed with the statement that women should stay at home and let men run the country.

Television viewers are bombarded one moment with commercials for high calorie junk food and the next moment with images of skinny women models.

Gerbner found that people over the age of sixty-five were conspicuously underrepresented on TV. They were often portrayed as weak, politically powerless, or physically ill. In reality, the elderly form America's most rapidly expanding age group and are powerful political lobby. They are healthier than any previous older generation. Yet the more Gerbner's respondents watched TV, the more they agreed that the elderly were a shrinking part of the population, politically powerless, and far less healthy today than in previous times.

Frequent TV users grossly overestimated the percentage of Americans employed as doctors, lawyers, athletes, and entertainers. All four of those professions dominate the prime time professional field, whereas blue-collar and service jobs on television are almost invisible, in spite of the fact that they compose about 60 percent of the real world work force. Gerbner's research suggests that television aggrandizes the professions that are the most out of reach for the majority of young people and neglects the occupations that most young people will have opportunities in. Gerbner charges that there are some dangers in this distorted version of the labor force: "You almost never see the farmer, the factory worker or the small businessman . . . Thus not only do lawyers and other professionals find they cannot measure up to the image TV projects of them, but children's occupational aspirations are channeled in unrealistic directions."[3] It is little wonder, according to Gerbner, that American TV viewers are dissatisfied with the less glamorous occupations many hold in life.

In televisionland, Gerbner found eating habits left much to be desired. Although television characters lived almost entirely on junk food and guzzled alcohol fifteen times more often than they drank water, he notes most managed to keep thin, healthy, and attractive in spite of it. Not surprisingly, the Annenberg team of investigators found that habitual TV viewers ate more, used alcohol more, exercised less, and possessed what he characterized as an "almost mystical faith" in the ability of medical science to restore health. Gerbner concludes: "Television may well be the single most pervasive source of health information. And its over-idealized images of medical people, coupled with complacency about unhealthy lifestyles, leaves both patients and doctors vulnerable to disappointment, frustration and even litigation."[4]

Health care experts have long linked obesity in both children and adults with TV viewing. Yet the Annenberg studies' findings on health contradictions raise even more disturbing questions in my mind about the relatively recent phenomenon of eating disorders. Could anorexia nervosa and bulimia be one tragic side effect of both programs and commercials, which sell tantalizing food and "perfect" bodies simultaneously? NBC news anchor Connie Chung observed on a special news report about weight: "We send our children conflicting messages on TV—eat fat and look thin."[5]

She's got a point. Television viewers are bombarded one moment with commercials for high calorie junk food and the next moment with images of skinny women models. Several million young American women now suffer serious eating disorders from what experts say is mounting pressure to stay thin. Where is that pressure coming from? Much of it comes from idealized images offered up constantly by media to today's young women, suggesting what the norm should be. Such conflicting messages find a home in impressionable young minds. Some experts claim that thousands of youngsters, mostly female, are alternately gorging themselves and starving themselves to death, while millions more induce vomiting to keep the calories off. Some medical experts attribute the rise in the severe and sometimes fatal eating disorders to the "commercialized cult of thinness" delivered through visual mediums.[6] They promote eating disorders by portraying slenderness as the desired ideal, charges James Kreisle, Jr., a psychiatrist who treats the problem.[7] If she doesn't look like the emaciated model of the commercial or skinny heroine of the program, a young girl gets the clear message that something is wrong. Many resort to extreme diets and exercise routines—programs that frequently fail, leaving them frustrated and unhappy.

Although media images are not the only factor behind such problems, they can contribute significantly, and serious psychological and physical harm is being done, conclude the experts. They point out that the problem burgeoned in the eighties, about the time the first generation of children heavily exposed to television were coming of age. "I attribute the problem a lot to the media," Arizona psychologist Connie Copenhaver, who specializes in treating dieting disorders, told me in a recent interview. She observed that for years we never saw an overweight woman on television. "Now with 'Oprah Winfrey' and 'Roseanne,' things are changing a little, but we still seldom see anything but thin women on TV in a starring or appealing role," she notes. Copenhaver complains that women are bombarded with visual suggestions of thinness in ads, movies, TV—role models that most women can never attain or maintain: "It's very unhealthy and unrealistic. Most of my patients have a totally distorted body image."

Copenhaver notes that made-for-TV movies and news reports about eating disorders have actually seemed to encourage the problem in some of her patients. "I really get unhappy with movies like *Pretty Woman*," notes Copenhaver, "where the body of leading lady Julia Roberts wasn't good enough for the bathtub scene, so the carefully made-up body of another model was used instead and the scenes edited to make it look like one woman instead of two different women. Women look at such totally unrealistic visual illusions and ask, 'Why can't I be that way?' Men see it and ask women, 'Why can't you look this way?' Yet the *whole thing is an illusion.*" The result, says Copenhaver, is discontent with real life and totally unrealistic sexual expectations.[8] The growing epidemic of anorexia nervosa and bulimia may be one of the strongest testimonies yet to the suggestive power of artificial imagery.

The Annenberg studies found that, with only a few exceptions, many minorities on television were employed in subordinate or supporting roles—typically as a white male hero's comic sidekick. The subliminal message, whether intentional or not, according to Gerbner, is that minorities should accept an inferior social or economic status as being both inevitable and deserved. A similar message apparently comes through subtly but powerfully to heavy TV viewers, who were asked whether whites should legally be able to keep blacks out of their neighborhoods or if there should be laws against interracial marriage. Gerbner found that the greater the number of hours viewers watched, the more they answered yes to both questions.[9]

Even when minorities are portrayed as leaders, they are often portrayed as crime fighters. An even more disturbing observation, notes Carlos Cortes, author of a book on ethnic images, is that many television minorities are cast as criminals, hustlers, or gang members. He points out that in TV-land racially complex America, especially in the cities, is a tough, dangerous, and deadly place. He notes that in the world of "Miami Vice" "a multiracial vice-squad, led by a Latino, wages war against black pimps, Latino drug dealers, Asian smugglers, and white killers. Minorities also lined up on both sides of the law-and-order struggle in TV's American Everycity of "Hill Street Blues."[10]

The message is subtle but strong. Whether they portray law-breakers or law enforcers, notes Cortes, in the world of television the one thing a minority is, is an expert in violence. Even when the force portrayed by TV-land cops is legal or justified, it is often portrayed excessively and unrealistically. The result is to paint an unsettling stereotype of minorities as people who enjoy "living by the sword." How do such images contribute to America's continuing struggles with racial polarization and distrust? Is it harder to love your neighbor if you are convinced that he might kill you?

> *Vast portions of the Old Testament contain stern warnings about the importance of a just legal system, and Christians especially should be interested in maintaining one out of sheer obedience to God's Word. However . . . Christian perceptions of our criminal justice system are deeply polluted by TV fantasy.*

The Annenberg studies found that perceptions of crime in general are greatly affected by television. TV depicts ten times more criminal violence than actually happens in real life. On television, more than half of the characters were involved in some type of violence once a week, whereas in reality less than 1 percent of the total population at the time of Gerbner's studies were the victim of a crime. Almost half of the heavy TV viewers rated their fear of crime as "very serious." Avid television viewers exhibited paranoia, and especially fearful were those whom TV frequently depicts as victims: women, the elderly, nonwhites, foreigners, and lower-class citizens. TV entertainment, concludes Gerbner, is conditioning viewers to think of themselves as potential victims. He found that television creates what he calls the "mean-world syndrome" among heavy viewers who exhibited a deep distrust of strangers.[11]

Criminologists agree with Gerbner's findings about distorted views of crime. Some agree that both TV news reports and fictional programs create fear among the elderly, who are the least affected statistically by crime. In statistical reality, most crimes occur in low-income neighborhoods and affect people (especially males) who are fifteen to twenty-four years old. By focusing on the most grue-some or unusual crimes, the impression is left in the minds of viewers that most crimes committed are violent, when in fact only 10 percent of all crimes are of a violent nature. Newscast viewers often assume that the crimes reported on TV are not exceptions to the rule but representatives of the norm. For example, one crimi-nologist points out that a crime against the proverbial "little old lady" is more likely to be reported by the news media rather than a crime against a young member of a street gang in a tough section of town. I know from my own experience as a reporter that this is true. Yet statistically, the crime against the elderly lady is least like-ly to happen.[12] Confusion often results, partly because TV vacil-lates between showing exceptions to the rule at one moment and projecting representative norms the next. Distinctions between the two are difficult to draw. Both rules and exceptions are painted with extremely broad strokes at a rapid-fire pace, and fine distinc-tions between the two tend to blend together.

American teenagers know what a mean world it is—especially the world in Miami, Florida. One teen from rural Grants, New Mexico, who was interviewed for *TV Guide* several years ago, ad-mitted that she has never been to Miami but has seen all she wants to on "Miami Vice": "All there is is violence in Miami. Bystanders get shot in front of things happening. A lot of drug pushers all over. No way I'd want to live in that place."[13] Many kids in remote towns all across America have only television to provide them with knowledge of America's big cities.

One tragic result of artificially created fear is a pronounced willingness of heavy TV viewers to strongly favor more spending for military and police budgets at the expense of social services.

Still another result may be that it inclines us to make bad choices about how to run our system of justice. We vote and legislate based on what we have seen on "L.A. Law" instead of what actually is true. Harvard Law School professor Alan Dershowitz notes that many of the legal premises that underlie episodes of "Hill Street Blues," "Miami Vice," and other dramas are unrealistic, deceptively simple, or just plain wrong.

The danger of these shows, he insists, is that week after week millions of Americans are sent distorted perceptions of the criminal justice system, such as the notion that you've got to choose between safety in the streets and the Bill of Rights.[14] Dershowitz warns that such utter lack of realism about the law is dangerous: "The danger of these myths is that TV will become real life, even if it doesn't reflect real life . . . If millions of American TV viewers come to believe that the law as presented on the TV shoot-'em-ups reflects reality, then our most cherished constitutional rights will become seriously endangered."[15]

Is America's criminal justice system in trouble because TV imagery feeds our fears and influences our political decisions about criminal justice?

Vast portions of the Old Testament contain stern warnings about the importance of a just legal system, and Christians especially should be interested in maintaining one out of sheer obedience to God's Word. However, I discovered while serving on a citizen's task force for Justice Fellowship, the legislative action arm of Charles Colson's Prison Fellowship organization, that Christian perceptions of our criminal justice system are deeply polluted by TV fantasy.

Every year in America, thousands of nonviolent criminals—bad-check writers, tax evaders, and those guilty of so-called white collar crimes—inhabit prison cells at an astronomical cost to American taxpayers. It costs approximately $80,000 to build each cell and $17,000 a year to lock up one individual.[16] Some of these prisoners need to be locked up. However, according to Colson, nonviolent inmates constitute at least half of all prison inmates and are not dangerous to society. Many could be working in restitution programs outside prison walls that are not only far less costly, but, in some cases, actually pay back victims.

Even worse, Colson tells us, locking up nonviolent inmates quickly turns them into hateful and violent people who come out worse than they went in because of dangerous and overcrowded conditions. However, in my work with Justice Fellowship, I found that many Christians are not only reluctant to push for any substantive change but are sometimes suspicious and critical of other better-informed Christians who are working for reforms. I found the images of "Miami Vice" and "L.A. Law" difficult to argue with, even among believers. There is little doubt in my mind, after talking with dozens of these emotionally wrought individuals, that their perceptions of truth have been deeply damaged by fictional crime stories.

The current trends in television are toward more so-called docudramas and made-for-TV movies based on real-life stories (many of which never let the facts get in the way of a good plot), as well as the new "reality-based" programs, such as "A Current Affair," "America's Most Wanted," and "Unsolved Mysteries." The trend, at least for now, is definitely in the direction of "reality-based" shows, which I suspect may generate even more confusion about the real world than their dramatic counterparts.

Yet these "reality-based" programs share television's inherent bent toward deception. Screenwriter Loring Mandel calls television a betrayer and a liar. He observes:

> All those hours of distorted social messages beamed at us with the brilliance of exploding electrons . . . teach us that the world is violent but bloodless. That loss, pain and grief are not consequences of violence. That healing is instantaneous. That children are smarter than adults. That most women are bleeding hearts and most men are self-important. That no problem is so great that it can't be solved in a half-hour. Or an hour. These things are drummed at us. We hear laughter at words that don't evoke laughter and watch anger evoked only by the need for a cliff-hanger. We see human relationships built entirely upon false emotions. And we can't easily separate the fantasy from the real.[17]

Gerbner's studies were conducted in the eighties. If the same studies were conducted today, many of the results might be the same though some new and different societal stereotypes would emerge. What probably would not change is the degree that television distorts reality for a significant number of Americans.

What new social truths and stereotypes will TV offer us in the nineties? The picture is now an uncomfortable one for Christians and clergy. TV-land increasingly portrays them as villains, troublemakers, bumbling idiots, and fools, and the recent scandals in televangelism have given TV writers even more "reality-based" material to work with.

If social scientists like George Gerbner study the perceptions of TV viewers about Christianity in the nineties, will their research reveal that Christians are perceived by the general public the way they are now often portrayed on TV?

George Gerbner concludes: "If you can write a nation's stories, you needn't worry about who makes its laws. . . . Those who tell stories hold the power in society. Today television tells most of the stories to most of the people most of the time."[18]

NOTES

1. Jerry Mander, *Four Arguments for the Elimination of Television* (New York: William Morrow, 1978), pp. 240-42.
2. Harry F. Waters, "Life According to TV," pp. 136-38. From *Newsweek*, December 6, 1982. Copyright © 1982 Newsweek, Inc. All rights reserved. Reprinted by permission.
3. George Gerbner, quoted by Waters, "Life According to TV," p. 137.
4. Ibid., p. 138.
5. NBC-TV broadcast, June 3, 1987.
6. Susan Willard, NSW, BCSW, quoted by Priscilla F. Vayda, "Family Dysfunction at Root of Eating Disorders," *The Times-Picayune*, June 26, 1991, p. F-3.
7. James E. Kreisle, Jr., quoted by Lanie Tankard, "Can Parents Prevent Eating Disorders?" *Austin Family*, March, 1988, p. 42.
8. Telephone interview with Connie Copenhaver, July 2, 1991.
9. George Gerbner, quoted in Waters, "Life According," p. 137.
10. Carlos Cortes, "TV Stereotypes Ignore Dramas of Life," *Media and Values*, Summer/Fall 1987, p. 25.

11. Waters, "Life According," p. 138.

12. "TV Accounts 'Distort' News About Crime," *Arizona Republic*, December 3, 1984, p. A-6.

13. Quoted by Michael Leahy, "Our Cities Are Big, Bad Places—If You Believe Prime-Time TV," *TV Guide*, May 3, 1986, p. 5.

14. Alan Dershowitz, "The Cops Are All Guilty," *TV Guide*, May 25, 1985, pp. 5-7.

15. Ibid., p. 7.

16. Charles Colson, Prison Fellowship fund raising letter.

17. Loring Mandel, "How I'd Save Television," *Parade Magazine*, May 11, 1986, p. 7. Copyright 1986 by Loring Mandel. From his article "How I'd Save Television." Originally appeared in *Parade Magazine*. Reprinted with permission from Parade, copyright © 1986.

18. Waters, "Life According," p. 136, and George Gerbner, "Television: Modern Mythmaker," *Media and Values*, Summer/Fall, 1987, p. 9.

13

GRAVEN IMAGES: WE ARE WHAT WE SEE

An uncomfortable truth about television is well summarized in a biting film satire from the seventies, *Network*. In one scene, an aging network program executive named Max Schumacher tells Diana, a young, ruthless program director: "Television isn't the truth; it's an amusement park. We're in the boredom killing business. We'll tell you anything you want to hear. We deal in illusions; none of it is true, but we're the only thing [the viewer knows] and you're beginning to believe it." After Schumacher is romantically dumped by Diana, he dismisses her incapacity for affection and commitment by pointing out: "I don't think she's capable of loving anyone. . . . She's the television generation . . . she learned life from 'Bugs Bunny.'"[1]

The television generation has indeed learned life from "Bugs Bunny." And from "General Hospital," "All My Children," "The Love Boat," "Dallas," and a host of other illusionary portrayals of human relationships. All across the country, day after day, even in Christian homes, individuals and entire families sit transfixed before the set, absorbed in fabricated scenes and imaginary relational conflicts portrayed in television dramas and soap operas.

Once, while witnessing such a scenario in a Christian home I was visiting, I asked if the family didn't see any problem, from a Christian perspective, with the sexually explicit soap opera they were engrossed in. Their teenage daughter flippantly replied: "I just watch to see the good looking guys! There aren't any in my town or in my life!"

Was it possible, I asked, that such programs might give her false ideas about what real relationships were all about? She looked puzzled for a moment, as though she had never considered the idea, then shrugged and turned back to the screen. Her mother, sensing the point of my remark, hastily added: "We only allow this because we think it generates family discussion." But I saw no discussion going on—only the glazed eyes of four mesmerized people staring into the tube, drinking in the fantasy world of the soap opera.

Television is common ground between believers and nonbelievers. Studies show there is little difference between the viewing habits of the two groups. Perhaps that is part of the reason there seems to be little difference today between the thinking and behavior of Christians and nonbelievers on matters of sexuality, romance, marriage, divorce, and family life. Quite simply, both groups watch the same TV programs and emulate the same behavior patterns.

Reality seldom lives up to the dream world TV offers. Television preaches a gospel of self-fulfillment that does not exist and will forever elude us in reality. Many people are unhappy or are frustrated in their search for happiness but cannot pinpoint the source of their discontentment. Real life seems flat to them compared with the diet of unreal imagery that dominates their thought processes. What woman wouldn't feel inadequate after unconsciously comparing herself to the "perfect" women presented on the tube? Why should anyone persevere through problems when there are quick and easy resolutions to life as TV presents it? We drink it all in, unaware of how what we see influences us in dozens of ways.

What about those economically trapped beyond reach of the American dream TV so vividly portrays? As one writer put it, TV "taunts and teases and jabs at the poor with sports events they'll never attend, clothes they'll never wear, game shows they'll never be on, food they'll never eat and cars they'll never drive (unless they steal them)."[2] What influence does it exert on those inner city youth who opt to peddle illegal drugs because they see such activity as the shortest and best option for grabbing their share of the American dream?

Television also haunts those who have the money to buy the American dream. Many who live in beautiful homes and have an abundance of whatever television has convinced them they must have are often depressed, vaguely restless, and yearning for something they cannot express. To what degree, I wonder, are many viewers unconsciously haunted by the gap between TV's version of reality and the real-life version?

The hundreds of hours of images that make up soap operas, sitcoms, and movie specials are almost completely fictional, yet the people and situations on the programs "look" real and even become real to many people. This pseudoreality has a strong impact. Studies of TV and social behavior made over the past twenty years suggest that adults and children are heavily influenced by TV in the way they handle life's problems. A federal study released in the late seventies concluded that television influenced the way people developed human relationships: family routines, relationships with co-workers on the job, moral and ethical values, and dealing with rebellious children. Viewers relied on TV for their understanding of deviations from the social norm sexually, politically, socially, and interpersonally.

Many people live by the fare of TV fiction, researchers found. They copy and act out the imagery they carry in their minds—in a more subtle and sophisticated version of the way children play "pretend" with the fictional characters of TV. When these people face family problems they tend to recall and act out the way the problem was solved in a similar fictional setting on TV. They see TV drama as directly relevant to their own lives and take the fictional content of programs more seriously and literally than most social thinkers and behavioral scientists had previously realized.

The fact that TV and movies are fictional did not stop people from patterning their own lives after the people and situations they watched on the tube.[3]

A group of mental health experts aware of this phenomenon has actually petitioned soap opera writers and producers to work nonviolent and emotionally healthy ways of managing anger into plot lines in an effort to influence viewers in high-risk categories where violence and abuse are concerned.[4]

A particularly bizarre example of this "adult emulation" was discovered by New York State Attorney General Rudolph Giulini. He found that the powerful stereotypes in the movie *The Godfather* and its successors subliminally influenced the behavior and self-image of mobsters. When Giulini compared tape recorded testimony taken both before and after the release of the movie, he found that the vocal patterns of his suspects had changed. The suspects interviewed after the movie's release sounded more like the characters in the movie than they had before seeing it. One suspect was so impressed by the film that he played a tape of its theme over and over in his car.[5]

American mobsters aren't the only ones to try to live in the illusion of the *Godfather* characters. Judith Miller and Laurie Mylroie, the authors of *Saddam Hussein and the Crisis in the Gulf*, mention that Saddam Hussein is reportedly obsessed with the movie—it is apparently his favorite, and he watches it repeatedly. They note: "The iron-willed character of the Don may perhaps be the most telling model for the [puzzling] figure that rules Iraq."[6]

A second study released in the early eighties by the National Institute of Mental Health concluded that there exists what one behavioral science expert described as a "general learning effect from television viewing which is important in the development and functioning of many viewers, particularly children." The report concluded that, along with other social factors, "[television] may play a significant role in shaping behavioral lifestyle."[7]

Viewers not only emulate the behavior of TV characters but unconsciously regard many characters as "real." Christian author Tim Kimmel tells of an incident related to him by a friend of his in the pastorate: a woman in the friend's congregation actually re-quested prayer in church for one of the couples on her favorite soap opera. Kimmel suggests that when Christians can't tell fiction from reality society is in more trouble than we think.[8]

As ludicrous and extreme as that example may seem, it is not as isolated as we would like to believe. David Hellerstein, a New York psychiatrist who has studied the way people regard television entertainment, discovered that quite a few grownups have imagi-nary friends in TV-land. One highly educated couple he knew had an extremely close, imaginary friendship with the characters on one particular evening soap opera. This couple referred to the characters by their nicknames and frequently discussed them. "I was preparing to question my friend's sanity," confessed the psy-chiatrist, "but then I realized that my wife and I have an imaginary friendship with the local newscasters on Channel 2—so I kept my mouth shut." He went on to say: "TV characters provide the illu-sion of intimacy—and couples can choose from thousands of TV characters to find those few they most would like to emulate. And there's the added advantage that these 'friends' will never snub you and never bring their bratty kids over to your house."[9]

> *The shattered marriages of this generation and the searching, disillusioned men and women of this age who drift from one ro-mantic relationship to another suggest that many may be searching for a "reality" they have been electronically conditioned to see.*

While anchoring early morning local television news, I experi-enced a little of this "illusion of intimacy" that Hellerstein speaks of every time I went to the grocery store. Even if I went stripped of makeup and in an old T-shirt and faded jeans, inevitably some stranger would accost me in the frozen foods section. Regardless of my casual appearance, the person would note the similarity between my facial features and the image he was accustomed to looking at as he drank his early morning coffee. His face would light up, and he would cry, "I know you!" or, "I watch you every morning!" Often he would grasp my hand, look at me in amazement, and say, "Why you're taller than I thought!" or, "You look younger in person!" He would stare quizzically as we talked, trying to differentiate between the one-dimensional image he had mentally carried before and the new multidimensional impression he now had from seeing me in person.

I discovered that when people carry your image around inside their heads, it can evoke some unusual responses. They will talk with you as though they have known you all their lives. As we stood in the grocery isle surrounded with bags of frozen peas and corn, often these same people would begin to tell me their personal problems, or what they thought of me or my colleagues, or how they thought I should improve my personal appearance—things that most people would normally never dream of walking up to a total stranger and saying in a grocery store.

Their behavior was terribly disconcerting to me until I understood that these people perceived me as an intimate friend. It never dawned on them that watching me anchor the news every morning as they munched bites of toast or sipped orange juice at the kitchen table was not at all tantamount to knowing me personally. Most were completely oblivious to the jarring effect their approach had on me. They were total strangers to me, but my image frequented their bedroom or kitchen, so they assumed that our television relationship earned them the right to converse with me or criticize me as though I were one of their children.

In spite of the apparent links between television and behavior, many continue to underestimate TV's influence in the sexual revolution and in the mushrooming phenomena of divorce and remarriage. Yet the shattered marriages of this generation and the searching, disillusioned men and women of this age who drift from one romantic relationship to another suggest that many may be searching for a "reality" they have been electronically conditioned to see.

Today's viewers are subjected to hundreds of hours of unrealistically presented sexual situations, male-female relationships, and marital situations. The images of those situations remain in the mind, acting as standards of what should be. Since many live in these fantasy worlds for hours, is it any wonder that so many in this generation are confused about what is truth? Conflict and dissatisfaction result when real life does not measure up to a movie or soap opera plot.

Psychiatrist David Hellerstein found many couples gauging the success of their marriages by what they saw on TV. One woman told him, "I always compare how my husband deals with a situation with what Bill Cosby would do."[10] She admitted feeling angry and cheated when her husband fails to measure up to Cosby.

Since many Christians are reservoirs of the same fantasies, Christian marriages now suffer in much the same way. In her book *Dreams and Delusions* (Bantam/Doubleday/Dell), Christian counselor and author Mari Hanes relates a counselee's confession: "I had a real problem with fantasies and daydreams for 13 years of my 17-year marriage. I dreamed of a more comfortable lifestyle with more money and nicer clothes. These daydreams often included more recognition and romance." Hanes notes that this woman almost ruined her marriage but finally overcame her unhappiness after she realized her daydreams were not her own, but instead the artificial suggestions of mediated imagery.[11]

Marriage counselors confirm that such expectations are a major cause of marital disharmony. One counselor told me that constantly he has to challenge his clients as to the source of their sexual expectations of each other. It is not surprising that sex within the daily routine of marriage might begin to look boring if our marital expectations spring unconsciously from the fantasy sexual situations offered on the screen. Real-life experience is bound to suffer in comparison, yet couples are frequently unaware of this powerful influence. Psychiatrist David Hellerstein concludes that many American marriages now have three partners, two human and one electronic:

Television has profound effects on married couples at their most intimate moments. It is deeply incorporated into their relationships and into their fantasies and dreams. . . . Appealing characters on sitcoms and on dramatic series often become "friends" for couples, and these imagined relationships can lead people to model their lives after them, for better or worse. At worst, TV can be an escape from problems that desperately need to be dealt with directly. And an "affair" with TV watching can kill a marriage.[12]

The fast pace and slickness of the TV world can, according to author and researcher Miriam Arond, "promote unrealistic expectations of passionate romance, that life should have a pace of passion that your own life doesn't have." She concludes: "People are less good at weathering problems than they were in the old days."[13] Says California psychiatrist Dr. Pierre Mornell: "The images people see on TV are so unreal that they make working on a real marriage seem about as much fun as painting a battleship."[14] Some counselors and researchers agree that the quick fixes suggested by many TV shows can reinforce one's impulse in real life to get out fast.

The aim of the Christian life should be not to escape into the fantasy world that TV affords but to live deeply and thoroughly for God in whatever circumstances we find ourselves.

Perhaps Sheila is an example. She divorced her husband Joe on the grounds of extreme boredom ten years ago. Their lovemaking had been tepid; their conversations infrequent and unstimulating. After Sean, an old college classmate whom Sheila found to be more handsome and sexy, arrived on the scene, Sheila left Joe for Sean. Looking back now, Sheila admits that she misses Joe's solid, although mild, presence in her life. Her expectations for their life together were, by her admission, "absurdly unrealistic." She admits: "I craved romance and excitement and felt that they were the only important criteria by which to judge a union." Now she realizes, too late, that they are not.[15]

More than a million divorces take place each year in this country—that's a breakup of one out of every two marriages. Yet a recent study conducted on divorce showed than in only 10 percent of the cases studied did either partner feel that a second marriage had improved or bettered their lives.[16] The statistics on divorce bear testimony to the fact that when the endings are not as happy as an old-time Western, where couples rode off into the sunset and lived happily ever after, they often change horses and continue a futile search for a sunset that might be merely the fabrication of a television or movie producer.

I heard an author of a book about prisons say he discovered in his research that convicts have their own code of behavior—a code based on the lifestyle and ethics of the prison system. One of the reasons released prisoners have such a tough adjustment back into society is that they try to make the code of behavior that worked inside the prison walls work in their new life outside. There is an analogy here to those who have made themselves prisoners of television. When they spend hours a day watching television they are unconscious prisoners of the unrealistic code of social behavior based in pseudosituations and fictional lifestyles. Like convicts, the prisoners of television imagery carry their fantasy code back into real life when the set is turned off. Many find to their frustration that the code does not work in reality. A deep gap emerges between the way life resolves itself on "Dallas" and the way life really is in the actual city of Dallas.

I once heard a pastor say that true fulfillment in life is found in the everyday, not in the exotic. The aim of the Christian life should be not to escape into the fantasy world that TV affords but to live deeply and thoroughly for God in whatever circumstances we find ourselves. That is reality. Television is a false escape.

Can Christians be effective servants of the truth that the Bible presents if their mental processes are torn between the truth that the Scriptures present and what the fantasy world of TV offers? To say that Christians can consume hour after hour of illusion and not be affected in some way is like saying: "I'm going to eat four banana cream pies, but I just won't let the calories affect me!" The Bible tells us what truth really is, but televised fantasy often paints a vividly deceptive picture of "truth" in our minds. The scriptural challenge to Christians from the apostle Paul is: "Do not conform any longer to the pattern of this world, but be transformed by the renewing of your mind" (Romans 12:2). But today, television is doing much of the mental transformation and renewal. Somehow I doubt that is what Paul had in mind.

Back to the movie *Network*. Observes TV screen writer Lloyd Billingsley: "There is something to be said for the counsel of Howard Beale," the mad prophet-anchorman who was another central character in the Academy Award winning movie. "If you want truth," he screams to his audience, "don't come to us. We'll tell you anything but the truth. Go to God. Go to your gurus. Go to yourselves. But don't come to us."[17] Television, Beale knows, is incapable of conveying truth. He reminds the television generation that "your lives are real, we are the illusion." But, concludes Billingsley, far too many people have it the other way around.[18]

NOTES

1. From the movie *Network*.
2. Terry Galanoy, "And Now—This Timely Message," *Coping with Television*, ed. J. F. Littell (Evanston, Ill.: McDougal Littell, 1973), p. 199, quoted in "Growing with Television," The Media Action Research Center (Seabury, New York, 1980), Unit I, p. 2.
3. *Television and Social Behavior*, vol. 4, quoted by Jerry Mander, *Four Arguments for the Elimination of Television* (New York: William Morrow, 1978), p. 254.
4. Sandy Rovner, "Soap Operas Can Help Viewers Manage Anger," *The Washington Post*, reprinted in *The Times-Picayune*, March 29, 1991, p. E-1.
5. "Media Watch," *Media and Values*, Spring 1988, p. 23.
6. Judith Miller and Laurie Mylroie, *Saddam Hussein and the Crisis in the Gulf* (New York: Random House-Times Books, 1990), p. 24.
7. "Networks Voice Views on Violence Research," *Media and Values*, Fall 1985, p. 11.

8. Tim Kimmel, *Little House on the Freeway* (Portland, Oreg.: Multnomah, 1987), p. 153.

9. David Hellerstein, "Can TV Cause Divorce?" *TV Guide*, September 26, 1987, p. 6. Reprinted with permission from TV Guide® Magazine, Copyright © 1987 by News America Publications Inc., Radnor, Pennsylvania.

10. Ibid.

11. Mari Hanes, *Dreams and Delusions* (New York: Bantam/Doubleday/Dell, 1991), p. 33.

12. Hellerstein, "Divorce," p. 7.

13. Miriam Arond, quoted by Hellerstein, "Divorce," p. 7.

14. Nina Combs, "Is Your Love Life Going Down 'The Tube'?" condensed from *Redbook*, reprinted in *The Reader's Digest*, October 1987, pp. 147-48.

15. Dalma Heyn, "When Divorce Is Not the Answer," *McCall's*, August 1987, p. 28.

16. Ibid.

17. The movie *Network*, quoted by Lloyd Billingsley, "TV: Where the Girls Are Good Looking and the Good Guys Always Win," *Christianity Today*, October 4, 1985, p. 41. Copyright © 1985 by *Christianity Today*. Used by permission.

18. Ibid.

14

THE "VID-KID" GENERATION

I reach for the knob on the nursery door, and it opens to a semi-darkened room where my two year old lies sleeping in his crib. "Good morning, son." He stirs at the sound of my voice. Struggling to his feet, with eyes full of sleep, he reaches to me with outstretched hands. As I lift him from the crib to hold him in my arms, he mumbles his first audible words of the day: "Big Bird."

It is the first thought on his mind. Not me, not even toast or Cheerios®, but the giant yellow canary of "Sesame Street." We hurry down the stairs and into the dining room, where he points to the darkened TV set, crying again for Big Bird. A mere flick of the switch pacifies him into mesmerized silence. Gone are the nagging cries for cereal, the demands for juice—in fact, I can ask several times about what he wants to eat, but he is now so engrossed that my inquiries about breakfast bounce back to me without answer, like echoes from an empty canyon. It will be this way for the next hour. Or the hour after that or the hour after that, if I permit it.

It is the ultimate temptation for the parents of young children to plop them in front of the tube, where they are physically safe, quiet, and out of our way. Every moment spent there buys us a precious moment of uninterrupted peace—a rare commodity for a busy mom or dad. It is an easy habit to cultivate—and what can it hurt, we argue?

However, if adults are impacted as strongly as I have already suggested, then what about our children? Kids are even more vulnerable to the fantasized version of life presented on the screen than are adults. Children, especially young children, don't view television the same way that adults do because children have very little in terms of life experience to bring to viewing.

Preschoolers lack a fully developed frame of reference with which to evaluate what they see. They are less able to call up other mental information or values to balance out the impressions that TV leaves. Toddlers and preschoolers, especially, absorb and store TV imagery like a sponge, with little or no capacity to interpret what they see beyond its face value. As one critic points out: "Very young children are unable to distinguish fantasy from reality on the television screen. They do not know what is fact and what is opinion. They do not understand the basis of many of the events that occur. They are exposed to the whole world—as seen through the eyes of a TV screen—before they have developed the ability to understand and to cope with the larger society."[1] A young child will be frightened by a monster movie, for example, not only because it leaves a lasting mental residue to haunt him again and again but because he cannot mentally distinguish between reality or make-believe by himself.

The powerful effect of some of these artificial memories is vividly illustrated by a phenomenon some fire fighters call the "Darth Vader Syndrome." Increasingly, masked fire fighters are noticing that many small children caught in burning homes are running from, hiding from, or furiously fighting and resisting rescuers instead of cooperating with them in the middle of life-threatening situations.

Subsequent interviews with small survivors pinpoint the problem. "I thought you were a spaceman," or, "I thought you were Darth Vadar," they confess. The gas masks and protective helmets worn by fire fighters are reminiscent of images of TV monsters or villains deeply embedded in the child's subconscious. Fire officials say the tragic juxtaposition of imagery may be costing some children and fire fighters their lives in the critical moments of rescue.[2] This problem also vividly illustrates the powerful effects that TV imagery can leave on children.

In what other ways are children being shaped by television? One dilemma TV presents for children is that it is turning them into adults before they are ready. Children now carry many adult images in their minds that they consider to be both reliable depictions of reality and something to model.

> *Author Neil Postman declares that "television all by itself may bring an end to childhood."*

There is a lively debate over the quality of children's programming, and parents should be concerned about it. However, regardless of the rhetoric over more and better children's programs, some surveys suggest that kids watch adult TV programs more often than they watch children's programs[3] and that many children prefer adult programming over kiddie shows. For example, the program "Dallas," along with several other prime time adult programs, ranked among the most popular programs in all age groups, including ages two to eleven.[4] That isn't surprising, since it is hard for adults to insulate children from what they watch. Too few parents consider carefully enough the potential impact of adult programming on children or seem willing to modify their own viewing habits for the sake of their kids.

Consequently, childhood as it once was no longer exists, points out communications professor Joshua Meyrowitz. Why? Because human development is based on more than just a series of biological stages. It is based as well on patterns of access to social knowledge. It used to be, according to Meyrowitz, that kids learned the "secrets" of adulthood slowly and in stages. They could be shielded from material they were too immature to handle. There were things appropriate for the sixth grader that parents would keep hidden from the first grader or the toddler. But no longer, writes Meyrowitz, because today "a secret revelation machine" is now a part of the living room. He notes:

> Communication through print allows for a great deal of control over the social information to which children have access. Reading and writing involve a complex code of symbols that must be memorized and practiced. Children must read simple books before they can read adult books.
>
> On TV, however, there is no complex code to exclude young viewers. . . . Even two-year-old children, unable to read or write their own names, find television accessible and absorbing.[5]

The ability to read and the level of skill are no longer buffers for social information revealed to children. "Television undermines behavioral distinctions," he observes, "because it encompasses both children and adults in a single informational sphere or environment."[6] Since we can't censor our children's viewing without censoring our own, Meyrowitz points out that television takes our children across the globe even before we give them permission to cross the street.[7]

Television transported both parents and children to the Persian Gulf War, despite the fact that few children could put what television showed them into a meaningful context. One eight-year-old boy who watched coverage from the Persian Gulf expressed his feelings about what he saw this way: "I feel scared that they might blow up my block and—boom!—My mom and everybody would be gone and then there would just be me."[8] This child had difficulty conceptualizing the vast distance between Arabia and America and putting it into a meaningful perspective.

Glen Sparks, a Purdue University communications professor who has extensively researched the emotional effects of visual imagery on children, says such a response is typical for a child of eight. He says kids ages six to twelve are especially vulnerable in less obvious ways, not only to fantasy violence and horror movies but also to news coverage of real disasters and wars.[9] After seeing TV reports of collapsed bridges in San Francisco during the major earthquake of 1989, my own six-year-old son became repeatedly panicky each time we drove across the Mississippi River bridge at home in New Orleans.

Children in the six- to twelve-year-old age range, says Sparks, are old enough to distinguish news events from "pretend" but lack the emotional maturity to mentally cope with either. Many are deeply troubled by what they see but are sometimes afraid to express their feelings, especially if they are ridiculed by adults. Sparks says many unsuspecting parents expose young children through television to images of war and disaster that they still need protection from until they have a chance to catch up emotionally.[10]

Author Neil Postman declares that "television all by itself may bring an end to childhood."[11] Increasingly, in homes where both parents work, the latchkey child who comes home to an empty house now has unlimited access to whatever TV serves up. Experts warn that children of divorce are especially vulnerable to the effects of TV distortion, because it can become a frequent and welcome escape from the pain of losing a parent. In such cases where divorce results in a latchkey situation, the combination is not a healthy one.

Psychiatrist David Elkind also warns that TV is a major vehicle for thrusting premature adulthood on teens: "Teenagers now are expected to confront life's challenges with the maturity once expected only of the middle-aged, without any time for preparation."[12]

A second way television changes children is through the behavior it models. Perhaps nowhere is the power of artificial imagery more obvious than in a child's behavior. We know that children copy and emulate what they see modeled before them. It does not take a mental giant to figure out that much of what children now copy and act out is from television. Characters and scenes pressed a thousand times into the memory bank can replace and stifle a child's own creative thought patterns. Someone else's view of life becomes a subliminal part of his psyche.

Children also copy what they see modeled in the home. We sometimes joke about the danger of children becoming like their parents. It is certainly true that parents exert tremendous power over their children, if the child has ample opportunity to observe and imitate parental behavior. We know that they often clone us in ways that we would rather they miss, picking up traits and habits that we wish they wouldn't notice. We have a tremendous opportunity to influence our children's behavior and beliefs through our own conduct, unless of course, they spend more time gazing at another role model. Are parents unwittingly allowing TV to usurp their authority as chief role models?

But many children now spend more time with fantasy television characters than they do interacting with their parents. The important job of modeling behavior is now shared with, or, in some cases, delegated to television. TV is increasingly the major competitor with parental influence. The risk in this is that children will be more influenced by the unrealistic view of life offered by TV than with the real-life experience they encounter in the family sphere.

Home is the boot camp of life—the place where children need to learn about good and to be protected from evil. However, when TV becomes the mediator between parents and children, it sometimes reverses that process. When our children are watching the tube, they are often learning the opposite of what we as parents may wish. Current trends in programs and commercials that portray kids as free-wheeling, savvy, independent spirits in control of their own little spheres have strong appeal to immature minds. Communications professor Jay Rosen of New York University notes that because TV sells consumption as a way to happiness, "TV [tries] to sell children on a way of life . . . their parents may not want for them. . . . One way is to present [images of] kids who are independent, who have nothing to learn from their parents, because then children have a right to consume the way they want to consume and parents have no basis on which to say no."[13]

TV sets up a conflict in the home between the view of the world that parents may wish their children to have on a variety of matters and the phony world that television presents so convincingly. Observes Alvin Poussaint, psychiatrist and consultant for "The Cosby Show," TV parents "are overly permissive, always understanding; they never get very angry. There are no boundaries or limits set."[14] What effect do such images of parental perfection have on real relationships between kids and parents?

The problem may be particularly critical in the first five years of life, which are especially strategic. Experts tell us that that is when the core of a child's personality is formed. Yet since that is the time when children are the most demanding, it is also the most tempting time to use TV as a baby-sitter. Since both of my children were in this age category while I wrote this book, I know firsthand how tempting it can be to let TV do the baby-sitting!

Nielsen figures show that children ages two to five now watch TV an average of about twenty-eight hours a week.[15] Remember, that's only an average. That means that those most vulnerable to television are spending a significant amount of time in the most critical developmental phase of their life learning "reality" from a medium that has a serious problem presenting it. Subtly the personalities of our children are being refashioned to some degree in whatever images TV provides.

What are some of the most damaging messages that I see children getting? That aggression is the way to become powerful and significant; that violence and crime are the norm, not the exception; that the world is an immoral, dishonest, unethical place and if you can't lick 'em, you might as well join 'em; that it is hopeless to try to change society; that materialism brings contentment; that casual sex satisfies and is guilt-free; that drinking is a solution to problems; that women are second-class citizens; that kids are smarter than adults; that life should be fun all the time; that if information isn't entertaining, it's not worth knowing. Are we coming to grips with the long-term impact of these kinds of messages on kids?

The problem is not confined to the under-twelve crowd. What impressions do teenagers embrace from a steady diet of unreality? Researchers who studied TV's effect on the ethnic attitudes of more than a thousand New York City high school students found that many teens regard TV as both a learning tool and an accurate reflection of the real world. One in four agreed that "TV shows what life is really like" and that "people on TV are like real life," and 40 percent agreed that they learned a lot from the tube. The research also showed that blacks (who watch significantly more TV than whites) were the group most likely to see television as a reflection of real life.[16]

Even the more wholesome programs present unrealistic expectations of life convincingly.

Columnist Herbert London played clips of "Dallas," "Dynasty," and some other evening soaps with big business themes to a group of teens and then asked them to what lengths they would go to save a failing enterprise. Most told him they would do anything short of harming a family member to stay afloat. When asked if they would engage in immoral behavior to stay on top, as do the characters in the shows, not one teenager said no. When they were asked if they thought the behavior of businessmen on such shows was typical of American businessmen, most of the students said yes. However, when London asked if the teens actually knew any businessmen personally who behaved like J. R., most admitted that they did not.[17]

Although surveys suggest that Americans think parents should control their children's TV selections, two-thirds of those asked admit that not enough parental guidance is being applied.[18] I think there are a variety of reasons for this. As I mentioned previously, it is hard to restrict children's viewing without restricting your own, and TV is too tempting a baby-sitter for the busy, overstressed parent of today. Peer pressure from other children that breaks down the resistance of parents to some shows is another factor. Still another, less obvious, reason TV is hard to regulate is that the modern home, in many ways, is now boring compared to the home of a hundred years ago. Observes pastor and author Kevin Perrotta: "Home is less a center of activity than formerly. In many ways, it is a less interesting place to be."[19]

In many neighborhoods the open fields and wooded areas where I spent hours playing as a child have given way to the narrow streets and postage-stamp yards of subdivisions. Because many children are in day-care, subdivision streets and playgrounds are now ghost towns for the few children who remain home in the daytime. Today, it is harder in some ways to amuse and stimulate children at home, which also may be why many parents send children to preschool at a younger age.

I have talked with some Christian parents who exhibit concern about sending small children away at a young age for a few hours a day. Yet some of those same Christian mothers I know who distrust preschool will keep their children confined inside the home and in front of the TV set for hours on end. Some never realize that their children, especially the young preschooler, can be mentally more detached and further from parental influence when they are watching the TV at home than if they were at a school miles away.

Even the more wholesome programs present unrealistic expectations of life convincingly. Quickly resolving plots, instant gratification, and simplistic solutions foster an unnatural, unbalanced view of how the world really is. Someday our children will have to learn the difference between the two—and it will be painful. Warns one researcher, the terrible "toos" now inflict children of all ages—too many expectations, too many media images of perfection and achievement, too many fears, and too much guilt from too many shoulds. The result, according to Joseph Procaccini of Loyola College in Baltimore, is a growing number of children burned out from too many unrealistic expectations of life. He claims that what begins as lethargic and irritable behavior and progresses to mental exhaustion and forgetfulness can end up in anger or paranoia, or, in extreme cases, a dropout attitude or suicide threat. Procaccini blames "constant images of perfection and impossible achievement" in the mass media as a major factor in child burnout.[20]

Since Christianity fares poorly on TV, and children watch people on TV resolve problems day after day without bringing religious or moral belief systems into play, it doesn't surprise me that an increasing number of children and teens I know seem to feel that religious experience is confined to whatever happens on Sunday morning and has no bearing on behavior the rest of the week.

Unfortunately, Eastern religious concepts lend themselves well to the TV theater, and some children's programs are riddled with them. Children now learn the dualistic concept of evil equally matched against good, which is Eastern, instead of the concept of the sovereign God of Christianity who has evil on a leash. Cartoons preach the human ability to possess "superpowers" and to become "masters of the universe." Many of these fantasy concepts reflect Eastern religious philosophies, but Christian parents, many of whom have a hazy understanding of their own theological beliefs, much less those of Eastern religions, are unaware of the implications. Impressionable children can now go "ghost busting" on a program that encourages them to exert power over the occult in a cute and humorous context. Yet many parents are oblivious to the messages in these disarmingly "cute" programs, and consequently some make no attempt to refute or shield children from such ideas in the most formative years of their lives.

Years ago Walt Whitman wrote:

> There was a child went forth every day
> and the first object he look'd upon,
> that object he became
> and that object became a part of him for the day
>   or a certain part of the day
> or for many years or stretching cycles of years.[21]

A generation later, while real life passes by, the adults of tomorrow sit watching, passive and unprotected, as strange and mixed messages pour into the living room. The result could be mass behavior modification to an unprecedented degree.

When I was growing up, we used to sing a little song in Sunday school that went something like this:

> Be careful little eyes what you see
> Be careful little eyes what you see
> For the Father up above is looking down in love
> So be careful little eyes what you see.

Perhaps there was far more urgency in that simple little verse than most of us could ever have imagined.

NOTES

1. Patricia Skalka, "Take Control of Your TV," *Friendly Exchange*, Spring 1983, p. 26.
2. Lee Dalton, "The Monster in the Mask," *Friendly Exchange*, May 1986, p. 46.
3. Joanmarie Kalter, "How TV Is Shaking Up the American Family," *TV Guide*, July 23, 1988, p. 5. Reprinted with permission from TV Guide® Magazine. Copyright © 1988 by New America Publications Inc., Radnor, Pennsylvania.
4. Joshua Meyrowitz, "Where Have All the Children Gone?" *Newsweek*, August 30, 1982, p. 13.
5. Ibid.
6. Ibid.
7. Joshua Meyrowitz, "Is TV Keeping Us Too Well-Informed?" *TV Guide*, January 9, 1988, p. 5.
8. Glen Sparks, interview on WWL Radio, New Orleans, Louisiana, February 11, 1991.
9. Ibid.
10. Ibid.
11. Neil Postman in *Teaching as a Conserving Activity*, quoted by Jim Trelease in *The Read Aloud Handbook* (New York: Penguin, 1982), p. 99.
12. David Elkind, "Teens in Crisis: All Grown Up and No Place to Go," *Focus on the Family*, April 1985, p. 2.
13. Kalter, "How TV Is," p. 11.
14. Ibid.
15. *The Nielsen Report*, 1990, p. 8.
16. S. Robert and Lynda S. Lichter, "Does TV Shape Ethnic Images?" *Media and Values*, Spring 1988, p. 6.

17. "What Is the Impact of Violent and Sexually Explicit TV on America's Children?" *Concerned Women*, May 1990, p. 20.
18. *America's Watching*, The Television Information Office/Roper Report, 1987, pp. 12-13.
19. Kevin Perrotta, "Watching While Life Goes By," *Christianity Today*, April 18, 1980, p. 17. Adapted from *Taming the TV Habit* (Ann Arbor, Mich.: Servant, 1982). Copyright © 1982 by Kevin Perrotta. Used by permission.
20. Joseph Procaccini, quoted by Mary Maushard, "Kids Suffer Burnout, Researcher Warns," *The Baltimore Times Sun*, reprinted in *The Times Picayune*, October 15, 1990, p. D-8.
21. Walt Whitman, in Edward E. Ford and Steven Englund, *For the Love of Children* (Garden City, N.Y.: Anchor Press/Doubleday, 1977), p. 3.

15

TELEVISION GONE TABLOID

A former pastor of mine once asked in a sermon if, in reality, there were enough jail cells to hold all of the violent characters that now parade across American television screens or enough sheets and pillowcases in American stores to make all the beds set up for sexual situations currently portrayed in TV and movies. With each passing year television seems to break more social taboos and stretch more limits. As one writer in a recent issue of the *Wall Street Journal* put it, "Television has gone tabloid."[1] Notes a critic for the *Washington Post*, "There is something unsettling about the way television has abdicated the old values. It's as if, somewhere along the way, the Judeo-Christian ethic became 'controversial.' Or at least unfashionable."[2]

One excuse for the permissive direction that many of today's miniseries and sitcoms are moving in is an expressed desire on the part of producers to come up with more "realistic" shows. "I feel realism is good," said David Chase, the executive producer of "Almost Grown," a CBS sitcom which, in one episode, depicted characters in the middle of having sex.[3]

In "Married . . . With Children" the main themes of the controversial Fox network program run the gamut of sexual preoccupation, tackling everything from masturbation, to obsession with body functions, to partial nudity and kinky sex, all presented in a raunchy "family" context. Ron Leavitt, who produces the controversial program, claims his show brings a badly needed dose of realism to a medium he says is dominated by boring, one-dimensional stories simply too good to be true.[4]

I wouldn't argue with Mr. Leavitt's accusation that much of television entertainment is one-dimensional and unrealistic, for such problems are inherent in the very fabric of TV imagery. But boredom is an intrinsic part of "real" life—so how can TV be "not boring" and "realistic" simultaneously? Exactly how does the sharp increase in vulgar or sexual themes to create controversy and titillate viewers bring prime time any closer to "reality" than it has ever been?

Just as in television news, a relatively small group of people in Hollywood produce the vast majority of all programs that Americans have to choose from, and, like their journalistic counterparts, the majority of those people hail from the ideological left, surveys show. Just as in news, the content of televised entertainment programs and movies will reflect to some degree the values of those who create them. But in entertainment, just as in the news, it is important to understand that the demands of TV technology and the institutional framework of television play an influential role in slanting the direction of programming. That is because certain themes are better suited to the televised format than others.

Sex and violence are popular themes in a visual medium because they conform so well to TV's narrow format requirements. Violence translates easily onto film or tape and is an uncomplicated way to accommodate the camera's need to show drama, action, or the human struggle for power. Sex is obviously very visual and far quicker and easier to communicate in a visual medium such as television than the more subtle and invisible aspects of love, kindness, and caring. Sex serves as a superficial, one-dimensional symbol of the deeper, more complex emotions of love and caring that are hard to visualize.

Sexual or violent themes also satisfy TV's need for compelling emotion or cosmetic attractiveness. Violence serves as a visual symbol of a person's struggle for control over human relationships and the environment. Sex and violence readily meet TV's criteria for plots that are tangible and dramatic, easily resolvable within stringent time limits, relatively easy and cheap to produce, and compelling to watch. Since TV cannot easily establish context or convey complexity, random violence and casual sexual relationships work extremely well in a medium that must establish immediate audience interest and solve conflict within a half hour. So the same biases that influence and manipulate television news exert a measure of control over entertainment production, too.

> *Theoretically, television can show anything it wants. However, it is pointless to broadcast (especially at enormous cost) if no one will watch.*

The dramatic and visual action of conflict and hostility in the Persian Gulf or the fictional street wars of "L.A. Law" will fare much better on TV than peaceful international solutions and tranquil neighborhoods ever would. Controversy among people works much better than consensus since agreement is dangerously boring; in entertainment, just as in news, simple, uncomplicated plots are much easier to resolve in thirty minutes than complicated ones; the tangible materialism of "Lifestyles of the Rich and Famous" is easier to depict visually than the "best things in life," which may be free but also happen to be invisible; the ambitions of J. R. are much more emotionally compelling to audiences than the contented humanitarianism of Mother Teresa.

Entertainment must be emotional if we are to be moved by it; it must be cosmetically pleasing in order to catch our eye. Consequently, passion and power-mongering among the beautiful play well in the TV theater because they lend themselves so naturally to the bent of TV and satisfy its visual appetite so easily; they are visual vehicles capable of conveying conflict, hostility, passion, and other emotions on camera.

I offer this observation not as an excuse for the direction in which TV is moving or as a way of discounting the liberal agenda of many producers, but as a partial explanation of why such a disproportionate amount of TV is dominated by sexual and violent themes. If we can recognize how accommodating these themes are to the need to produce imagery that holds attention, then we might begin to analyze our own viewing habits and become more conscious of how TV exploits those themes to coax us to the set.

We might also have more sympathy for those producers who are attempting to steer programming in a different direction if we recognize what they are up against technologically as well as morally. They are beleaguered not only by working in a climate fostered by many who push the moral limits for profit but by the inherent nature of TV. Steering programming away from something that works for any reason is risky business in an industry where job security is directly tied to the last Nielsen rating book. Producer Norman Lear is right in saying that "commercial television's moral north star, from which nearly all bearings are set, is quite simply: 'How do I win Tuesday night at eight o'clock?' That is the name of the game, the only thing that matters."[5]

Theoretically, television can show anything it wants. However, it is pointless to broadcast (especially at enormous cost) if no one will watch. Television cannot deal effectively with subject matter that does not conform to its rigid format requirements and entertain or it risks losing audience. In its earliest days, the major networks enjoyed a monopoly on TV programming and reaped the benefits of their status as a novelty. Viewers watched TV for its uniqueness. That climate is long gone. Not only has the novelty of television worn off, but now cable and satellite dishes, movie and video rentals, and other forms of competition are taking a bite out of the audience the major networks once held hostage.

Television networks are addicted to their own past successes. Now that they have savored years of success and generated huge profits, they are terrified by the prospect of losing it to cable, video rentals, and other new technologies. The greater the competition becomes, the more desperate television networks and stations become for a share of the audience. The bent inevitably moves toward doing what TV does best and away from what it does not do well, as well as fulfilling its inherent need to stimulate in order to hold attention.

> *Is TV's fascination with violence and
> sex . . . a distorted attempt to tap
> into humanity's natural longing for
> paradise lost? . . . TV producers, many
> who know nothing about the Bible, seem
> to sense innately those deep-seated
> human longings outlined in Scripture.*

One of the easiest and cheapest ways to stimulate is to tackle the forbidden. Both television and movie producers pick at social taboos not only to break them but because, as I discovered as a TV journalist, tackling forbidden or negative subjects is a proved way to heighten viewer interest. But since TV has an inherent problem with establishing context, the moral context that must accompany any social problem can easily suffer. So although TV has been commended for tackling social taboos, because it is inherently a poor reflector of reality the result has often been more distortion than solution. Hollywood's stabs at painting a picture of real life problems in recent years have produced a dark, deformed portrait of America. The visual canvas of TV drama is littered with wife abuse, child molestation, teen suicide, rape, incest, and other topics that manipulate the innate curiosity of viewers for the unusual.

Are such topics approached out of proportion to their existence in real life? Are emotion-charged visual portrayals helpful in
creating awareness of a problem? Or do they encourage such behavior among those perpetrators who are already predisposed to it?
Do the programs shock audiences into caring about such problems, or in the long run do they desensitize audiences through
overexposure? The difficulty lies in the fact that the answer to all of
those questions may be yes.

However, the most dangerous distortions occur when good
and evil lose their moral context. Writer Simone Weil once remarked: "Nothing is so beautiful and sweet as the good. No desert
is so dreary, monotonous and boring as evil. But fictional good is
boring and flat, while fictional evil is varied, intriguing and full of
charm."[6] Perhaps this is true because fiction in any form is an escape to some degree from daily existence. The tendency for Weil's
observation to be true in televised fiction is perhaps because, in
entertainment just as in news, interest and accuracy are often irrecon-
cilable partners.

A recent *TV Guide* poll suggests that viewers overwhelmingly
agree that there is too much sex and violence in television entertainment.[7] That this is true and that viewers recognize it is hardly a
revelation. However, I think the question of why this is so is worth
contemplating. The answer may lie in part in the truth about our
human nature as depicted in the Bible.

In spite of their nonreligious orientation, the creators of television entertainment seem to have an intuitive grasp of what the Bible tells us people naturally gravitate to in their fallen condition.
Much of the trend toward sex and violence is rooted in the fact that
such themes appeal deeply to fallen human nature. What is violence anyway, but the visual expression of one person's attempt to
control or subdue another and to gain power? Sexuality, especially
outside the context of commitment, can also be a visual expression
of an attempt at intimacy, as well as of our fallen desire to manipulate and control another human being.

What we often see in televised portrayals of sex or violence is a
blurred version of the human dilemma portrayed in the first three

chapters of Genesis. On those pages we find a man and a woman who were once commanded to share a joint rulership over creation (Genesis 1:28) later condemned to a struggle with each other and the world around them because of their disobedience and resulting alienation from God (3:8-19). Instead of the mutual balance of power (God-given dominion) and the climate of intimacy (nakedness without shame) enjoyed before the Fall, another pattern emerges. Life after the Fall becomes a struggle.

Part of the curse in the third chapter of Genesis for the man is to grapple for power and control over his surroundings (Genesis 3:1-19). Some interpreters suggest that part of the curse of sin for the woman is the man's desire for power over her and her often unreciprocated longing for intimacy with him[8] as well her endeavor to achieve lost dominion with him. The man and the woman search for lost dominion and intimacy. Is TV's fascination with violence and sex in part a distorted attempt to tap into humanity's natural craving for paradise lost?

It fascinates me that TV producers, many who know nothing about the Bible, innately seem to sense those deep-seated human longings outlined in Scripture. Through sexual and violent themes, they subsequently convert those longings into imagery they suspend on the screen before viewers like the proverbial carrot is dangled before the donkey. It is no coincidence that both Nielsen ratings and studies on TV viewing habits show that male audiences in general are predominantly drawn to action, violence, and TV shows that feature strong and overpowering male characters. Why? George Gerbner suggests: "[The predominantly] male cast makes the [TV] world revolve mostly around questions of power. That is why television is so violent: The best, quickest demonstration of power is a showdown that resolves the issue of who can get away with what against whom."[9]

The same data suggests that female audiences in general, particularly the less educated or nonprofessional women, lean strongly toward soap operas and programs with romantic themes and characters searching for an often elusive mirage of intimacy with others.[10] Soap operas, note two University of California professors, offer stories "dominated by feminine values, creating male characters as unlike real males as possible, but very much like what women think they want males to be, displaying a far greater degree of interpersonal competency and intimacy than most men are capable of."[11]

If we understand what Scripture teaches about humanity's fallen nature and our subsequent search for power and intimacy, we understand a little more why sexuality and violence, and the increasing mix of both, are effective tools to lure us into the prime time versions of "real life." Such shows are attractive not so much because they are "real" as because they exploit real needs within us that few are consciously in touch with. As long as the standards of television are governed only by viewer interest, the temptation for the TV industry to exploit our fallen nature will be great.

Just as interest and accuracy work against each other in TV journalism, amusement and reality work against each other in TV entertainment. There is little evidence that the current wave of permissive shows have achieved "reality" by stretching the bounds of what is acceptable on the airwaves for the sake of viewer curiosity. Such programs claim to be a kind of backlash against the rosy but unrealistic outlook of sitcoms and dramas of the earlier years of TV, but they have failed as miserably on the permissive side of the spectrum at conveying reality as their earlier counterparts. The dramatic alterations that inevitably take place when real life problems are tailored to fit the televised format will inevitably leave viewers with grossly caricatured ideas about complex and difficult to understand issues and human relationships.

Combine television's inherent inability to be "real" with the current wave of permissiveness and the predictable result is a world where sexual situations, violence, profanity, and a host of negative sense-bombardment techniques appear to be more prevalent, more casual, and less complex than they are in reality. The same inherent weaknesses blend together in both news and entertainment, leaving viewers with the same misleading impressions of the world. Yet for millions, those same stories will form their concept of social reality. The old adage that "what we don't know won't hurt us" doesn't hold up, especially when we apply it to the truth about sexuality.

NOTES

1. Dennis Kneale, *The Wall Street Journal*, quoted by Randall Murphree, *American Family Association Journal*, July 1988, p. 5.
2. Tom Shales, quoted in "Television Is No Angel of Light," *The Washington Post*, November 12, 1982, p. 24.
3. Mike Yorkey, "TV's Prime Time—Rated R?" *Focus on the Family Citizen*, February 1989, p. 2.
4. Ibid.
5. Norman Lear, quoted by Les Brown, "Reading TV's Balance Sheet," *Media and Values*, Summer/Fall, 1987, p. 13.
6. Simone Weil, quoted by Lloyd Billingsley, "TV: Where the Girls Are Good Looking and the Good Guys Win," *Christianity Today*, October 4, 1985, p. 40. Copyright © 1985 by *Christianity Today*. Used by permission.
7. Michael Lipton, "Television in the Nineties: What You Want to See in the New Decade," *TV Guide*, January 20, 1990, pp. 13-14.
8. Gilbert Bilezikian, quoted by Mary Stewart Van Leeuwen, "Life After Eden," *Christianity Today*, July 16, 1990, p. 20. The Scripture reference is Genesis 3:16.
9. George Gerbner, "Television: Modern Mythmaker," *Media and Values*, Summer/Fall, 1987, p. 9.
10. Robert Spier, "We Are What We Watch: We Watch What We Are," *Media and Values*, Summer/Fall 1987, p. 6.
11. Warren Bennis and Ian Mitroff, quoted by Stephen Goode, "The World in a Fun House Mirror," *Insight*, November 27, 1989, p. 46.

16

SEX, LIES, AND VIDEOTAPE

Sexuality sells" a network executive admits. "It's a fact of TV life."[1] The most recent federal study on television and behavior concurs that sex is indeed a major commodity of prime time. "Entertainment television has become an important sex educator" but not necessarily a very good one, the report concludes. Extramarital affairs were portrayed on television five times more often than sexual relationships between married couples in the early eighties.[2] In the nineties, the normal married couple seems on the verge of television extinction.

A study conducted several years ago found that Americans are bombarded by twenty-seven sexual messages an hour on television—that adds up to sixty-five thousand references a year in the prime time and evening hours.[3] Another study released by the American Academy of Pediatrics estimates that teens see and hear fourteen thousand sexual references and innuendos on TV a year.[4] What such statistics underscore is how out of proportion to real life sexual situations on television during the past ten years have been.

Sexual satisfaction for many Americans is now an elusive mental mirage created in the image of TV or movie fantasy. Many today pursue its illusion of intimacy relentlessly from one hollow relationship to another. Pastor Randy Alcorn, author of *Christians in the Wake of the Sexual Revolution,* counsels both married and unmarried couples. He suggests that because of media imagery

> millions now live under the burden of sexual expectations and pressures to perform in a prescribed manner. Victims of the tyranny of the orgasm, they feel that unless their sexual experience is what they see in the media—where everyone is effortlessly erotic and every encounter is comparable to nuclear fission—they're being robbed, or they're not a real man or a real woman. . . . Throats parched, lips cracked and bleeding, we are nomads in search of a sexual oasis that forever eludes us.[5]

Is it any wonder that sexual promiscuity is now a social epidemic among the young, when casual sex according to television is not only a prime source of contentment but is portrayed as simple, guilt-free, and capable of making us healthy, wealthy, and wise—and, most important, powerful?

The consequences of sexuality are often more fabricated than the portrayals, or are simply nonexistent. People who have sex on TV or in movies rarely get pregnant, and if they do the depiction is unrealistically sanguine. Even in the rare moments that programs offer a glimpse into the aftermath of sexuality outside of marriage, those involved are either unaffected, or live happily ever after, or get an abortion. If TV now offers any solution to the problems of sexuality outside the framework of commitment, it is predictably simple, visual, and commercial: buy a condom.

Although a host of network executives and civil libertarians continue to insist that TV's sexual imagery is protected free speech and is not responsible for the well-documented rise of sexual activity among teens, in some cases teens themselves acknowledge the link. Michelle, who became pregnant at age fifteen, confessed: "Our families and teachers tell us to say 'no' to sex, but often TV movies and commercials say 'yes' to sex. It's made so glamorous."[6] Unfortunately, not enough sexually active teens may yet make the conscious link Michelle did between TV's unrealistic sexuality and their subsequent real-life behavior.

However, those involved in combating the problem of teen pregnancy express little doubt about the connection. Daphne Busby, head of an organization for black teenagers who are pregnant, agrees that even unwed motherhood is now presented on TV as glamorous. Kids watch the girlfriends of rock stars on talk shows talking about their children out of wedlock. The perception left, says Busby, is what a wonderful life it is.[7]

A school nurse at a large Southside Chicago high school attributes much of the sexual activity among teens to commercials, movies, and TV, all of which paint the picture that "it's cool to have sex before twelve."[8] Abortion is now the legacy of the teen pregnancy epidemic in America, and those who profit from it focus little attention on the possible link between TV's sexual preoccupation and subsequent behavior patterns.

Are Christians breaking stride at crucial points of difference with our culture, or are we too enthusiastic consumers of the latest barrage of subliminally suggestive imagery?

Since retiring from television to raise my own children, I've developed an awareness of how many young children at home are now regular watchers of soap operas with their mothers or baby-sitters. They apparently assume that their children don't really understand what they are seeing. That is true, but it is part of the problem, not the solution. Young children lack the maturity required to put such imagery into some type of moral framework. A former neighbor of mine, who watched soaps in front of her five-year-old son, confessed to me that she was shocked when he told her one day that he has a girlfriend but they haven't "taken a nap together yet." She couldn't understand where her five year old got the idea that girlfriends and boyfriends should take "naps" together.

It never occurred to her that he had seen dozens of such "naps" in his own living room.

Randy Alcorn points out that Christians who permit their children to watch such programs or who enjoy these types of shows in front of their kids should hardly be surprised if they find their teenagers acting out of the reservoir of their mediated imagery. He admonishes: "We are hopelessly naive to think that Christians do not watch such programs—or that watching them we are somehow immune to their effects. . . . Like the frog boiled to death by degrees, many Christians have been desensitized to sexual sin."[9]

Alcorn observes that dozens of professing Christians feel the freedom to miss church but wouldn't dream of missing soaps and sitcoms peppered with sexual immorality and innuendo.[10] He relates some frightening examples from his personal counseling experience of what he believes is the legacy of Christians who welcome TV's version of sexual reality into the home: a man comes home from a business trip to find his seventeen-year-old daughter in bed with a boy she's been dating for three weeks; a woman finds her six-year-old daughter and a neighbor boy together naked and fondling each other; a high school boy admits to his parents that he's a prostitute. Writes Alcorn: "These things just didn't happen; they happened in Christian families. I know, because they came to me for help."[11]

Some surveys reinforce Alcorn's suggestion that professing Christians are part of the problem, not the solution. During the eighties, Nielsen conducted a poll of viewers of "Dallas," a leader at the time in terms of sexual innuendo. The results showed that more than half of the regular viewers also identified themselves as born-again Christians.[12] Yet some professing Christians who are regular supporters of popular programs where the leading characters commit adultery or live together without the benefit of marriage seem genuinely horrified and confused when their own children move in with a boyfriend or girlfriend.

Are Christians breaking stride at crucial points of difference with our culture, or are we too enthusiastic consumers of the latest barrage of subliminally suggestive imagery? Theologian Donald

Bloesch put it this way: "Before the church can make an impact on the culture, it must break with the idolatries and misconceptions that dominate the culture."[13] But Charles Colson suggests that "the 'real' world (now for many of us) is that which flashes across the electron tube each night in the family living room."[14] Where is the Christian sense of outrage over what is happening in the culture around us? asks Colson. He answers: "Perhaps our moral sensibilities have been dulled because of today's dazzling instant communications. We sit mesmerized in front of our TVs, unable to turn the sets off, so we turn our minds off instead."[15] He's right, except that the evidence is compelling that the set itself possesses the ability to turn off our minds, turn on our desires, and revolutionize our values.

Although many TV executives deny any link between television and behavioral influence, a few producers at least inadvertently admit to a link. The producer of the daytime soap "Bold and Beautiful" claims that soap producers in the nineties have now toned down the bed hopping themes of the eighties because of the AIDS epidemic. He admits: "We all feel the need to be more responsible in our story telling [now]."[16] Why the concern for sexual "responsibility" if no one's behavior is being influenced?

Even if a barrage of sexually explicit imagery or sexual innuendo doesn't influence actions, it can take a subtle but powerful toll on attitudes. Overexposure to anything desensitizes us. One executive in Program Practices at CBS, perhaps unintentionally, concedes that long-term familiarity breeds acceptance instead of contempt for sexually explicit programs: "Some people who tune in to certain shows infrequently may be shocked or disturbed by what they see because it's not what they're accustomed to."[17]

The issue of desensitization should be an important one for anyone who claims to take Scripture seriously. Peter tells us that one of the reasons God spared Lot in the Old Testament from destruction with the immoral culture around him was because, in spite of his circumstances, Lot had managed not to lose his sensitivity to sin. The apostle Peter commended Lot for being disturbed by the sin in the culture around him (2 Peter 2:7-8). The Bible warns that a loss of moral sensitivity in society is a serious problem.

Christians need to ask themselves—am I disturbed about, intrigued by, or apathetic to the current depictions of sexuality on TV? Or am I oblivious and accepting—able to shrug off almost anything now?

We dare not underestimate the power of imagery to influence both actions and attitudes. We imitate or learn to accept what we contemplate for long periods of time. Slowly we are influenced by what we see and absorb over the period of our lifetime. If we understand this, should we be surprised that what often begins as a fabricated TV image eventually becomes a social reality?

NOTES

1. Jason Bonderoff, "Sex, Lies and Videotape," *Soap Opera Digest*, March 5, 1991, p. 24.
2. "TV Bombs Out in New Federal Study," *U.S. News and World Report*, May 17, 1982, p. 17.
3. "27 Times Each Hour, Sex Is the Focus of Network TV," *The Arizona Republic*, January 28, 1988, p. E-5.
4. "Movies, TV Bombard Viewers with Sex," *The American Family Association Journal*, January 1991, p. 4.
5. Randy Alcorn, *Christians in the Wake of the Sexual Revolution* (Portland: Multnomah, 1985), pp. 21-22.
6. Marvin Scott, "How Adults Could Have Helped Me," *Parade*, August 21, 1988, p. 5.
7. Claudia Wallis, "The Tragic Costs of Teenage Pregnancy," condensed from *Time*, reprinted in *The Reader's Digest*, April 1986, p. 101.
8. Louise McCurry, quoted by Randy Frame, "School-based Health Clinics: An Idea Whose Time Has Come?" *Christianity Today*, March 7, 1986, p. 43.
9. Alcorn, *Christians*, p. 25.
10. Ibid., p. 24.
11. Ibid., p. 25.
12. Viewers participating in the survey were asked a number of questions about their religious beliefs to identify them as born-again Christians. "Opinion Roundup: Dukes of Hazard vs. Dallas," *Public Opinion*, October/November 1981, p. 38.
13. Donald Bloesch, quoted by Charles Colson, *Who Speaks for God?* (Westchester, Ill.: Crossway, 1985), Introduction.
14. Ibid., p. 24.
15. Ibid., p. 67.
16. John Zak, quoted by Bonderoff, "Sex, Lies," p. 27.
17. George Dessart, quoted by Doug Hill, "Is TV Sex Getting Bolder?" *TV Guide*, August 8, 1987, p. 4.

17

THE "MEAN WORLD" LEGACY

J ust as television "has gone tabloid," as the *Washington Post* put it, so "mayhem has gone mainstream." The latter is the conclusion of *Newsweek* magazine, which also notes: "If artists, as (poet) Ezra Pound said, are 'the antennae of the race,' they're picking up some plenty bad vibes these days."[1] TV and movie violence is not only becoming more graphic, it is increasingly presented as both amusing and beyond any boundaries of right or wrong.

"Television didn't invent violence," notes George Gerbner, "it just put it on the assembly line."[2] The assembly line on American TV has jacked up production on several fronts. Both real and make-believe savagery now seem to flow from the screen faster than Detroit auto makers crank out cars. Like pizza, much of the product is delivered conveniently to our doorstep via the tube.

As I pointed out earlier, since negative stimuli exploit our natural human curiosity about the unpleasant, there is increasing concern among social scientists that this curiosity can become emotionally compulsive. *Newsweek* warns: "America's addiction to make-believe violence is like any other addiction: it takes more and more to accomplish less and less."[3] The "thrills" must escalate in order to provide viewers with a continuing sense of stimulation, satisfaction and motivation to come back for more. For those who border on mental instability, some experts argue, repeated exposure to such stimulation through TV or movies can push them over the brink into some type of antisocial or criminal act.[4] However, some express concern about the effects of violence on society's fringe element yet deny any influence on themselves, because they discount the importance of their own mental imagery.

Although many believe that media violence contributes to real-life violence, there appears to be an embarrassing gap between profession and practice. In a recent *Newsweek* poll, 68 percent of those asked saw media violence as a significant influence in behavior. Yet, "even as we express such heartfelt concerns," the magazine observes, American audiences are packing into movie theaters and onto living room couches, "lapping up the fictive blood."[5]

TV did not invent violence, as Gerbner pointed out, any more than it invented sin. It is not the only factor behind violence in our society. However, it can join with other factors to serve as a significant catalyst to behavior because it provides the imagery—the role model of imagination. The TV and movie industry often underscores its power to persuade until it becomes convenient to disavow. The industry continues to deny the link between excessive or graphic violence on television and antisocial behavior, just as the tobacco industry denied the link between cancer and smoking for years before the proof became conclusive. Although the networks are correct that one cannot conclusively prove the link yet, a prima facie case certainly seems to exist. After all, sponsors pay millions for TV commercials because of what television claims is its extraordinary ability to affect behavior. The industry can't have it both ways. Can TV executives continue to suggest that their medium's power of persuasion is phenomenal one minute and merits the highest price, while denying any influence on social behavior the next?

There are now thousands of studies to document the relationship between violence and television that common sense should tell us are valid to some degree. In 1972 and again in 1982, the *Surgeon General's Report on TV and Social Behavior* claimed definite links between TV violence and aggression. The 1982 report bluntly insisted that there is overwhelming evidence that excessive violence on television causes aggressive behavior in adults and children.[6] Statistical studies by one sociologist reveal that murder rates go up immediately after televised prize fights, and suicides climb after media-publicized suicides.[7] Other statistical studies claim that at least half the murders in the United States and Canada can be attributed to the influence of television on impressionable youth. The research shows a dramatic rise in homicides in both countries about a decade after the advent of TV, compared with other countries where TV was banned during the same time period.[8]

The American Medical Association has long insisted that televised violence encourages real-life violence and is a threat to the health and welfare of Americans.[9] While in office, former Surgeon General C. Everett Koop blamed TV violence for contributing to an abnormal increase in assaults, child and spouse abuse, murders, and suicides. TV violence, declared Koop, made people feel more threatened in real life. The legacy of the "mean world syndrome" that George Gerbner spoke of, according to Koop, is that people are both frightened by and desensitized to TV brutality and are less likely to get involved in stopping or preventing real-life violence in their midst.[10]

If fantasy images of violence pose a threat to adults, how much more vulnerable are children who lack the discernment that comes from a well-developed moral frame of reference? Children today are exposed to televised violence to an unprecedented degree. Psychiatrist Thomas Radecki, of the National Coalition of Television Violence, warns: "To teach children to see war as exciting fun (as many programs now do) is extremely dangerous. Our research shows that it increases the acceptance of and use of violence in their everyday lives."[11] Radecki warns that we are training kids to see their opponents as subhuman monsters who can only be dealt with through violence and aggression.[12] Two University of Illinois psychologists who studied one set of children for over twenty years found that kids who watched significant amounts of violence at the age of eight were consistently more likely to commit violent crimes or to engage in child or spouse abuse at age thirty. They concluded that although exposure to media violence was not the only cause, it was "one of the very important factors" they had identified, adding that "if we don't do something [about media violence], we are contributing to a society that will be more and more violent."[13]

Televised violence not only models negative behavior but often ignores by necessity the real consequences of violence altogether or paints unrealistic impressions of them.

I discovered very quickly with my own sons that children are naturally born with a bent toward aggression that hardly needs further cultivation. Some TV cartoons are vehicles to promote violent toys designed for children to act out the images they see. A recent Columbia University study concludes that TV violence is changing the way children play by increasing aggressive behavior and aimlessness and reducing creativity in play patterns. The study concludes: "Many children no longer seem to be in control of their play."[14] Perhaps that is because they are no longer in control of their own mental imagery. Such studies simply support what any attentive mother or father can see.

According to a recent classroom survey, teachers overwhelming agreed that some cartoon characters "encourage violent and anti-social behavior among young children and have a disturbing effect on learning, behavior and play."[15] The popular "Teenage Mutant Ninja Turtles" were most frequently cited for ushering in the most recent wave of classroom aggression. Meanwhile, a newly released study shows that violence in children's weekend programming is on the upswing—up to twenty-five acts of violence an hour on some shows. The study also underscored that much of the violence in children's programs is presented in a humorous context.[16]

Far more unsettling than the effects of children's TV programs are surveys showing that very young children are watching adult programs or movies. Children are now being exposed to levels of violence far beyond what they see in cartoons and kiddie shows. We should not be surprised when young children who grow up on "L.A. Law" and "Hill Street Blues" are ready for much more by the time they become teenagers.

Televised violence not only models negative behavior but often ignores by necessity the real consequences of violence altogether or paints unrealistic impressions of them. The visual shorthand and time constraints of television leave no time to chronicle extended hospital stays and sufferings of victims lucky enough to survive. Even if such details could be visually portrayed, producers might commit the ultimate TV sin and bore their viewers in the process. The internal grief of both victims and loved ones is invisible to the camera's eye. The context of violence is completely lost on television and in movies. Is violence the exception to the rule—or the rule in our society? Such questions are raised but remain unanswered when context is lacking. Consequently, what we don't know for sure frightens us.

Since artificial savagery takes the viewer out of touch with the realities of actual violence, through lack of exposure to what is real we loose our ability to care. Notes *Newsweek:* "Our ability to feel compassion is brutalized by excessive brutality, especially when it's given that Hollywood sheen."[17]

I witnessed the practical result of this effect while covering crime as a reporter. I remember being on the scene of a fatal shooting that occurred during a coin shop robbery. I was interviewing bystanders who had witnessed a man brutally gun down the young store manager. There were quite a few witnesses, and as I pressed them for information, many kept saying over and over, "I feel like I've been watching television," or, "It was just like watching TV. It didn't seem real." Several confessed that they stood paralyzed as they watched the crime. Several told me they were having a genuine difficulty feeling any sense of horror or disgust over the crime they had just witnessed because "it just seemed like a movie."

They complained of a numbness—a detachment from what they had seen with their own eyes. I suspect that the barrage of crime stories seen repeatedly on the news, combined with hundreds of movie and TV images absorbed over the years, was so deeply impressed on their minds that when they watched a real crime taking place they could no longer make a mental distinction between reality and fantasy.

Violence in visual media tends to be a gray area for many Christians. Notes a writer for *Christianity Today:* "Evangelicals . . . are far quicker to protest nudity than violence. This is partly because the issue of violence is not as clear cut as pornography. We cannot categorically dismiss all violent actions as immoral. Most evangelicals believe some forms of violence are occasionally appropriate, as in certain police actions or for national defense.[18] The confusion is understandable since the issue of televised violence is morally complicated because of gray areas and questions of context.

This chapter is a meager forum to adequately explore the issues surrounding televised violence. However, I hope it can serve as a warning flag to Christians who are perhaps too accepting of violence in whatever form or context that it now exists. The failure of many Christians to distinguish between the just war philosophy and violence for fun and profit may have serious long-term consequences. Yet some Christians are inconsistent in their attitudes toward media violence. Many decry the violence of abortion one minute then line up the next minute to watch Arnold Schwarzenegger machine gun seventeen policemen in *The Terminator* or blow his wife away in *Total Recall.*

Is it possible that our protests against the violence in abortion clinics have yet to impress the non-Christian public partly because Christians fail to take the question of violence seriously enough in other areas? If Christians are in fact the "salt" of our society, as Christ declared, how does our obedience to God in this area impact our culture? If Christians are as indiscriminate in their consumption of media mayhem as non-Christians, then television conditioning may be a reason behind the difficulty of the visible professing church to stand for Christ at the places where the rest of society is denying His Lordship.

The Scriptures warn repeatedly about the importance of what occupies the recesses of our mind. Jesus reminds us: "The good man brings good things out of the good stored up in his heart, and the evil man brings evil things out of the evil stored up in his heart" (Luke 6:45). But today, millions are mentally storing up hundreds of hours of negative artificial imagery and are failing miserably to recognize both the significance and the consequences of it.

Although we see violence in the Bible, it is always within some kind of moral context, such as justice or self-defense.

The God who created our minds knows and understands the powerful effect of image creating on the mental process. The tedious rituals chronicled in the early Old Testament books may seem puzzling and irrelevant today until we realize that through such carefully recorded symbolic rituals God visualized truth to an illiterate people. God wisely denies His people the power to make any graven image of Him. He allows for no limited, visual fabrications of His unlimited and invisible nature. The only images He permits of Himself are the inspired verbal images revealed in His Holy Word. And even when God finally made Himself visible in history in the person of Jesus Christ, the Lord Himself warned us about the importance of what our eyes bring into our minds. "The eye is the lamp of the body," declared Christ. "If your eyes are good, your whole body will be full of light. But if your eyes are bad, your whole body will be full of darkness. If then the light within you is darkness, how great is that darkness!" (Matthew 6:22-23). Can any Christian who reveres the words of Christ seriously suggest that we are not affected by what we carry in our mental storehouse?

The apostle Paul encouraged us to think on "whatever is true, whatever is nobel, whatever is right, whatever is pure, whatever is lovely, whatever is admirable" (Philippians 4:8). Note especially that Paul was concerned about focusing on what was true. Paul knew through the inspiration of the Holy Spirit that positive, wholesome thought and imagination linked with a firm grasp on reality are important ingredients in Christian living. In the book of Proverbs, we are warned: "Above all else, guard your heart, for it is the wellspring of life"(Proverbs 4:23).

Watching violence may not push most Christians to violent acts, but hundreds of scenes that trivialize death condition a casual, passive attitude toward human life that Christians are not to have. A steady diet of such fare desensitizes us to something we need to be sensitive to. Scripture makes clear that God does not take the shedding of human blood or the loss of human life lightly. Do we? Although we see violence in the Bible, it is always within some kind of moral context, such as justice or self-defense. Its purpose in Scripture is not to merely entertain or titillate but to warn or instruct.

The effectiveness of Christ's life was characterized by his personal purity. Our effectiveness as Christians will be neutralized by the content of our thinking. We will hardly be motivated to tackle problems of immorality, or even avoid them, if acceptance of them is deeply ingrained in the recesses of our minds.

A disturbing new trend is emerging on both TV and movie screens: the increasing mix of violence with eroticism. The TV wives and mothers who dominated the tube ten years ago are giving way to a different breed of women who are now the prime-time targets of brutality. Notes one TV critic, the murder victims in many popular crime shows are increasingly women of ill repute—prostitutes, centerfold models, oversexed teenage runaways, and beauty contest winners—all of whom have something in common: they are women of easy virtue who are easily disposable. Why? On TV, according to one female producer, "It's a crime to kill a man; it's sexy to kill a woman."[19] A TV scriptwriter admits that female victims on TV "have to be people who don't matter." The reason fits right in with TV's narrow format requirements: "That kind of plot is easy. You don't have to [take time to] explain why such a person should die."[20] Christian viewers who might find themselves more comfortable with and accepting of the demise of the TV "bad girl" might stop to ponder the contrast of that message with Christ's attitude toward the prostitutes of his day.

Still another popular way to fuse eroticism and brutality is to turn rapists into romantic heroes. In the early eighties, soap opera fans saw Luke of "General Hospital" rape Laura, who eventually fell in love with him and married him. Several other soaps, including the popular "Dynasty," followed suit with rape plots that sent a clear message that instead of being a crime of violence rape was something a woman enjoyed and wanted to happen. A number of rapists in soap operas emerged as sexy leading men, giving the crime of rape an unrealistic appeal.[21]

Even more recent shows and movies that claim an antirape theme may in fact promote it because of sophisticated photographic techniques. Playwright Steve Tesich notes: "I haven't seen a single anti-rape movie that doesn't promote rape. The very manner in which sexual scenes are shot causes rape to look like an activity that is energizing."[22]

It's no secret that these movies, along with soap operas, slasher films, and other explicit videos that combine sexual and violent themes are popular viewing fare among American college students. Perhaps it is no coincidence that date rape, according to a recent study, has now reached epidemic proportions on American campuses. The study revealed that one out of six college women had been the victim of a rape or attempted rape within the year she was surveyed. The overwhelming majority of the victims—80 to 90 percent, were victimized by fellow college students. One out of every fifteen men who participated in the study admitted to committing sexual assault against a date.[23] Although alcohol is primarily blamed by some rape counselors, college students have been using alcohol for decades before this most recent epidemic of rape incidents. Perhaps someone should take a closer look at the subliminal messages of erotic violence in TV and movies.

Neil Malamuth of the University of California and Edward Donnerstein of the University of Wisconsin did just that. They showed young male subjects clips of films depicting a woman responding positively to a rapist. They found that the men interviewed became significantly more accepting of the idea of rape after seeing the films, and were aroused by them. The men were also more likely to minimize the guilt of a rapist in a mock trial after watching the films. The researchers also discovered that a surprising number of "normal" men described themselves as highly inclined toward rape: 25 to 30 percent of the group they studied. Those who responded that way were identified in the study as "normal" men whose personalities were more aggressively inclined to begin with, who were most likely to be influenced by media stimuli, and who were more likely to be accepting of violence in the real world. The researchers concluded that sexually violent material can affect the attitudes of sensitive individuals.[24] As Dr. Donnerstein put it: "If you take a young man and constantly and repeatedly expose him to material that portrays women responding positively to rape, should you be surprised if he begins to believe that women want to be forced into sexual relationships?"[25]

The researchers also found that, although their viewers were initially depressed and bothered by the content of graphic sex and violence, the more their subjects watched, not only did they become desensitized to the material but they began to enjoy it.[26]

One female writer, disturbed by the alarming escalation of sexual violence against women in visual media and other art forms, asks:

> Why this escalation at the same moment in history when women are finally asserting their equal dignity and equality as persons in all areas of life? Is there a connection?
>
> We know that rape is not an act of passion; it is an act of aggression in order to show domination. Are the images and lyrics of women chained, beaten and raped a media expression of a deep cultural need to dominate women, to keep them in their place?[27]

Is such imagery one more warped visual expression of the consequences of fallen human nature that Genesis 3 warns of? Does the Bible's prophecy against the male tendency to seek power over women shed light on why this type of material can easily become popular among young men?

Adolescents are now the prime target audience of so-called slasher movies containing unbelievably graphic scenes linking sexual explicitness with violent assault. Such movies often feature a common central figure—a deranged man who searches the night for victims, mostly women, whom he proceeds to stalk, dismember, and slaughter. Often the female victims are seized while engaged in sexual trysts or suggestive settings and are murdered in the nude. A horrible array of knives, axes, and chain saws are used to accomplish the job. The cameras pause to celebrate the display of carnage.[28] This scene is typical of any number of slasher films, such as *Friday the Thirteenth, Halloween,* or *Nightmare on Elm Street,* which are often shown on cable channels or independent stations hungry to steal away network audiences.

Why are such movies so successful in luring and addicting teens? One movie producer offers the answer: "I find that youth doesn't seem to be bothered as much by violence as adults are . . . older audiences are grossed out by the scenes the younger audiences enjoy. They've been raised watching a lot of violence on TV."[29] Such films exploit the natural peak of curiosity and sexual desire in the teen years. But some parents are not concerned, because they claim their children don't seem to be "bothered" by what they see in such films. They fail to realize that their children's lack of sensitivity might be the problem, not the solution.

It is bad enough that teenagers see such films; however, 20 twenty percent of children age five to seven who were surveyed several years ago in suburban Cleveland admitted that they had already seen *Friday the Thirteenth*—in almost all cases watching it on cable.[30]

In the nineties, as both TV and film producers strive increasingly for their art to imitate "real life," real life continues to bear a growing resemblance to such art. At the time of this writing, *The Silence of the Lambs*, a movie about serial killers who do unspeakably horrible things to their female victims, is the runaway box office hit at American theaters. How soon will it come to cable television? At other movie theaters, *New Jack City*, a film about inner-city violence and street gangs, plays inside theaters while outside the theater real gangs rumble with each other in front of the box office.

Meanwhile, a newly released U.S. Senate report paints a bleak picture of life resembling art in the United States: a record number of murders, rapes and robberies in 1990. Statistics show, in particular, that violence against women is more pervasive now than in any other time in history—with more rapes committed in 1990 than in any previous year. The report declared the United States to be "the most violent and self-destructive nation on earth."[31]

Policemen now faced with the staggering task of curbing the escalating tide of violence talk about what they face. The role for many has shifted from prevention to self-preservation. "The main objective when you go to work is to go home at night," admits a patrolman from El Dorado, Arkansas. "Just live through the day and make it home."[32]

At the same time, the eyes of America witnessed the beating of a drunk driving suspect by several Los Angeles police officers, who joked about the incident. Unbeknownst to the officers, a witness had videotaped the event. The American Civil Liberties Union, which unflaggingly defends and protects the creators of the graphically sexual and violent imagery that now haunts American memories, led the outcry on television against Los Angeles police brutality. The news departments of the TV networks—who broadcast a significant share of fantasized brutality—accommodatingly echoed and magnified the ACLU's protests. It was a schizophrenic picture of life imitating the "art" that now inhabits the TV screen. In the nineties, are we merely victims of the mean-world syndrome of the eighties, where life in TV-land makes us feel more threatened than we really are? Or is the mean-syndrome becoming a reality as fantasy imagery becomes a role model for real life?

There seems no end to the real life scenarios of violence in the news these days that resemble movie and TV plots. After profiling three bizarre murder cases, the writer of an article in *Time* magazine pointed out that all three crimes resembled "dramas that seem ready-made for TV." [33] What a coincidence. Or is it?

What is a not a coincidence is the truth French churchman Bernard of Clairvaux noted about human nature almost a thousand years ago: "What we love we shall grow to resemble." The bodies that lie scattered on the landscapes of both TV-land and real-life America suggest that what many now savor as entertainment is rapidly becoming the new reality. Historically, cultures that feed on violence have a short track record. What television is increasingly "free" to sell may be coming at an astronomically high price to its consumers.

NOTES

1. Peter Plagens, Mark Miller, Donna Foote, and Emily Yoffe, "Violence in Our Culture." From *Newsweek*, April 1, 1991, p. 46. Copyright © 1991 Newsweek, Inc. All rights reserved. Reprinted by permission.
2. George Gerbner, quoted by William Fore, "Where Do You Draw the Line?" *Media and Values*, Fall 1985, p. 10.
3. Plagens et al., "Violence in Our Culture," p. 48.
4. Jack Haskins, "The Morbid Seducers," *Channels of Communication*, January/February 1986, p. 79.
5. Plagens et al., "Violence in Our Culture," p. 48.
6. "Warning from Washington," *Time*, May 17, 1982, p. 77.
7. "Media Coverage of Prizefighting Bouts Linked to Homicides," *The Los Angeles Times*, reprinted in *The Arizona Republic*, August 14, 1983, p. AA-1.
8. Brandon Centerwall, quoted by Luke Hill, "Research Says Rising Murder Rate Related to TV," United Press International, reprinted in *American Family Journal*, May 1989, p. 3.
9. "As TV Violence Grows, the Campaign Against It Alters Course," *Christianity Today*, November 25, 1983, p. 34.
10. Ibid.
11. Thomas Radecki, M.D., "The TV War on Children," *The Christian Reader*, July/August 1986, p. 17.
12. Ibid., p. 16.
13. Plagens et al., "Violence in Our Culture," p. 51.

14. Nancy Carlson-Page and Diane E. Levin, quoted by Patricia McCormack, "Violence of TV Shows for Kids Is Blamed for Unhealthful Play," *The Arizona Republic*, November 7, 1987, p. C-11.
15. Eve Epstein, "Ninja Turtles Get Shelled," *The Arizona Republic*, March 18, 1991, p. A-7.
16. Jeff Barker, "Kids' TV Violence, Deregulation Linked," *The Arizona Republic*, January 26, 1990, p. D-11.
17. Plagens et al., "Violence in Our Culture," p. 49.
18. Randy Frame, "Violence for Fun," *Christianity Today*, February 21, 1986, p. 16.
19. Linda Bloodworth-Thomason, quoted by Judy Flander, "Television Targets Women as Victims," *Media and Values*, Fall 1985, p. 12.
20. Ibid., p. 13.
21. Gerald Waggett, "Let's Stop Turning Rapists into Heros," *TV Guide*, May 27, 1989, pp. 10-11.
22. Steve Tesich, quoted by Plagans et al., "Violence in Our Culture," p. 51.
23. Marybeth Roden, "Acquaintance Rape: What Men Need to Know," *Signet*, Winter 1991, p. 6.
24. Edward Donnerstein, quoted in "Media's New Mood: Sexual Violence," *Media and Values*, Fall 1985, pp. 3-5.
25. Ibid., p. 4
26. Ibid., p. 5.
27. Maria Riley, O.P., "Enough Is Enough!" *Media and Values*, Fall 1985, p. 20.
28. Roy Anker, "Yikes! Nightmares from Hollywood," *Christianity Today*, June 16, 1989, p. 19.
29. Richard Tuggle, quoted in "Violence Sells Film to Teens," *The Arizona Republic*, July 23, 1986, p. G-1.
30. Plagens et al., "Violence in Our Culture," p. 51.
31. Knight-Ridder Newspapers, "U.S. Leads the World in Violent Crimes, Panel Says," reprinted in *The Times-Picayune*, March 13, 1991, p. A-3.
32. Donald Curole, "Quotelines," *U.S.A. Today*, March 19, 1991, p. 10-A.
33. Nancy Gibbs, "Murders They Wrote," *Time*, April 1, 1991, p. 29.

18

THE SELLING OF
THE AMERICAN MIND

On a return flight from Ireland several years ago, my husband and I sat next to a friendly young native of Shannon. While chatting, we learned that his work took him back and forth to the United States frequently. After conversing for a while, my husband finally asked the young man: "Tell us—what do you really think of Americans?" Our acquaintance answered: "Oh, I like Americans very much, although it puzzles me—why is it that they always seem to be so interested in *buying* something?"

A good question, and an interesting observation from a native of a country where television advertising, for the most part, was nonexistent until recently and is now only in its infancy. The native of the impoverished Emerald Isle saw something in Americans that is so pervasive most of us are oblivious to it—our obsession to buy. It's hardly surprising considering that from the moment we are born we are bombarded with sales appeals—a significant number of them from the TV screen. According to the Television Advertising Bureau, 89 percent of American adults are reached by TV commercials each day, and most Americans spent substantially more time watching TV advertising than seeing or hearing all other media ads combined.[1]

The evidence that this is true is all around us and *in* us. If you doubt TV's ability to commercially indoctrinate, listen to what your children now parrot. My own children, who saw little more than an hour or two a day at the most, could sing jingles before they could compose a full sentence.

Children are particularly vulnerable to TV's commercial Pied Piper. Notes pediatrician Victor Strasburger, children are not only uniquely receptive to its messages because of their innocence, they are particularly attentive to TV advertising because of its visual gimmickry.[2] A 1987 study by the American Automobile Association's Foundation for Traffic Safety, which analyzed the content of television beer commercials, points out that their heightened decibel level, quick pace of change in visual content, and happy, smiling faces appeal to children. Several studies have shown that for those reasons, children pay closer attention to commercials than to programming.[3]

Many children's shows are now nothing more than lengthy toy commercials designed to transform children into addicted materialists before most are old enough to count pennies or have an allowance. One critic of TV points out that commercials exploit a child's desire for instant gratification often at the age when both child and parents are struggling to control such urges. Studies show that children want what they have most recently seen on TV.[4] One study showed that Americans spend close to four billion dollars a year in addition to grocery bills by giving in to their children's requests for products or specific brands.[5]

Advertisers are well aware of that, and they exploit it. A Federal Trade Commission investigation found that TV commercials undermine parent-child relationships by causing conflicts over food, generate resentment against parents who deny their children advertised products, and manipulate children into becoming little sales agents for the advertisers.[6] Boasts one article in *Advertising Age,* a major advertising trade magazine, "If you truly want big sales, you will use the child as your assistant salesman. He sells, he nags, until he breaks down the sales resistance of his mother and father."[7] Ironically, around 2250 B.C. the Code of Hammurabi made selling something to a child without power of attorney a crime punishable by death.[8] Perhaps that ancient law should tell us something.

Children now see between a quarter of a million to a half million TV commercials by the time they turn eighteen. Adults, who often complain of an inability to remember important things, can easily regurgitate dozens of commercial slogans and jingles at the drop of a hat—a testimony to the significance of advertising's staying power.

When I worked in television, people would sometimes complain to me that the television commercials were better, louder, and more interesting than the programs. That is not a coincidence. It is indicative of something that sociologist Todd Gitlin once noted, to which most Americans are inattentive. The priority of most of American television is not to provide programs that entertain or inform. The preeminent purpose of TV is to sell products. The commercial, observed Gitlin, is the reason for it all; programs only exist to package commercials in.[9]

If programs ever became more interesting than the ads, notes former advertising executive Jerry Mander, it would be the end of TV, because programs are shown in America as an excuse to get the public to watch ads and buy products. He notes: "Advertising exists only to purvey what people don't need. Whatever people do need they will find without advertising, if it is available. This is so obvious and so simple that it continues to stagger my mind that the ad industry has succeeded in muddying the point."[10]

Mander points out that advertising works by intervening between people and their needs, urging them to believe that satisfaction can be obtained only through the purchase of more and more commodities. The need for the product is enhanced by linking those products with other, deeper human needs.[11] Vance Packard pointed this out thirty years ago, before TV imagery in advertising reached the level of potency it has today. Packard noted that ads did more than highlight products; they were marketing answers for the deeper human needs of a sense of self-worth, ego gratification, and the desire for power over people and life circumstances.[12]

Advertising doesn't stop at offering a product at face value. Its basic goal is to deliberately create discontent where there previously was none by linking what we don't need with what we emotionally crave. That is why Americans now can "have it your way," or why "you deserve a break today," or why "you never looked so good." Advertisers exploit our fears, loneliness, and self-doubt, and spur our desire to compete. TV ads enter what Mander calls "our inner sanctum" to pull those feelings up and out of ourselves, displaying them on the screen before us and then selling them back to us as commodities. He concludes: "We desperately seek to get them back and pay high prices for the privilege. . . . Whenever we buy a product we are paying for the recovery of our own feelings."[13]

Beer commercials in particular are a prime example of this. A 1987 Michelob commercial, which imitated a rock video, linked the human desire for pleasure, escapism, and thrills with beer by the use of fast-moving, colorful, blurred imagery of night clubs, blinking neon signs, and the visual sensation of travel in a fast moving car. The background lyrics of the accompanying jingle were poetically suggestive of the thrill of high speed driving after dark. The ad clearly touted barhopping and alcohol as an essential part of having an exciting time. Researchers for the AAA Foundation for Traffic Safety also charged that it subliminally linked drinking with driving, a dangerous combination, not just for adults but for teenagers in particular, since half of all auto accidents involve alcohol.[14]

TV beer ads also offer alluring images of encounters between the sexes in bars and night spots, sending the message to youth that the random, casual sexual encounters of adults are "cool" and worth imitating. Some pediatricians charge that the ads, whether intentional or not, sell much more than beer. They point out that such illusions encourage promiscuity and consequently leave both sexes vulnerable to sexually transmitted diseases and young women vulnerable to sexual assault. By linking beer to sexual success, the ads encourage drinking as a means of lowering inhibitions. They also encourage teenagers, through drinking, to diminish their ability to make wise sexual decisions.[15]

In both candidates and hamburgers,
it's the sizzle that sells.

Television ads also distort reality by breeding discontent with our real-life situations. It is the greatest instigator of the "I-could-be-happy-if-only" syndrome in America. Since it enjoys the advantage of moving imagery, it simply does this better than other media, providing the product can be skillfully molded to meet TV's visual criterion. Commodities lend themselves better to TV's inherent production needs than anything else, which is why Jerry Mander rates TV as a better salesman than a news reporter: "Nothing works better as telecommunication than images of products."[16]

TV is the best of all preachers of the gospel of materialism and is the major perpetrator of a fundamental assumption underlying our culture—the idea that products are the solution to our problems. Commercials are inherently the most biased part of TV, yet America's obsession with materialism testifies to how readily we accept artificial imagery as real, in spite of the fact that ads are completely one-sided in presentation.

Many would argue that advertising is an important staple of capitalism, but communications professor Neil Postman disagrees, pointing out that "television commercials are an assault on capitalist ideology. Advertising has been devastating to capitalism because the belief that I needed to produce a better product than my competition—is now completely irrelevant. Instead of investing in improving a product, companies put their money into improving their image."[17]

The American penchant for buying images has spilled out of the supermarket and into the political arena. TV advertising is being used more and more to package and sell candidates. In both candidates and hamburgers, it's the sizzle that sells. Candidates for the presidency and the Senate are being marketed like hamburgers and laundry soap in thirty- to sixty-second blips. The bulk of campaign advertising spending now goes to television ads because candidates and parties have good reason to believe that voters are more influenced by images than by mere information about candidates. Americans are now conditioned to buy anything, even leaders, through commercials. The American people may be the losers in such image-dominated campaigns. The sure winners are the major networks, who during major political campaigns rake in millions.

The significance of TV advertising to Christians is paramount. The very nature of television, which thrives on creating discontent for the sake of commercial prosperity, flies in the face of biblical commands: "You shall not covet" (Exodus 20:17); "be content with what you have" (Hebrews 13:5). Christians need a more conscious realization that commercialization is not necessarily the next thing to godliness. We need greater awareness of how commercials work to enslave us to artificial need, and in both a material and spiritual sense, leave us less than free.

Yet, in spite of the myriad of biblical commands and warnings about the love and use of money, materialism is as much a plague to many American Christians as it is to non-Christians. Despite God's commands to die to self, deny oneself, and seek God's kingdom first, professing believers whose attitudes actually reflect the Book they claim to believe may be an unsettling minority.

Some surveys reveal how deeply conditioned professing Christians are to hedonism and materialism. For example, a national survey several years ago by Christian opinion pollsters George Barna and William Paul McKay found that seven out of ten professing believers were in agreement with the hedonistic idea left over from the sixties that a person is free to do whatever he pleases as long as he doesn't hurt anyone else, in spite of clear biblical teaching to the contrary. Three out of ten Christians surveyed agreed that "nothing in life was more important than having fun and being happy."[18]

Surveys by Barna and McKay in regard to materialistic attitudes produced almost identical results. Two out of three Christians asked expressed a strong desire for more money and possessions. Half said that they would never have enough to buy what they thought they needed. One out of four agreed that material possessions are the principal indicator of a successful life.

The survey showed that the number of people who professed faith in biblical truth yet affirmed these antibiblical concepts was almost identical to the ratio of nonbelievers who gave the same answers. The researchers concluded that only less than 5 percent of Americans who claimed to be born-again Christians gave answers that did not reflect the values of hedonism or materialism to some significant degree.[19] Do such results indicate that the gospel of self-fulfillment, with television as a prime time preacher, is more deeply entrenched in the professing Christian's mind in America than the gospel of Jesus Christ?

The love of money is as old as money itself. Jesus spoke of it repeatedly, and Barna and McKay note that Christ foretold of its seduction. He warned that its pursuit would steal our attention, distort our priorities, prevent our acceptance of the spirit of true belief, generate weak faith, and cause a disparity between what men say and what they do.[20] Are we more tuned into advertising slogans than to Scripture?

Television did not create the love of money, but the principal preacher of prosperity to a culture immersed in hedonism and materialism is the glimmering box that chatters and flashes material illusion at us for hours on end.

The tragic side effects of the endlessly absorbed commercial messages can be seen in many ways, not the least of which is the debt and financial pressure that many American families have brought on themselves. One chain of banks in the Pacific Northwest, apparently in response to this problem, has begun a counter-advertising campaign with the message to consumers that "you don't have to buy everything you see." "How to get out of debt and stay out of debt" ranks among the most popular topics now being offered at Christian conferences and seminars.

I once heard someone say that our earning capacity never quite seems to keep up with our yearning capacity. Why should we be happy with our possessions after watching hundreds of hours of commercials designed to make us discontent with what we have? We gripe and react negatively to church sermons that implore us to tithe money yet passively accept without a whimper the hundreds of commercials that pour into our heads, compelling us to squander our dollars on objects of far less long-term value than the work of the church. Research also shows that two out of three Christians do not give the scripturally mandated tithe.[21] Some who are in debt and who give less than a full tithe to the church spend money on luxury items, including more television, by paying expensive monthly fees to have extra movie and entertainment channels pumped into their homes via cable or satellite.

By allowing a machine and those who use it to determine the desires that haunt our imagination, we have given it the power to decide to a far greater extent than many realize our very motives and pursuits in real life. We have allowed it to propagate a unique kind of religion. Former Idaho school superintendent Roy Truby, testifying at a PTA hearing on TV's impact, observed: "There is what we might call a 'theology of television' developing as a prevailing influence on American society. The ads constantly tell us to seek greater pleasure through more consumption . . . somehow the ads make us feel that to have nothing less than too much is un-American."[22]

American advertisers, armed with television and its media cousins, have spawned a curious new set of "beatitudes":

> Blessed are those who buy—for they shall not be lonely.
> Blessed are those who buy—for they shall not be hungry.
> Blessed are those who buy—for they shall be popular.
> Blessed are those who buy—for they shall experience no pain.
> Blessed are those who buy—for they shall appear young.
> Blessed are those who buy—for they shall appear more beautiful.
> Blessed are those who buy—for there shall be no odor about them.
> Blessed are those who buy—for they shall be called successful.[23]

Since television successfully sells products, some have used it to "sell" Jesus. In light of what we know about TV's inherent weaknesses, how should we regard the "electronic pulpit"? That is the subject of the next chapter.

NOTES

1. "Media Comparisons," *The Television Bureau of Advertising Research Report,* Bruskin Associates, 1990, p. 3.
2. Victor Strasburger, quoted by Barbara Borsch, "How Madison Avenue Seduces Children," *Pediatric Management,* March 1991, pp. 14-15.
3. Ibid., p. 14.
4. Diane Bogosian, "How Advertising Sucks Kids In," *Growing Parent,* June 1986, p. 2.
5. Ibid.
6. Ibid.
7. Ibid.
8. Gregg Lewis, "TV Advertising's Double Threat," *Christianity Today,* September 20, 1985, p. 10.
9. Todd Gitlin, "Sixteen Notes on Television," *Literature in Revolution,* quoted by Jerry Mander, *Four Arguments for the Elimination of Television* (New York: William Morrow, 1978), p. 307.
10. Ibid., p. 126.
11. Ibid., pp. 127-29.
12. Lewis, "TV Advertising's Double Threat," p. 10.
13. Mander, *Four Arguments,* pp. 130-31.
14. Borsch, "Madison Avenue," pp. 19-20.
15. Ibid., p. 20.
16. Mander, *Four Arguments,* p. 42.
17. Neil Postman, quoted by Alvin P. Sanoff, "TV Has Culture by the Throat," *U.S. News and World Report,* January 23, 1986, p. 59. Copyright © 1985, U.S. News and World Report.
18. George Barna and William Paul McKay, *Vital Signs* (Westchester, Ill.: Crossway, 1984), p. 141.
19. Ibid., pp. 142-43.
20. Barna and McKay, *Vital Signs,* p. 137. Relevant Scripture texts are Matthew 19:16-22; 23:2-12; 24:45-51; Mark 7:6-13; 8:34-38; Luke 8:5-15.
21. Ibid., p. 115.
22. Lewis, "TV Advertising's Double Threat," p. 10.
23. "Blessed Are Ye if Ye Buy." Reprinted from *Growing with Television: The Study of Biblical Values and the Television Experience,* Adult Level, Unit 2 (United Methodist Communications, 475 Riverside Drive, New York, N.Y. 10115), p. 4. Originally publshed by Seabury (New York, 1980).

19

THE DILEMMA OF THE ELECTRONIC PULPIT

t's good to leave our evangelical cocoons periodically and find out what people really think of us," wrote author Charles Colson, after a promotional book tour several years ago. In one of his columns, he related a sobering experience with a radio talk show host that he claimed was typical of his reception in secular media. The red "on the air" light flashed, Colson remembered, and the interviewer began: "Today we're interviewing Charles Colson," said the host smoothly. "But first, let's hear from 'God's little goofballs.'"

With that, Colson said, the host flipped a switch and a prerecorded message from Jim and Tammy Bakker filled the studio. "I'm not sure," Colson reminisced, "but I think the inspirational recording included Tammy's recipe for three-layer bean dip." The interviewer grinned at the end of the recording and segued, "And now, we have another evangelist with us today. Let's hear what Chuck Colson has to say." "The majority of my 100 interviews," Colson concluded, "began in a discouragingly similar manner. . . . It's cold out there," he notes.[1]

Electronic preacher-bashing has become a popular pastime in both secular and Christian circles for the past few years, thanks to well-publicized scandal within the electronic church. Much rhetoric has been generated about what Christians are doing to television. However, after considering the spectrum of weaknesses inherent in television production, perhaps we should reverse the question and ask, What is television doing to Christianity?

The answer, of course, is that TV is doing to Christianity what it does to everything else. The same weaknesses of television—human, technological, and institutional—afflict televised Christianity. The scandals of recent years have established that the electronic church is not immune to ideological bias and power lust—such problems plague preachers as well as journalists. Ignorance is a problem for reporters and preachers alike. As one Christian station manager notes, some Christian broadcasters have drifted into theological never-never land because they are professional personalities and theological amateurs.[2]

Certainly not all Christians agree on doctrines and issues, and Christian television inevitably reflects to some degree the particular ideological views of the handful who control it, to the exclusion of ideas held by those who don't. But, more important, Christian television, like its secular counterpart, is at the mercy of TV's technological limits and demands, which remold the message in the image of the medium. In the TV age, warns author Virginia Stem Owens, the tool becomes the master. She warns: "We are in great danger of allowing communications tools to dictate our theology, a theology that must be reducible to a telex message or taken from headlines composed for the sake of sensation and guaranteed to change tomorrow. Scripture is whittled into slogans."[3] Robert McNeil was right—television alters everything it consumes. Nothing goes into television and comes out quite the same, including the gospel.

It is not my purpose in a single chapter to critically analyze television evangelism but to simply underscore the dilemma of the electronic pulpit. The TV evangelist faces the same limits of a secular producer. He must either start with a message simple enough to fit the narrow confines of TV communication or take his theology and adapt it for survival on the tube. The message must be geared toward broad appeal, because mass communication is dependent on audience numbers to survive. The need to build interest and hold viewers, the demand for visual attractiveness—all such production demands exert their influence in the realm of Christian TV.

For example, one reason charismatics dominate much of Christian TV is that charismatic expression is simply more theatrical and visual than the worship style of some other Protestant groups. Charismatic theology also tends to be less preoccupied with complex theological concepts and systematized theology. Since it is less complicated, it tends to work better on television.

Because TV communicates visually and emotionally, it was inevitable that televised religion would become a Christianized cult of personalities. It was unavoidable also that TV's lust for the visual would shift the attention away from an invisible, mysterious, incomprehensible, highly complex God and elevate the personality attempting to communicate the message.

> *Does the preacher dare risk boring*
> *the very audience he wants to reach*
> *when so much money is invested*
> *in technology and air time?*

Since emphasis on TV shifts inevitably from content to style, what the preacher has to say becomes secondary to his technique, cosmetic appearance, and personal charisma in saying it. Some of the emerging stars of the evangelical TV screen are not necessarily the best and brightest theologians but the most magnetic personalities and the best entertainers. They succeed, not so much because of theological prowess, but because of their story-telling ability and their skill at visually holding our battered attention spans.

Since TV can't convey complexity, it automatically does a complex subject such as Christian theology an injustice. Preachers who achieve any degree of audience success have discovered they must keep their message short and simple. The Christian programmer must conform the gospel message to fit the television format, if it is to find an audience.

Robert Schuller is an example of a television preacher whose message has been successfully molded for the medium. His message has been criticized heavily within evangelical circles, but few seem to recognize that Schuller is a TV preacher who thoroughly understands the medium. He is one of the few TV evangelists who attracts viewers outside the Christian ghetto (his books are best-sellers in the secular market). He knows Hollywood, and he understands the secular audience, but he has undertaken a sizeable theological risk in the way he tailors his television appeal.

I see Schuller as an intelligent and well-educated preacher who is not uninformed about orthodox theology. However, at least part of his problem may be that he knows Christian theology is far too complicated and unwieldy for television. Schuller knows that words and phrases such as *saved, sanctified, justified, sin,* and *under the blood* just don't communicate well to contemporary audiences, so he substitutes words that do, but meaning is lost in the process. Content becomes the sacrificial lamb of the style and simplicity necessary to use television effectively.

It can't be any other way if one is to hold an audience in a highly compressed audio-visual medium. The biblical message he preaches undergoes an enormous face-lift in the process. Some would claim it has been irreparably damaged. Even if this is so, from the perspective of a TV producer I think that his critics may spend too much time blaming Schuller himself and not enough time recognizing how television refashions his content.

The TV preacher can overwhelm, confuse, or turn off a listener or viewer with technical Christian jargon. He can stick doggedly to terms such as *sin, sanctification,* and *justification,* saying all he wants in a no-frills setting. But he will communicate only to a select few, most of whom are probably already predisposed to the message. Or he can simplify his message, add the crystal cathedral, lush greenery, and sparkling fountains, and suddenly he has a larger and more diverse audience. Such elements create interest. The chief sin of man may be to be separated from God—but the chief sin in TV is *to be boring*. Boredom is the sin that separates the programmer from viewer. Does the preacher dare risk boring the very audience he wants to reach when so much money is invested in technology and air time? God may own the cattle on a thousand hills, but would He slaughter the entire herd for a feast no one is attending? It is a difficult question indeed.

I see nothing wrong with and *much to be desired* in putting a new contemporary face on sound old theology. However, it must be realized that an inherent hazard of TV is that it can do more than just make the message contemporary. It sometimes creates a new theological hybrid, molded and altered to fit the confines of the expensive technology attempting to preach it.

Communications professor and author Neil Postman underscores the danger of using TV to convey religion. Television, contends Postman, is the enemy of religious experience because it presents religion just the way it presents everything else—as entertainment. In the transition onto the tube, Postman observes, religion loses context just as does news: it is stripped of everything that is historic, profound, and sacred. The aura, or reverence, withers away. On television, offers Postman, "there is no ritual, no dogma, no tradition, no theology and above all, no sense of spiritual transcendence."[4] In addition, Postman says, the television screen itself has a strong bias toward secularism: "The screen is so saturated with our memories of profane events, so deeply associated with the commercial and entertainment worlds that it is difficult for it to be recreated as a frame for sacred events."[5]

As we have already seen, on TV the emphasis shifts inevitably to the seen at the expense of the unseen. On religious TV shows, notes Postman, "the preacher is tops. God comes out the second banana."[6] In an image-oriented medium, the invisible God of the Bible will be shortchanged to some degree every time.

Postman charges that no great religious leader, from Moses to Luther to Jesus Himself, offered people what they wanted—only what they needed. "But television," points out Postman, "is not well suited to offering people what they need." It's too easy to turn off.[7] He concludes: "As a consequence, what is preached on television is not anything like the Sermon on the Mount. Religious programs are filled with good cheer. They celebrate affluence. Their featured players become celebrities. . . . Christianity is a demanding and serious religion. When it is delivered as easy and amusing, it is another kind of religion altogether."[8]

The dilemma of the electronic preacher is similar to that of Howard Beale, one of the central characters in the film *Network*. *Network* is a ludicrous, sometimes vulgar, portrayal of the inner workings of a fictitious major TV network called UBS. UBS is the poor fourth position competitor to ABC, CBS, and NBC, and a loser in both programming and ratings. In a last-ditch effort to improve audience share, UBS adopts a no-holds-barred policy toward programming. Howard Beale, of UBS, is a TV personality's "Everyman": an aging news anchor who finds his hair thinning along with his audience. What transforms him from a mundane news reader who teeters on the brink of being retired to the number one personality of UBS's "Howard Beale News Hour" is that he alters his delivery and his message to play to the masses. He becomes the "mad prophet of the airwaves," the cheerleader of network news. He chants and rants the things the public wants to hear and understands. All of a sudden his ratings begin to climb, and he is an overnight success. He has the masses in his palm as long as he tells them what they want to hear.

At the peak of his success poor Howard Beale, the "mad prophet," discovers that he has not been communicating reality to his viewers. Truth is not all cheerleading about life, liberty, democracy, and the importance of the individual, a UBS company executive convinces him. It is also death, destruction, and the eroding value of the person in society. So Howard Beale, struck by his newfound understanding of the truth, changes his style and message. He lowers his voice and attempts to tackle the complexity of the human condition.

Immediately the ratings drop. The public loved him as a cheerleader, but he bores them or scares them in the role of doomsday prophet. Howard Beale has committed the ultimate TV sin.

He loses his audience. In the irreverent and absurd plot of the movie, the network executives decide that Howard Beale must be assassinated on the air. The movie closes with Howard's epithet: "This was the story of Howard Beale. The first known instance of an anchor man who was killed because of his lousy ratings." The ever-changing faces on network and local newscasts are testimony to the fact that Howard was the embodiment of many TV personalities who "died" due to low audience numbers.

Howard Beale, Robert MacNeil, Robert Schuller, and I—along with other TV producers—have learned this the hard, frustrating way. After wrestling with the medium, we discovered that we could not tame TV; it tamed us, time and time again. TV cannot and will not effectively convey anything we want, any way we want it, as truthfully as we want it, if we just work hard enough and spend enough money. Like Howard Beale, the TV preacher can either run the risk of becoming a Christian cheerleader to the masses, in order to hold his audience, or he can uncompromisingly preach against the grain of the medium he uses and risk becoming like Howard Beale, the first known instance of a once-popular TV preacher who "died" on the screen because of lousy ratings.

NOTES

1. Charles Colson, "Reflections on a Book Tour: It's Cold Out There," *Jubilee*, February 1988, p. 7.
2. J. Thomas Bisset, "Religious Broadcasting: Assessing the State of the Art," *Christianity Today*, December 12, 1980, p. 29.
3. Virginia Stem Owens, "The Jesus Technique," *Christianity Today*, September 21, 1984, p. 55.
4. Neil Postman, *Amusing Ourselves to Death* (New York: Penguin, 1985), pp. 116-17.
5. Ibid., p. 119.
6. Ibid., p. 117.
7. Ibid., p. 121.
8. Ibid.

20

WHY CHRIST CAME BEFORE TV

W hy did Christ miss the "age of television"? It is a question worth pondering. Modern day religious leaders are certainly enamored with its potential. Pope John XXIII once called television "God's greatest modern gift for communicating the Gospel."[1] More and more Christian groups now rush headlong into the electronic video arena in an effort to fulfill the Great Commission. Some proclaimed television to be "a tool used of God to present the Gospel into homes of millions who otherwise would never set foot in the doors of the church," and "a perpetual advertisement for local churches."[2] One particular denomination predicted that Christian television would provide churches with a constant flow of people responding to the national and local programs his denomination planned to produce.[3] Cardinal John O'Connor once told a group of New York state broadcasters: "With 30 seconds of time given to me free on television or radio, I reach more people than Christ reached in a lifetime—in 33 years."[4]

As a child, I remember wondering why Christ hadn't come when television was available to beam His message to the four corners of the earth. Going into all the world to preach the gospel to every living creature sounded like a big job for just twelve people. Wouldn't it have been easier and far more effective if Jesus had just founded the Christian Broadcasting Network? His arrival could have been announced before millions, just as was Justice O'Conner's appointment to the Supreme Court.

I now know that television is best at creating illusions, not at communicating truth. Since Jesus was in the truth business, television might have presented some very perplexing problems for Him.

I wonder what kind of treatment Jesus Christ would have received at the hands of twentieth-century producers had He chosen to come at a time when television was the prevailing medium of communication. Would He have been the target of biased interpretation? In his book *Christ and the Media*, Malcolm Muggeridge muses about a fictional Fourth Temptation. While wandering in the desert for forty days, Jesus is offered free prime time television coverage by the devil but turns it down.[5] Notes television writer Lloyd Billingsley, "[Christ] knew that through the miracle of editing, the network illusionists could make him appear however they chose, something they frequently do with his more outspoken followers [these days]."[6] Or, perhaps worse, as they did the babies in the Southern California storage container, would the media just have *ignored* Him altogether?

If Christ had come for TV, would He have waited to perform His miracles until the cameras arrived? Would He have repeated them for the benefit of a network crew that arrived late or whose camera suffered a technical failure? Would He have jumped off the Temple as Satan suggested—something really visual and spectacular—to attract the "right" kind of coverage?

Which one of the twelve disciples would have made the best press secretary? The outspoken Peter, who would have blasted the press like Spiro Agnew, or the wily Judas Iscariot?

Would Christ have risked the integrity of His ministry to a medium that inevitably generates illusion? Would He have catered to a medium where the premium is on visual performance rather than on unseen attitudes of the heart? If Jesus' message had come under the excruciating time constraints of television, would we have heard only one of the nine Beatitudes?

Would we have rated Jesus on how warm, witty, and dynamic He was on the tube? We pick our politicians this way—and certainly our news anchors. I wonder, would we have chosen a Savior that way?

Would the man Isaiah described as "having no beauty that we should desire Him" have been just too ordinary and mundane looking to capture the hearts of the sophisticated TV generation? Would we have based our choice to follow on how charismatic or entertaining He was? Would we have held the Lord up to some of the same shallow standards of performance that we use to evaluate our Christian leaders and speakers today—good looks; dynamic, humorous delivery; and engaging smile? Would His TV image have overshadowed His words, which He declared were the source of all life? Would television have rendered Jesus into just another media performer competing for a share of the available audience?

Jesus' way of communicating stands in stark contrast to twentieth-century sophistication. His words traveled beyond the crowds in Galilee simply by the faithful repetition of His disciples, who repeated them countless times with others. Unaided by modern methods of communication, those words finally came to rest in handwritten manuscripts, copies of which have survived the ages. Jesus had no electronic tools for broadcasting, but how profound and far-reaching His communication was and continues to be! Jesus may have "missed" modern media technology, but He was not without powerful ways of getting His message across. In fact, He employed the two most effective ways to communicate truths, even by today's standards.

One of the first lessons I learned in basic college communications theory is that delivering a message in person is considered to be the most lasting and effective way to communicate accurate information, even in this advanced electronic age. One-to-one communication breaks down barriers to understanding by establishing a system of feedback and exchange. Electronic devices masquerade as personal communication, but in reality they create a distance between sender and receiver. I once interviewed evangelist Billy Graham and and found him to be far more awe-inspiring in person than on television. Although he had impressed me before by his powerful on-camera presence, he conveyed a warmth, humility, and serenity in person that was lost on the TV screen.

Cult leaders understand the power of personal contact, which perhaps explains why various sects still grow by leaps and bounds without the benefit of mass media devices. Politicians comprehend the value of personal communication. In spite of televised debates and commercials, those who seek the highest and the lowest offices in the land still go door-to-door, meeting-to-meeting, shaking hands and kissing babies.

Someone once said that the best way to send an idea into the world is to wrap it up in a person. God understood the power of person-to-person communication, so He met and made His disciples face-to-face—one at a time. Perhaps ABC anchor Ted Koppel was partly correct when he referred to Jesus Christ as "the Ultimate E. T.—the ultimate Extra-terrestrial." Yet Christ was far more than a visitor from outer space. He was the Infinite penetrating the finite. God became a human being, dying and delivering the good news of forgiveness person-to-person.

Far from "missing" the modern media,
the Scriptures insist that Jesus
arrived at the ripest possible
moment in history to communicate.

In this electronic age, we should be careful not to lose sight of the effectiveness of God's approach. Christianity is far more than simply broadcasting a message over a mass medium. It is living the gospel out in multidimensional detail before the eyes of the world and personally reaching people at their point of deepest need. Chuck Colson reminds us: "While we are creating sophisticated organizations and employing the latest technology to win the world to Christ, let us not forget that our neighbor judges Jesus Christ by what he sees in us."[7] Modern man can flick off the Christian broadcast, but he cannot rid himself so easily of the witness lived out at the desk next to him at work, or in the home next door.

The second most effective means of communicating is the book. Printed words on a page have potential to communicate truth accurately in a way that lasts. Listen to this statement from my college communications textbook: "Books provide a permanence characteristic of no other communications medium. The newspaper reporter and the radio-television commentator speak to [a short-lived] audience. Books, however, such as the superb copies of the Bible produced by Gutenberg in the fifteenth century, live always."[8]

Words on a page cry out to us again and again, speaking and influencing us long after the people who wrote them have gone to their graves. The oxide images of videotape will fade, crack, and deteriorate over time, but words recorded on a page have the potential to live and speak for all time, through all ages, to be copied and recopied forever. Although books lack the immediacy possessed by radio and TV, what is lost in speed is often balanced by the potential for accuracy. Writers have the ability to check and recheck facts and rewrite information. Books are capable of what mass communications experts refer to as "sustained and systematic exposition."[9]

Words on a page—inspired by the Wisdom behind the universe and unhampered by cosmetic distractions—such words are life and the light of men. God, the master communicator, as we say in the news business, has gone on record. He guided the thoughts of His chosen authors and wrote a Book that has changed history. In a culture fascinated with the toys of electronic communication, we dare not neglect the power of its pages. Although Jesus Christ made a profound impact in person, it could have been as though He never lived were it not for the recorded, inspired words written about Him and left for posterity.

God not only used the two most effective ways to communicate truth, but Scripture reminds us that Jesus came at the most effective time for communication. The Bible tells us that "when the time had fully come" God sent His Son into the world (Galatians 4:4). Far from "missing" the modern media, the Scriptures insist that Jesus arrived at the ripest possible moment in history to communicate.

In *The Life and Teachings of Jesus Christ*, Scottish minister James Stewart builds a beautiful case for the "fullness of time" in terms of communication. Stewart points out that when Christ came, Jerusalem was the literal center of the world—the best possible place geographically to launch a worldwide movement.

It was the fullness of time politically. The world was in relative peace. No major wars were in progress. Good roads were available for travel almost anywhere. Greek was a universal language at the time, and almost everyone was bilingual.

It was the fullness of time economically, a time of great prosperity in the midst of great economic distress. Taxes were high, and the economic system was in decline. People were in despair over a coming economic crisis. They were searching for answers— looking for truth.

It was the fullness of time morally and religiously. Stewart notes that it was a time of great moral despair. Old religions were dying out, and moral standards were breaking down. Men and women were grasping for something to believe in. The time was ripe for the spread of truth. God could not have picked a better time or a better way to communicate with lost mankind. Stewart concludes:

> So the Redeemer came. Somewhere in the mind and heart of God from the very foundation of the earth the Christ had been waiting, hidden in the counsels of eternity until the great bell of the ages should strike; and when at last everything in the world and in the souls of men was ready and prepared, he came, the Word of God made flesh, not a moment early and not a moment late, but exactly on the stroke of the hour. It was the day of the Lord.[10]

Perhaps the vast array of modern communication devices would only have served to obscure the message of the One sent to redeem us. So the Word became flesh (not videotape or a graven image on a screen)[11] at just the right moment. God became man and lived among us, "full of grace and truth" (John 1:14). He arrived unobtrusively in the chilly silence of a Bethlehem night. No glaring camera lights were available to illumine the darkness of the dirty stable for the Minicams® to record the light of the world—the ultimate communication link between Holy God and sinful man. No major media promotions of His arrival or commercials heralded His coming. The event would have been too humble and unspectacular.

The only reporters on the scene were a handful of shepherds. "I am" Himself was born to be one of us and yet be fully God at the same time. It is a mystery no network commentator could analyze, no journalist could capsulize in a minute and thirty seconds, no camera could begin to convey. No theologian can fully explain it, and no heart can fully comprehend it.

David Worley . . . suggests that perhaps TV is better suited "to the work of John the Baptist than the work of Jesus."

Jesus probably had good reasons for avoiding television. However, TV is a part of our culture that the church cannot ignore. There are some who argue that Christians dare not fail to make use of television. TV evangelist Pat Robertson declares: "It would be folly for the church not to get involved with the most formative force in America."[12] He's probably right. But the questions of what it is used for and how are paramount. How can we use television for evangelism? Can Christians make effective use of its power? It is a question I wrestle with frequently. I do believe that part of the answer is not in whether television is used for evangelism, but in how. To use it ineffectively may be worse than not using it at all.

I have had access to the Nielsen ratings of religious programming in several different cities during my career, and I saw little to convince me that much of current television evangelism is, in fact, evangelism in the sense that it reaches a significant number of peo-

ple outside the established church and impacts them with a trans-
forming message. If success in television is defined in audience
numbers or, more significantly, in attracting those unreached by
the traditional church, all of the data and analysis I have seen suggests that the returns for the millions of dollars being spent have
been minimal.

When I observe much of Christian broadcasting on both a national and a local level, I am left with the feeling that Christian
broadcasters have sincerely but naively tried to make television do
what it does not do well. Many have tried with the best intentions
to use TV to transmit abstract and detailed information in some
meaningful context, which is unfortunately what TV does poorly.
Others have succumbed to creating nothing more than what Charles
Colson has called "entertainment for the faithful,"[13] tailoring their
appeal only to those who already agree with the message. I believe
one of the weakest spots of so-called Christian television is that
many its perpetrators seem to speak completely out of the frame of
reference of those they claim to be reaching for. I suspect that part
of the reason for TV's lack of true evangelism is that the vast majority of its potential audience cannot understand what is being said
or apply it to their own lives, even if they wished to.

It is my guess that the majority of those involved in Christian
television have spent little or no time in the secular side of broadcasting. Perhaps some have spent their entire professional life within the sterile confines of the church. If I had the power to do so, I
would make a rule that every Christian broadcaster must spend
five years in secular television before entering Christian television.
They could learn much, as I did, in the secular television world
about the need to "contextualize" their faith—to make it understandable and relevant to a skeptical world.

The image projected by some inadvertently frightens some not
conditioned to speaking the Christian "lingo" or to certain cultural
styles. Several years ago a young, sophisticated, broadcasting executive came to my home for Bible study. Hungry for meaning and
purpose and searching for answers to tough questions, we poured
over Scripture together for hour after hour. After several months

she seemed open to making a personal commitment to Christ, but was still noticeably wrestling with something. "What's holding you back?" I queried. Her answer was disturbing: "If I take this step of faith," she offered, with tears in her eyes, "will I eventually end up looking like those people on Christian TV?" This woman had confused the substance of Christianity with the provincial style of a particular evangelist. Unfortunately, in a cosmetic, image-oriented mass medium the style of delivery perceived as credible in the Deep South may not be received the same way in Boston, New York City, or Los Angeles. Does such imagery actually subvert the message of the gospel in some places?

One *New York Times* writer notes that when Christians have organized boycotts against major networks, their complaints were "dismissed as coming from outside or mainstream American opinion." Evangelicals were characterized as people "on the fringes of the establishment."[14] Before dismissing such labels as mere secular bigotry, should we not reexamine the way Christian broadcasting has defined the Christian image for the majority? Are broadcasters who have failed to contextualize faith to a modern culture guilty of creating caricatures that impede evangelism?

Can a medium that elevates style over substance and is capable of portraying only partial truth evangelize effectively? David Worley, a Christian friend and broadcast entrepreneur who has struggled together with me on this question, suggests that perhaps TV is better suited "to the work of John the Baptist than the work of Jesus." I agree with David. Perhaps television is a better seed planter than savior. The right kind of imagery might help to soften the hard ground in the hearts of those who need Christ. The question remains: Is the "right" kind of imagery traditional preaching or contemporary storytelling? Do we need more storytellers and fewer preachers?

In one instance, I know of a person who was uneasy in traditional evangelical church settings and turned off by the image of most TV preachers but who was willing to listen to Robert Schuller because his message was contemporary looking and nonintimidating in approach. He eventually explored the church option a little further because Schuller projected an image of credibility to this particular individual.

However, the Institute for American Church Growth, reminds us that it is personal encouragement, not the mass evangelism, that often makes the biggest difference. In a survey of by the Institute of almost 40,000 church attenders, less than 1 percent asked said they attended church because of mass media evangelism. However, 85 percent said they came to Christ through a personal relationship with a friend, relative, or associate.[15]

Whatever use Christians make of television, we must first define it strictly along the lines of the strengths and weaknesses of the medium or it will not be effective. First, *we must recognize the dilemmas of the electronic pulpit and resist trying to make television do what it is incapable of.* Second, *we must identify our audience.* Who are the people we want to reach, and what will they respond to? The answer is not just the unchurched or unsaved. Who *are* these people really? Christian broadcasters must recognize that we now live in a post-Christian culture that does not understand our spiritual terminology, church traditions, or cultural mannerisms. Today's unchurched audiences are far more discriminating than many would-be evangelists realize. They are deeply conditioned to salivate to a particular type of imagery with a certain look and feel to it. They have been trained subliminally by highly polished advertising and programs. The production standards by which Christian TV programs are measured in the minds of audiences are those set by the major networks and professional production companies.

The vast majority of unchurched people do not respond favorably to oratorical styles of bygone eras. The new standard-bearers of what constitutes a credible personal image are Dan Rather, Tom Brokaw, and Peter Jennings. Unfortunately, some of what I see labeled "Christian TV evangelism" does not come anywhere close to projecting the kind of credible image that the majority of secular people might respond to. Those who produce and fund some Christian programming apparently make their decisions based on what they themselves respond to, with little or no real knowledge of or sensitivity to the style of message that would most effectively penetrate the mainstream of thought in secular culture.

I suspect that most of those who do watch Christian television are not newcomers who would never darken the door of a church, but those who are already predisposed to accept its traditional cultural entrapments, music, message, and style. Charles Colson warns: "We talk in our own language to like-minded friends, and the world is content to let us put on our own show, so long as we don't bother anyone."[16]

Third, *we need to learn what we can from secular television producers.* Norman Lear, the highly successful producer of *All in the Family* and other prime time hits who has been preaching his own gospel of social values for years via TV, says that ideas are more convincing when they come gift-wrapped in drama and humor: "People, he points out," accept information more readily when they're being entertained."[17] Is it possible that we need to "preach" less directly and more subliminally?

If I could use TV any way I wanted to preach, I would use it to tell more stories and preach fewer sermons. I am excited about the prospect of seeing Frank Peretti's *This Present Darkness* come to the movie theater (although I know the best-selling book will lose much rich detail in its transformation to film). I have been personally more enthralled by the beauty of the movie *Chariots of Fire,* more moved by the emotion of *Shadowlands* (the award-winning TV drama about Christian author C. S. Lewis), more convicted by the powerful Christian symbolism of the TV movie *The Doll Maker* (starring Jane Fonda!), and more instructed by the moral lessons of Walt Disney's *Pinocchio* than by much of the evangelism I have seen on TV. One of the most powerful pieces of "TV evangelism" I have ever seen was a recent "20/20" interview by Barbara Walters with former baseball star and Christian Dave Dravecky about the tragic amputation of his pitching arm.

Am I saying there is no place on TV for preachers? Not if they are good speakers with a contemporary style and if they possess a strong sense of how to relate Christianity to the felt needs of secular culture. But if Christians are to use a mass medium like television with any degree of success in terms of changing the audience, they must move out of merely broadcasting church services and sermons and into the storytelling business in a significant way. To spend millions to merely broadcast speakers, is to use TV's power only in a limited, secondary sense.

And, finally, *the electronic church must face the fact of what it is competing against.* Currently, much of existing Christian broadcasting is merely competing against itself for the same audience already agreeable to its present style. There is much duplication of effort. We need to stop rivaling each other for a share of the "already convinced" and design programming that will compete with secular programming for the "unconvinced."

Frankly, I am more impressed with the way the Mormon church has used mass media advertising to create a desirable public relations image of itself by linking its name with felt needs, such as family togetherness and antidrugs, than with the image created by some Christian broadcasters, especially those who seem to exist in some type of time warp in terms of their ability to relate to mainstream America. The images projected by the Mormons in their TV and radio commercials are the kind that leave a favorable emotional impression, arouse interest, and stimulate curiosity. The Mormons are using the media effectively to preevangelize and condition positive impressions without ever uttering a word of theology. They seem to understand the strengths and weaknesses, as well as the limits, of the medium they are using.

In spite of millions of dollars spent to "evangelize" America via the airwaves, a survey by Christian pollster George Barna suggests that confidence in the local church continues to decline. The perceived relevance of Christianity is in a downward spiral in America.[18] According to Barna, only 38 percent of Americans believe that the church is relevant for today.[19] One positive use for television would be to use it to build audiovisual images that link Christian beliefs with the felt needs of the culture. But in many cases, millions of dollars are spent on amusing the already saved with images they are comfortable with, while those same images intimidate, confuse, and, in some cases, repulse those who are beyond the boundaries of the established church and who, sadly, are the ones most desperately in need of a change of heart about Christianity.

Christian television must be more than a man reading the King James Version of Scripture into a TV camera. We cannot treat television as though it were merely radio with a picture. But we dare not to continue to use it, as some do, blindly or ineffectively if we are to meet the felt needs of our culture, project an image of credibility on behalf of our Lord, and penetrate the skepticism of this age.

NOTES

1. "The Electric Family," *Christianity Today,* April 19, 1985, p. 77.
2. Charles Page and Nelson Price, quoted in "When ACTS Comes to Town," a brochure of the Broadcast Services Department: Radio and Television Commission of the Southern Baptist Convention.
3. Ibid.
4. "Speakers Take the High Road in Addressing NY Broadcasters," *Broadcasting,* July 22, 1985, p. 90.
5. Malcolm Muggeridge, *Christ and the Media* (Grand Rapids: Eerdmans, 1977), p. 30.
6. Lloyd Billingsley, "TV: Where the Girls Are Good Looking and the Good Guys Win," *Christianity Today,* October 4, 1985, p. 39. Copyright © 1985 by *Christianity Today.* Used by permission.
7. From a speech given by Charles Colson to a 1984 Evangelical Press Association convention. This speech was published by Victor Books, Wheaton, Illinois, copyright © 1986, under the title *Presenting Belief in an Age of Unbelief.* The quote is taken from page 29.
8. Warren K. Agee, Phillip H. Ault, and Edwin Emery, *Introduction to Mass Communications* (New York: Harper & Row, 1979), pp. 252-53.
9. Ibid., p. 253.
10. James S. Stewart, *The Life and Teaching of Jesus Christ* (Nashville: Abingdon, 1978), p. 19.
11. Muggeridge, *Christ and the Media,* p. 88.
12. Pat Robertson, quoted in "Religion in Broadcasting," by Robert Abelman and Kimberly Neuendorft, p. 27; quoted by Neil Postman, *Amusing Ourselves to Death* (New York: Penguin, 1985, p. 118.
13. Colson, *Presenting Belief,* p. 32.
14. Bill Carter, quoted by Esther Byle Bruland, "Voting with Your Checkbook," *Christianity Today,* August 19, 1991, p. 21.

15. Win Arn, quoted in "Is TV Appropriate for Mass Evangelism?" *Christianity To-day,* October 16, 1987, p. 50.
16. Colson, *Presenting Belief,* p. 32.
17. American Family Association Pass Along Sheet, 1991.
18. George Barna, "How We Lost the War in the Gulf," *Ministry Currents* 1, no. 1 (April 1991): 2.
19. George Barna, quoted in "North American Scene: Church's Influence Waning," *Christianity Today,* August 20, 1990, p. 41.

21

THE ELECTRONIC DRUG

According to Steven Bochco, creator of "Hill Street Blues" and "L.A. Law," what TV viewers want today is to be left in what he described as "a pleasant state of semiconsciousness before going to bed."[1] Most viewers would probably agree. One of the most popular reasons Americans give for spending leisure time before the TV set is that viewing is "relaxing." As discussed in chapter 13, there is scientific basis for the idea that TV does lull viewers into a passive mental state. Researchers confirm that activity in the part of the brain that processes complex information is reduced while viewing takes place.[2] However, it is a serious mistake to equate such passivity with relaxation. A second important behavior that TV may prevent is the relief from stress that many Americans crave.

Jerry Mander, author of *Four Arguments for the Elimination of Television*, suggested years ago that TV viewing was the opposite of relaxation. He observed that some experts believe TV viewing may be a major cause behind hyperactivity. Ironically, Mander noted, the very instrument parents may use to calm a hyperactive child could be contributing to the problem.[3] Viewing is a paradox, he claimed, because it does not rest the mind, since it occupies it with imagery, nor does it stimulate the mind, because it impedes the ability to think. The mind is empty, yet filled at the same time, which is exhaustive, yet strangely restful in a zombie-like sense.[4]

Drugs are a mind-altering way of fleeing from the realities of life. They cloud reality and affect our judgment. Television accomplishes many of those same things. The vast majority of professing Christians would never think of taking drugs or giving them to their children, but they fail to see that TV can be a type of drug.

The effect is both passivity and agitation simultaneously. Mander stated that TV adds to our stress level because it delivers too much, too fast, too powerfully. Although the initial effect is to lull us into a passive state, the long-range aftereffect may be stressful because of the overwhelming nature of much of what we watch. He predicted something more than a decade ago that should be particularly unsettling to Christians:

> It is little wonder, therefore, that we have seen the sudden growth of Eastern religious disciplines, yogic practices, martial arts, diverse exercise regimens and many forms of meditation. They help relieve the agony of uncalm minds pacing their narrow cages. They stop excessive thinking and open alternative mental awareness. They allow for the reception of new experiences. They encourage yielding as opposed to always driving forward. They teach people to take in rather than put out.[5]

Mander suggested that television would foster the use of Eastern meditation techniques, drugs, alcohol, Valium®, and sleeping potions, because it conditions people to escapism. He pointed out, "Drugs provide escape while passing for experience and relaxation. Television does as well."[6] He insisted that the only difference between TV and Eastern meditation is that in the latter one produces one's own internally generated imagery, whereas with television, we are focused on image that is imposed by a machine and a producer.[7]

Former CBS correspondent Daniel Schorr sensed the same uncanny parallel between TV and mystic experience when he wrote:

> By forging a magic electronic circle, coast to coast, television has created a national seance. Millions sit figuratively holding hands as they are exposed together to a stream of images and suggestions, mixed-up facts and fancies, playing more on their senses than their intellects. Television may be on its way to doing in America what religious mysticism has done in Asia—dulling the sense of the objective and tangible and making the perceived more important than the fact. There is at least a superficial similarity in the trancelike state that accompanies both experiences.[8]

The current climate in America suggests that both Mander's and Schorr's observations were prophetic. Americans are turning to drugs, alcohol, and Eastern mystical experience to relieve distress in unprecedented numbers. Even more turn to television. However, the newest and most comprehensive evidence on TV viewing suggests that although viewers experience something that feels like "relaxation" while viewing, the response is short-lived. Most end up feeling worse after viewing than they did before and fail to connect this with the viewing experience.

One of the most comprehensive studies on the effects of TV viewing was released in 1990 by the National Institute on Mental Health and several other private, nonprofit organizations. The research found that "heavy viewers use television like a drug—as an easy, available way to escape reality, loneliness, and boredom. But, as with a drug, its sought-after effects wear off, leaving the viewer less relaxed afterward."[9] Although most viewers said they felt more soothed while watching TV than they had been before they started, they ended up feeling worse once they stopped. After turning off the set viewers admitted they felt far less rested, less happy, and less able to concentrate on other activities than after they participated in sports, reading, or other leisure activities.[10]

Since the relief from stress that TV provides is only temporary, TV can be addictive. The idea of TV addiction was once a joke but now may be a clinical reality. In the early eighties, psychiatrists broadened their definition of addiction to include behaviors that people turn to for relief from distress and continue to rely on in spite of negative social or emotional effects. According to some psychiatrists, compulsive television viewing now fits under the new umbrella of addictive behaviors. The signs: using TV as a sedative, a lack of selectivity in what is viewed, feeling powerless to turn it off, feeling a loss of control over viewing, feeling angry for watching so much, and feeling miserable when not watching.[11]

Many Christians who would frown on drugs, alcohol, gambling, tobacco, or other obsessive behaviors fail to recognize that many of them would be hard-pressed to get through the week without turning on a TV set. Should the truth of this frighten us a little more than it does? The lives of some Christian families to some degree are controlled and scheduled around television. Yet nowhere does Scripture suggest that we are to be controlled by anything but the power of the Spirit of Christ. Is the mere fact that we are domineered by something besides the power of the Spirit something we need to examine more closely?

TV is compulsive to many because it is designed to be. Part of the television illusion is to hold you and keep you by appealing to your emotions and sense of curiosity. If you are addicted to soap operas, sitcoms, and dramas—or even news—and constantly look toward the "escapes" that TV offers, don't be shocked and confused if your children emulate that escapist mentality and begin to explore the wide range of illusionary escapes—drugs, sex, alcohol, overeating—that our culture offers. Christians should certainly face the fact that, at least in theory, we should be able to do without TV without feeling as though our leg has been amputated. Many Christians can easily go through the week without reading the Bible, but to spend a week free of television would be a challenge few could meet without great difficulty. That fact should open our eyes to the nature of what we are dealing with. We need to regard television the same way we regard industrial poison—something with limited usefulness and considerable hazard unless handled properly.

Because television encourages passivity, not relaxation, could it be snuffing out the kind of motivation necessary for people to make a difference in the world? Because it overexposes us now to an overwhelming flood of events, many of which we can do little about, does it lead us to feel powerless to change anything? Could

TV be part of the reason many feel frustrated, stressed, and apathetic about what is happening in society?

Consider a prevailing attitude among today's college students. According to Arthur Levine, author of *When Dreams and Heroes Died*, students today suffer from an acute sense of impotence and fatalism on the larger issues. When asked about the future of America or the world, they declare, "It's going down the tubes, and there's nothing we can do about it." Their subsequent reaction is to conclude that they might as well concentrate on enjoying themselves. Levine labels this fatalistic brand of hedonism "going first class on the Titanic."[12]

Is there a connection between the flood of news and "reality based" programming and the fatalistic worldview of the current television generation that induces feelings of social impotency, apathy, and preoccupation with trivial pursuits? Neil Postman thinks so: "Maybe it's a speculative guess, but I think self-help, self-improvement, jogging, dieting—this preoccupation with fixing oneself up—may be a manifestation of the fact that you can't do anything about Iran, Lebanon, the earthquake in Mexico, the volcano exploding in Columbia. So people turn inward."[13]

Television, warned the late British TV commentator Malcolm Muggeridge, discourages a balanced view of life. He warned:

> I think that diversions are more difficult to deal with than ever before because the fantasies of life have been given such extraordinary outward and visible shape, even to the point where you can see them on the TV screen for three or four hours a day, these fantasies of power, of leisure, of carnality. Western men and women live in the world of images almost as long as any other, and it is a fearful thing. That is why you find among the young this extraordinary despair, because they feel there is no escape for them—*no escape into reality.*[14]

Earlier I pointed out TV's inherent tendency to distort through overgeneralization. Such distortions may be more ominous than we think, for people of all ages. A news study group at the Massachusetts Institute of Technology, after a month's analysis of nightly

newscasts, issued a warning about the dangers of TV overgeneral-
izations, especially negative ones, in terms of contributing to an
unbalanced view of life. The uniform style of newscasts, they cautioned, gives the impression that all of our troubles flow from inept
individuals and political institutions, that big institutions are un-
feeling, and that we are all at the mercy of forces beyond our
control.

---

*We claim to believe in a God who is
sovereign, ultimately in control, but
we can't seem to apply such a concept
to the flood of bad news TV brings.*

Social psychologists worry that such a steady diet of pessimistic stereotype is making Americans doubt that they are in control of
their destinies. We grow frustrated, angry, and confused by what
we see and hear on TV. So many don't vote, dropping out of the
American political consensus while continuing to tune in for more
of what TV news offers. Such a misleading perception, concludes
the MIT study group, is not good news, but is a dangerous brand
of technologically conditioned fatalism.[15]

Suicide experts say that such feelings of hopelessness and lack
of control are prime reasons people take their own lives. Could it
be that the gap between reality and what is presented on TV contributes to the feelings of hopelessness from which suicidal individuals suffer? Researchers have solid evidence that when celebrity
suicides are media publicized, suicide rates immediately rise.[16]

Even some suicide experts, who fail to understand how TV
works on the mind, may be greatly underestimating the role of negative TV imagery in regard to feelings of depression and fatalism in
people who are already despondent to begin with. It's critical for
viewers to grasp that negative and overgeneralized impressions are
not simply the deliberate intent of news producers but the inevitable result of television's institutionalized format and technological
limitations.

Current trends in Christian books, magazines, and seminars reflect the same obsession with self-preoccupation present in the wider culture, suggesting that Christians are equally influenced by the negative, fatalistic illusion present in television. One of the side effects of the TV-conditioned attitude of fatalism and hedonism in the Christian community is that many Christians not only have no time for involvement in social causes but exhibit no desire to be involved, because they too believe that they are powerless to change the world around them.

This cancerous attitude among Christians is an embarrassing example of faulty theology. We claim to believe in a God who is sovereign, ultimately in control, but we can't seem to apply such a concept to the flood of bad news TV brings. The negative mental residue of television may actually erode our ambitions to change the world because we find it difficult to overcome impressions left in our minds by television imagery.

Christians must counter what television shows out of context with the abstract realization that we serve a God who sees all of history at once and controls it. Nothing is news to Him. He invites us to be threads in His tapestry of sovereignty—to take part in affecting history through involvement. Yet how many Christians now follow the electronically fashioned illusion of "there's nothing I can do about it"? Are we guilty of a Christianized brand of escapism—by simply "grabbing all the gusto I can get" or merely hiding in the Christian ghetto?

Pastors and other spiritual leaders who assessed the state of the church several years ago agreed that they saw no signs of revival in America and only limited signs of a positive impact of the church on individuals or society. The major obstacle, according to those asked, was not money or lack of material resources but what pastors characterized as passivity—an overwhelming "lack of spiritual commitment and maturity of the church population of this country."

In a survey by the Barna Research Group, spiritual immaturity among professing Christians was described as a "very serious" problem by 60 percent of pastors asked. The other problems identified by pastors, according to Barna: "The refusal of the laity to assume ministry responsibility, . . . the lack of spiritually mature lay leaders, . . . the lack of commitment to Christianity demonstrated by the body, . . . the worldly perspective and values of the laity, . . . and the inability and unwillingness of people to share their faith with non-believers."

The pastors interviewed cited these problems to be greater than the lack of resources, training, or preparation. The picture painted by pastors was one of "dedicated chiefs" whose uppermost struggle was with "lackadaisical indians." Many pastors interviewed were described as "psychologically, emotionally, and spiritually frustrated." Many felt "impotent as agents of spiritual growth." Most admitted the chief source of their frustration was their inability to motivate an increasingly passive laity that did not want to be involved but was instead content with being disinterested spectators to the process.[17]

Such attitudes are a complete denial of New Testament teaching in regard to the Body of Christ, where every single member has a responsibility—a function—and matters. Is the once joked about "church of anesthesia" now a product of the television age? Probably such problems can't be attributed exclusively to television, but neither should we underestimate the relationship between the amount of time spent before a machine that tranquilizes, anesthetizes, mesmerizes, desensitizes, pacifies, and overwhelms us and our unwillingness to roll up our sleeves and become directly involved in the spiritual battle. Until believers wake up to the true conditioning dangers of television, the church will fail to recognize it as a source of cancerous lethargy and desire to escape. Some churches, warns Charles Colson, are in danger of becoming nothing more than "places where people go for their one-hour a week inspirational fix."[18]

NOTES

1. Steven Bochco, quoted by Anne C. Roark, "An Ominous Side to Television," *The Los Angeles Times,* reprinted in *The Arizona Republic,* April 30, 1990, p. A-4.

2. Daniel Goleman, "Television Addicts," *The New York Times*, reprinted in *The Arizona Republic*, November 7, 1990, p. C-5.

3. Jerry Mander, *Four Arguments for the Elimination of Television* (New York: William Morrow, 1978), pp. 167-68.

4. Ibid, p. 214.

5. Ibid.

6. Ibid.

7. Ibid., pp. 213-14.

8. Daniel Schorr, *Clearing the Air* (Boston: Houghton Mifflin, 1977), p. 291.

9. Judy Folkenberg, "More Tube, Less Fun," *American Health*, January/February 1991, p. 82.

10. Ibid.

11. Goleman, "Television Addicts," p. C-5.

12. Arthur Levine, quoted by Dick Keyes, with Steve Garber, "Going First Class on the Titanic," *Christianity Today*, November 20, 1987, p. 25.

13. Neil Postman, quoted by Alvin P. Sanoff, "TV Has Culture by the Throat," *U.S. News and World Report*, December 23, 1985, p. 58. Copyright, 1985, U.S. News & World Report.

14. Malcolm Muggeridge, quoted by Kevin Perrotta, "Television's Mind-Boggling Danger," *Christianity Today*, May 7, 1982, p. 22. Adapted from *Taking the TV Habit*, by Kevin Perrotta (Ann Arbor, Mich.: Servant, 1982). Copyright © 1982 by Kevin Perrotta. Used by permission.

15. Edwin Diamond, Barry S. Surman, and Jack Link, "Network Reporting: Where the Bias Is," *TV Guide*, July 7, 1984, p. 5.

16. "Media Coverage of Major Bouts Linked to Homicides," *The Los Angeles Times*, reprinted in *The Arizona Republic*, August 14, 1983, p. AA-1.

17. George Barna, "The State of the Church, 1985: A View from the Pulpit," *Christian Marketing Perspective*, Barna Research Group, P.O. Box 4152, Glendale, Calif. 91222-0152, September 1985, pp. 1-2.

18. From a speech given by Charles Colson to a 1984 Evangelical Press Association convention. The speech was published by Victor Books, Wheaton, Illinois, copyright © 1986 under the title *Presenting Belief in an Age of Unbelief*. The quote is from page 35.

22

WATCHING WHILE LIFE PASSES BY

A *New York Times* reporter, after seeing television introduced at the 1939 World's Fair, wrote the following prediction about its future: "The problem with television, is that the people must sit and keep their eyes glued to a screen: the average American family hasn't time for it. Therefore . . . for this reason, if no other, television will never be a serious competitor of broadcasting."[1]

The reporter was correct in stating that the American family doesn't have time for it. Unfortunately, he failed to consider the possibility that they would make time for television anyway. The average American family now has had its eyes glued to the screen seven hours a day for most of the last decade.

We have spent a significant amount of time considering the question of what TV does to us as we watch. However, there is another angle to this question: what are we *not* doing because we watch? Research psychologist Urie Bronfenbrenner insisted long ago that the primary danger of television is not just in the behavior it *presents*, but the behavior it *prevents*. Consider for a moment what television often displaces in the lives of many.

A prime time casualty of TV viewing is socialization with others. Viewing robs families of precious time spent in strength-building contact with each other and with outsiders. Talking, game playing, discussions based on real events, not imaginary ones, and yes, even arguments, often vanish among family members when the set comes on. Urie Bronfenbrenner notes: "Like the sorcerer of old, the television set casts its magic spell, freezing speech and action, turning the living into silent statues so long as the enchantment lasts."[2] Many parents praise television as a wonderful way to pacify kids and eliminate conflict in the home, never realizing that the process of arguing and the subsequent resolution or working out of disputes is an important way for young children to learn to cope with life.

It is through human interaction (arguments included) with parents, siblings, and other children that a child forms his essential character. Warns Bronfenbrenner: "Turning on the television set can turn off the process that transforms children into people."[3] Author, family counselor, and juvenile delinquency expert Edward E. Ford blames TV for systematically depriving kids of the kind of socialization that makes the difference between a whole human being and one who systematically expresses an inability to handle life. "Excessive TV viewing" may not be the only factor, declares Ford, but it is "the singular hallmark [and] the most decisive and basic element in the cocktail of causes contributing to youth's inability to cope [in today's world]."[4] Children need direct interaction with others, Ford says, to develop what he calls "coping strength," which he describes as "the ability to figure out what to do when you don't know what to do." Such "coping strength" is essential in order to transform kids into mature people who can handle the pressures of the real world.

When young children spend hours with television, warns Ford, they are no longer engaged in the social skills of getting along, expressing oneself, listening and playing satisfyingly, nor are they sharpening their intellectual skills and capacity for creativity. Parents underestimate the importance of the interaction that takes place in eating and working in the home together, running errands, traveling, playing together, and visiting with friends. Such simple, seemingly mundane practices have enormous value in terms of teaching children the process of coping with others. TV's double-edged dilemma is that those who watch are immersed in unreality at the same time they are deprived of real-life experience.

As kids grow older and life becomes more difficult, Ed Ford predicts that "inner fissures and weaknesses" created by the lack of strength-building interaction in the early years will be exposed—and will explode in a variety of negative and antisocial ways that will be completely perplexing to parents. That will happen, Ford says, because few people recognize the dangers of the subtle breakdown in family socialization brought on by television and thus are not working to combat it. Even now, Ford warns, there are increasing signs of character weakness—escapism, excessive drinking and drug abuse, criminal behavior, materialism, and narcissism—that testify to a lack of socialization in the process of growing up.[5]

> *Poet T. S. Eliot once called television "a medium of entertainment which permits millions of people to listen to the same joke at the same time, yet remain lonesome."*

Minnesota-based researchers Merton and Irene Strommen found in their studies that children of close families are the most likely to develop healthy friendships and a deep religious faith and to involve themselves in helping others. They will be "significantly less likely" to involve themselves in drugs, premarital sex, and other antisocial, alienating behavior.[6] Some Christian parents fail to recognize the spiritual wedge that TV can drive between family members. Pastor Kevin Perrotta, author of *Taming the TV Habit*, points out that television competes with the process of natural spiritual instruction children used to get from parental interaction. "Television may be an effective narcotic for undisciplined children," warns Perrotta, "but the temporary peace brought by television may have long range side effects as children grow less compliant and parents less confident to deal with them."[7]

Children are not the only ones at risk. Something that the be-numbing silence of TV viewing has replaced is the type of conversation and interaction that builds marital relationships. More and more counselors are pointing to television as a major inhibitor of the type of intimacy in marriage that must be painstakingly developed through interaction over a long period of time. "TV watching is a passive habit that can serve as a substitute for intimacy," warns California psychiatrist Pierre Mornell.[8] According to Mornell, many American couples are now more tuned into the set than to each other. Every hour spent there is an hour not spent in the kind of strength-building interaction that cements marriages into life-time relationships. A *TV Guide* poll revealed that many get more satisfaction from TV than from their marriage, preferring it over talk or sexual activity.[9] In their book *The First Year of Marriage* two researchers studied more than 530 newlyweds and found that television played a major role in divorce, dominating the early evening hours when newly married couples are most in need of communication.[10]

Poet T. S. Eliot once called television "a medium of entertainment which permits millions of people to listen to the same joke at the same time, yet remain lonesome."[11] For the chronically lonely person, who has difficulty to begin with in building relationships, the temptation to use the television escape is overwhelmingly addictive. Louise Bernikow, the author of *Alone in America: The Search for Companionship,* points out the danger television presents to the lonely is that it can keep them passive, reducing whatever desire they might have to reach out or to deepen existing relationships. Like any other addictive substance, television allows people to escape instead of confront their problems. "The 'lifeline' television provides is in one sense quite dangerous," she notes.[12]

Many of the lonely develop pseudorelationships with imaginary characters of shows because such relationships are the least painful. According to psychiatrist Harvey Greenberg, such imaginary relationships all too often become substitutes for real ones.

Images seldom disappoint or aggravate us as real people do. The risk of hurt or rejection is minimal. Television is an escape, not from just the dull realities of life, but from other people, their imperfections, and their potential rejection.[13]

The glimmering box is also an escape for the elderly. Ratings show that the older people are, the more TV becomes an umbilical cord to the outside world—a primary source of companionship. "I prefer not to have any friends around [when I'm watching TV]," one elderly retirement community resident told a *TV Guide* journalist. "They talk too much, and I'd rather concentrate."[14] Many elderly speak of television characters as though they were real. Illusion is now the last and most faithful companion of America's oldest family members. The final moments of life that could be spent with family and friends and on volunteer projects, lending years of experience and insight, are now spent before the tube, watching while real life goes by.

Anthropologist Ben Logan, who remembers what life was like before the tube, points out that television brought us far more than just a technological revolution. He writes:

> In my background, gathering around a table at mealtime, with all its talk and laughter, had been the very heart of being a family. Yet people were casually giving that up, as though the mealtime had no purpose other than getting food into the body.
>
> TV was the new hearth, with the warmth and voices coming from the magic box, taking the place of talk with each other, taking the place, it seemed to me, of family itself.[15]

The social impact of TV's advent for him, says Logan, was subtle, but painful. He remembers:

> At the home of a favorite friend in Wisconsin, the set was never turned off. My good days of searching talk with that man were over, except for a time or two when I found him in the kitchen and quickly sat down there, ignoring the flickering light and strange voices from the next room.

I never fully recovered that friend from the TV screen. *Our relationship was a casualty of the revolution.*[16]

Decades later, such changes are so pervasive we no longer notice, because they are now the norm in all social circles. The way we talk with each other, what we do with each other, how and when we relate to our friends, when we attend church—all of these things have been altered to some degree by TV's hold on society.

Ben Logan concludes: "The most startling fact of all was the quietness of the revolution. *Almost no one was questioning the changes.*"[17] And few are doing so today, failing to ask themselves, *What am I not doing while I give three to four hours a day to television? How does it separate me from people? How does it restrain me from going places and doing things by monopolizing several hours of my day? What new areas in my life am I not exploring because of it?*

It never dawns on most of us that we are now more in touch with events thousands of miles away than with our neighbor next door. Observes communications professor Joshua Meyrowitz, we don't "live" in towns the same way we used to, or with people the same way we used to, because we have granted TV the power to redefine our social reality. He points out: "We pay more attention to, and talk more about, fires in California, starvation in Africa and sensational trials in Rhode Island than the troubles of nearly anyone except perhaps a handful of close family, friends and colleagues."[18]

In New York state a TV is now legally considered a necessity. The legislature passed a bill several years ago that made the TV set, along with clothing and furniture, immune from appropriation should a family go bankrupt. The bill declared that the television set is "a necessary utensil" for a family to survive in this society.[19] Yet to argue that TV is a necessary instrument of living belies something that should be more obvious to some—the fact that human beings survived for thousands of years on earth before television was invented. It is also a denial that real life is, and always has been, the best source of truth. Regardless of whether what comes across the screen each night is positive, negative, or neutral (and often it is all three at the same time), the bottom line is that much of what is reflected to us is only illusion—illusion that many are now lost in while real life passes by.

NOTES

1. Peggy Charren and Martin Sandler, *Changing Channels: Living (Sensibly) with Television* (Reading, Mass.: Addison-Welsley, 1983), p. 2.

2. Urie Bronfenbrenner, quoted by Kevin Perrotta, "Watching While Life Goes By," *Christianity Today*, April 18, 1980, p. 17. Adapted from *Taking the TV Habit*, by Kevin Perrotta (Ann Arbor, Mich.: Sevant, 1982). Copyright © 1982 by Kevin Perrotta. Used by permission.

3. Ibid.

4. Edward E. Ford and Steven Englund, *For the Love of Children* (Garden City, N.Y.: Anchor Press/Doubleday, 1977), p. 11.

5. Ibid., pp. 7-10.

6. Kristine Tomasik, "Teens Want to Talk," *Christianity Today*, September 20, 1985, p. 48.

7. Perrotta, "Watching While," p. 17.

8. Nina Combs, "Is Your Love Life Going Down 'The Tube'?" condensed from *Redbook*, reprinted in *The Reader's Digest*, October 1987, p. 148.

9. "More Enjoy TV Than Sex, Says Ad Agency Study," *TV Guide*, July 12, 1986, p. A-1.

10. Combs, "Love Life," p. 147.

11. T. S. Eliot, quoted by Louise Bernikow, "Is TV a Pal—or a Danger—for Lonely People?" *TV Guide*, October 25, 1986, p. 6.

12. Ibid., p. 5.

13. Ibid., pp. 5-6.

14. Joanmarie Kalter, "If It's Wednesday, It Must Be Dynasty," *TV Guide*, August 2, 1986, p. 6.

15. Ben Logan, *Television Awareness Training: The Viewer's Guide for Family and Community* (Nashville: Abingdon, 1979), p. 7.

16. Ibid.

17. Ibid.

18. Joshua Meyrowitz, "The 19-inch Neighborhood," *Newsweek*, July 22, 1985, p. 8.

19. "Media Watch with an Eye to Values," *Media and Values*, Summer/Fall 1987, p. 31.

23

THE PRIME TIME THIEF

woman in a Bible study I once participated in shared a growing conviction with our group about not continuing to watch soap operas. Although the Bible study content wasn't specifically related to the questionable moral content of many soaps, this woman was learning in our study that God makes some very definite demands on how Christians use time (see Ephesians 5:15-17; Psalm 90:12; 1 Corinthians 7:31; Philippians 4:8-9; Colossians 3:1-2; 1 Thessalonians 5:19-22; 1 John 2:15-16). After examining Scripture, she had finally begun to consider what television was displacing in her life. Slowly she began to make a mental connection between the priorities established by TV's addictiveness and the priorities established by the Word of God she claimed allegiance to.

The minutes of our lives are slipping through life's hourglass, and Scripture reminds us that we will be accountable for each grain. Charles Colson wonders: "When we arrive in heaven and account for the stewardship of our time, will Christ say, 'Well done' to, say, one and a half years of TV commercials?"[1] Or thousands of hours of game shows and sitcoms? Christ must be Lord of everything, Colson reminds us, including prime time.

I border on sounding as if God permits no leisure. That's not so, but God does demand control over the quality of our leisure. Christians need a clear realization of what our leisure may keep us from. Christians are commanded to be holy. That means more than just abstaining from evil. It means indulging in good. It means to be set apart in life for a different purpose. Some of the most important business TV can displace is the agenda that God calls Christians to assume. Far too many Christians remain uninvolved in biblically based social action, the pursuit of spiritual wisdom, and the refinement of personal character simply because they are too busy amusing themselves to pursue such mandates.

---

*Most Americans are barely aware that
TV has returned us to an oral society,
. . . but with one important difference.
The focus has now shifted primarily
to imagery instead of mere words.*

The Bible commands us to be salt and light in our society. Research suggests that involvement in social action may be one of the most crucial witnesses of the Christian to the current unchurched population of baby boomers. In *Woodstock Census* Rex Weiner and Dean Stillman argue that many church planners believe that the division between evangelism and social action is a major stumbling block to unbelievers today. Efforts to really help people, such as hunger relief, urban ministry, and housing for the poor, to name only a few, are the essence of an attractive witness to unchurched baby boomers who still cling to the idealism of the sixties and are looking for concrete answers to society's problems.[2] I know from my own experience that many newspeople are skeptical of organized religion because they see few links between professed belief and solutions to the overwhelming social problems they are constantly confronted with in their work. The Christianity my former colleagues were most impressed with is the faith that is married to social action.

Public television's Robert MacNeil calls television the "flypaper of life":

> I think of television as I do those gluey spirals of paper we used to hang in the summertime, on which hundreds of flies got their feet stuck and buzzed helplessly for a few hours until they died. . . .
>
> In our grandparents' eyes, such a prodigious waste of our God-given time would have been sinful because it was not using time constructively, for self-improvement, for building moral character. They would call it sloth, escapism. Yet they probably would have found television as difficult to resist as we do.[3]

The meaning of temptation, wrote German theologian Helmut Thielicke, is to allow oneself to be torn away from God. Years ago, he warned: "Through small and great events, little fondnesses and great passions, we can be brought to the point where we lose contact with the Father. We hardly ever sever our relationship to God standing up and shaking our fist at heaven . . . renouncing God with planned defiance. As a rule this decision against God is made in a far more tepid way; it occurs almost unnoticed by the apostate mind."[4]

Thielicke, who wrote prior to the invention of the tube, saw TV's forerunners as a subtle but insidious threat to true spirituality. He concludes:

> Radio, the movies, and other factors in our modern life have had far more influence upon the decision against God than anti-Christian ideologies and misguided philosophies. [They] take up so much of our lives that we no longer have opportunity to ask the question of eternity or listen to its question to us. . . . [These factors have] had far more to do with the dying away of our relationship with the Father than all the ideological programs. This is the tepid, almost unconscious way of deciding against God. Therefore, our way of life must be examined and controlled in the name of eternity.[5]

Television not only preempts our time but our silence. We
have lost the value of quiet in our sense-bombarded American culture. In fact, many of us are downright terrified of it. We play our
TV sets, radios, and Walkmans® constantly, addicted to the background chatter that they provide. What is it that we are afraid of
that we now compulsively block out by the sounds of TV and radio? Is it the hum of nature, or the echo of our own conscience?
Are we frightened of silence because it would enable or compel us
to hear the still, small voice of God within?

Theologian Carl F. H. Henry offers some "sound" advice for
stressed, sense-bombarded believers:

> We would profit from the silencing of today's media bar-
> rage. . . .
> As Christians we need to tune our spirits to God's heavenly
> Talk-Show: to the God who speaks his own word, the God who
> shows himself throughout the cosmos and history and who shows
> himself supremely in Jesus Christ. This Divine Speaker is waiting
> for people to converse with him, to spend unhurried time with him,
> the God of the Ages, and Eternal one who wants more than a three-
> minute long distance call or a five-minute parking stop for a "hello"
> and a "good-bye." Activism today so hurries worship, prayer and
> Bible reading, theological study and reflection, that we risk becom-
> ing practical atheists steeped in this-world priorities.[6]

There is perhaps no greater example of how to avoid the type
of pitfall that television presents to the Christian than to look at the
life of Christ Himself. He had an unswerving conviction that His
life's purpose was to do the will of the Father who sent Him and to
finish the work that God sent Him to do (John 4:34). Christ clearly
states than anyone who is truly a disciple has the same responsibility and the same set of priorities (John 8:31). No matter how innocent the program content, do we dare let such a priority become
displaced by the escapism of TV viewing?

Television imposes not only on our time and our silence but
on our literacy. Most Americans are barely aware that TV has returned us to an oral society, something like the one centuries ago

before the development of the printing press, but with one important difference. The focus has now shifted primarily to imagery instead of mere words. Information now consists of images to be passively absorbed along with spoken words, rather than concepts to be mentally wrestled with on a page. Researchers confirm that when we watch TV, we are developing the mental ability to simultaneously filter and process vast amounts of data in a wide variety of forms in a way that is directly opposite of the skill needed for absorbing information through print.[7] Because television conditions the mind in the opposite direction from reading, it deadens people's receptivity to the printed page.

TV has spawned what Librarian of Congress Daniel Boorstein calls the "aliterate"—the person who technically can read, but who doesn't.[8] The more we learn to love television, the less willing we seem to be to train our eyes to the printed page and the more willing we are to abandon any effort to understand abstract concepts that requires mental effort and imagination to grasp.

Critical judgment is best developed through reading, but reading, especially on a level that challenges the mind, is rapidly becoming a lost art. More and more people are systematically denying themselves access to the printed word, seemingly unaware that print enjoys a far greater capacity for content and ideas than televised imagery. In a Gallup poll on television several years ago, 46 percent of those asked admitted that if they watched less television, they would read more. In the same study, 52 percent of those asked said that they believed heir children would read more if they watched less TV. Less than half of those asked said that they read every day to their children under the age of seven.[9] The United States now rates twenty-fourth worldwide in per capita readership of books, and newspaper sales are also declining.[10]

One of the most obvious advantages of reading, observed Malcolm Muggeridge, is that the printed word is not subject to the same centralized control as television.[11] PBS news anchor Robert MacNeil paints a gloomy picture of the legacy of television for America. "What will happen is that the mass public will increasingly be the captive of television for its information," he warns.[12]

This trend will make an ever-increasing audience easier to manipulate. Concludes MacNeil, only "the small, elite, educated public will continue to be the consumers of print . . . you can almost see that happening [already]."[13] Unbeknownst to many, we are subtly being conditioned toward emotional manipulation and away from rational thought perhaps more now than any other time in history.

Television has not only discouraged reading, it has changed the way we read. Those who still read do so at a different level than previous generations. Some education critics charge that school textbooks and tests are being simplified to accommodate students who can no longer comprehend complex or abstract ideas.

The phenomena of aliteracy has forced TV's print competitors to change the way newspapers are being written and read. *USA Today*, with its brightly colored format of short, simply written, sometimes sensationalized stories, and emphasis on sports and entertainment, closely parallels the format of TV news. As Neil Postman points out, the paper can be purchased from a box on the street corner that bears an eerie resemblance to a TV set.[14] Color is now added more often to many newspapers, in spite of increased expense, to cater to the conditioned visual hunger of the TV viewer. Newspaper stories grow simpler and shorter, to pamper our battered attention spans.

The shift to visual imagery is also mirrored in the book market. More and more detail and dialogue are being left out of books today in order to compete with the rapid pace and attention getting techniques now established by TV. Writers are now forced to limit concepts to those that can be painted in visual word pictures and to spend less time trying to develop abstract ideas. Many books are now designed to pander to the same mental lethargy that causes us to flick the switch. Interest in serious books with any degree of complexity in content is on the decline. There is a subtle but observable drift from reading in young people today. *Publisher's Weekly* has ominously noted that book readers under the age of twenty-one are falling away at a rate the industry termed "threatening."[15] Fewer readers aspire anymore to any higher level of reading skill or taste than the elementary school level.

Yet the link between literacy and Christianity has always been important. The decline of Old Testament spiritual life among the people of Israel was parallel to a decline in their knowledge of the written law and the repentance it inspired. It was the written gospels and epistles that transformed the early church and lived on through the subsequent centuries. The Bible was the first book to come off Gutenberg's fifteenth-century printing press, and its accessibility fueled the Reformation. The American school movement began with Christians who recognized the importance of people's being able to read the Bible for themselves.

> *If the church only exists to provide eloquent speakers and capsulized tidbits of information . . . it is in danger of rendering the Bible into another mediated experience.*

However, an American Resource Bureau survey several years ago of those identifying themselves as born again Christians revealed that in the course of *a week*, the average amount of time spent reading the Bible is only about sixty-eight minutes,[16] compared to three or four hours *a day* watching TV.[17] A more recent study by the Barna Resource Group shows that 23 percent of professing born-again Christians admit that they never read the Bible and only 18-percent read it every day.[18] "Television, VCRS, motion pictures, and even computers have moved us from a literate to a visual society." admonishes theologian Haddon Robinson.[19]

The "blue glow" now overshadows spiritual literacy. Fewer professing Christians now seem able to grasp abstract Christian truths or even basic biblical facts. A survey several years ago by *Christianity Today* revealed that less than half who identified themselves as evangelicals were aware of or agreed with the key biblical doctrine that Jesus Christ was fully God and fully man.[20] In a Gallup poll, only 42 percent of professing Christians knew it was Jesus who delivered the Sermon on the Mount. Only 46 percent could name the four gospels.[21] It is the image, not the Word, warns Robinson, that emerges as the dominating force in our culture: "Traditionally Christians have believed spiritual growth came through reading and studying the Bible. In a culture that cannot or will not read, the influence of the Bible in printed form will continue to slip."[22]

Christians are quick to criticize cults for accepting only parts of the Bible as true, but how many believers act as though the whole Bible were true? How many of us have actually read through the entire Bible at least once? Many Christians focus only occasionally on a few select portions they find simple, or interesting enough, to hold their attention. They tune out to the rest—flicking the channel on vast portions of Scripture because they find them too boring, or too taxing, to read and understand.

The desire to passively listen and be entertained is prevalent in the church. Most of what many Christians now know about the Bible comes only from the short, oral capsules that they grab on Sunday morning or from Christian media. Yet biblical literacy must be more than just sermons, videotapes, or setting up satellite dishes to hear the oration of polished Bible teachers. Such devices are fine supplements to real Bible study, but if the church only exists to provide eloquent speakers and capsulized tidbits of information, then it is in danger of rendering the Bible into another mediated experience.

Many Christians "can't" memorize Scripture verses but can rattle off the commercial jingles of every major product advertised, with little effort. Many can regurgitate the punch lines of sitcoms, and some know every television character's name on each program and who plays who. Many Christians possess a good deal of information about the lives of rock music stars, actors, game show hosts, news anchors, and sports figures. Yet the majority of biblical characters are vague unknowns to them. The electronic Christian is a storehouse of the cultural trivia TV offers even though the Scriptures implore us to store up the commands of God within us (Proverbs 2:1).

What is it that really dominates our minds? Does TV trivia displace the serious and purposeful type of Bible knowledge that will penetrate our minds to the point where we act out what we believe in the world around us?

Shortly before his death, Christian author and publishing executive Joe Bayly implored Christians to guard their biblical literacy. He warned: "Thinking Christians, able to reason on the basis of God's Word, may become scarce in the future. Note how often the Apostle Paul speaks of the mind, of wisdom, of knowledge, and of understanding in his epistles. We understand true doctrine with our minds, not with our feelings."[23]

The apostle Peter cautioned believers to be "clear minded and self-controlled" (1 Peter 4:7) and "self-controlled and alert" (1 Peter 5:8). But are we? Or are we impotent and confused by a stream of electronic imagery?

Neil Postman points out that TV's spin in the direction of entertainment and away from a print-oriented culture fulfills the grim prophecy of English novelist Aldous Huxley in his novel *Brave New World*. Postman contrasts the prophecies made in George Orwell's classic novel *1984* with those of Huxley and asserts that America has not become the oppressed culture Orwell portrayed in *1984* but instead has become the trivial culture of Huxley's prediction.

In Orwell's vision of the future, people were controlled by inflicting pain. In Huxley's dark utopian vision they were controlled by inflicting pleasure. Huxley's prediction, Postman reminds us, is that people would become more and more distracted from what was important for their very survival because entertainment would come at them in every form—in their politics, in their education, in their religion—and they would succumb to it at every turn. Such people, Postman warns, lose the concentration, discipline, and rigor in thinking necessary for the greatness that we have come to associate with a literate culture. Such a vision of America is not an attractive one, argues Postman, but a frightening one.[24]

Perhaps there is a little of the truth in both of the utopian pictures described in *1984* and *Brave New World*. In *1984* every room contained an ever-present TV monitor that constantly flooded the minds of the people with the accomplishments of the prevailing dictatorship. There are no reading materials in this Orwell utilitarian society—no concrete evidence on a page to offer citizens a frame of reference for thinking and analysis. The people who live in Orwell's utopia have only the flickering fragments of information that blare constantly from the ever-present screen in the background. The blaring TV monitor "Newspeak" is their only contact with the outside world. All that is presented is out of context—to be mindlessly absorbed and accepted.

As we approach the end of this century, almost a decade beyond the real 1984, we find that nearly every home has one or two ever-present tubes that flicker for hours on end. What we find may bear more resemblance to the monopoly on information portrayed in Orwell's book than we would like to admit. Like the people of Orwell's *1984*, some today are prisoners of the tube, with one important distinction. In the novel, people were forced into this situation against their will. In America, we go willingly and freely, surrendering our option to participate in real-life experience, to read a diversity of views from a diversity of sources and to think about them, laying aside our liberty to discuss publicly and to participate directly and personally in government decision making, in exchange for "mediated" imagery.

"In the Huxleyan prophecy," warns Postman, "Big Brother does not watch us, by his choice. We watch him, by ours."[25] Most accept the exchange without the slightest flicker of realization of what they have lost in the process. Questions Robert MacNeil: "When before in human history has so much humanity collectively surrendered so much of its leisure to one toy, one mass diversion? When before has virtually an entire nation surrendered itself wholesale to a medium for selling?"[26]

I agree with Postman. In the end, Huxley was a better prophet than Orwell. In Orwell's *1984*, there were those who would ban a book. But in Huxley's *Brave New World*, Postman notes, the majority would be so distracted by trivia that there would be no reason to ban a book because there would be no one left who wished to read one.[27] Our conditioned addiction for entertainment technology has made a Big Brother conspiracy behind today's broadcasting industry completely unnecessary.

Each medium of communication has something unique to offer. To exalt TV over others as the best medium for information or to insist even unconsciously that newspapers, books, and magazines conform themselves to meet the visual expectations conditioned by television means losing touch with the abstract, the theoretical, and the intangible considerations of our culture. By permitting this, we forfeit another important avenue of awareness. Such conditioning is a form of powerful, self-imposed censorship. We need to reverse the trend by becoming what George Gerbner calls "hunters and gatherers" in the information age. That can be done by using many different media, not just television, and by learning, to some degree, to doubt them all.

NOTES

1. Charles Colson, *Who Speaks for God?* (Westchester, Ill.: Crossway, 1985), p. 131.
2. Ken Sidey, "A Generation on the Doorstep," *Moody Monthly,* January 1987, p. 23.
3. Robert MacNeil, "The Need for a Pause," *Vital Speeches of the Day* 45, August 1, 1979: 632.
4. Helmut Thielicke, "The Great Temptation," *Christianity Today,* July 12, 1985, p. 28.
5. Ibid.
6. Carl F. H. Henry, *The Christian Mindset in a Secular Society: Promoting Evangelical Renewal and National Righteousness* (Portland: Multnomah, 1984), p. 28.
7. Rushworth Kidder, "Videoculture 2: At Home with the Video Revolution," *The Christian Science Monitor,* June 11, 1985, p. 24.
8. Rushworth Kidder, "Videoculture 4: TV As Teacher: What Kind of Results?" *The Christian Science Monitor,* June 13, 1985, p. 22.
9. "Book Reviews," *Public Opinion,* October/November 1981, p. 39.
10. Frederick Case, "Tuning In and Turning Off Brainwashed," *The Seattle Times,* reprinted in *The Times-Picayune,* May 8, 1991, p. E-3.
11. Malcolm Muggeridge, *Christ and the Media* (Grand Rapids: Eerdmans, 1977), p. 106.

12. Rushworth M. Kidder, "Videoculture 3: Do 'Mediagenic' Candidates Make Good Leaders?" *The Christian Science Monitor,* June 12, 1985, p. 19. Reprinted by permission from *The Christian Science Monitor* © 1985 The Christian Science Publishing Society. All rights reserved.

13. Ibid.

14. Neil Postman, *Amusing Ourselves to Death* (New York: Penguin, 1985), p. 111.

15. John Baker, "1984: The Year in Publishing," *Publisher's Weekly,* March 15, 1985, p. 30.

16. George Barna and William Paul McKay, *Vital Signs* (Westchester, Ill.: Crossway, 1984), p. 110.

17. Ibid., p. 51.

18. "Bible Illiteracy in America," *The Church Around the World,* May 1989, p. 1.

19. Haddon Robinson, "More 'Religion,' Less Impact," *Christianity Today,* January 17, 1986, p. 4-I-5-I.

20. Colson, *Who Speaks,* p. 88.

21. Ibid.

22. Haddon Robinson, "More 'Religion,' Less Impact," pp. 4-I-5-I.

23. Joseph Bayly, "Ten Truths to Live By," *The Christian Reader,* September/October 1985, p. 24.

24. Neil Postman, quoted by Alvin P. Sanoff, "TV 'Has Culture by the Throat,'" *U.S. News and World Report,* December 23, 1985, p. 58.

25. Ibid., p. 155.

26. Robert MacNeil, "The Trouble with Television," *The Reader's Digest,* March 1985, p. 174.

27. Neil Postman, quoted by Reed Jolley, "Descent into Triviality," *Christianity Today,* March 7, 1986, p. 29.

24

TAMING THE TV TYRANT

Man invented television," two University of Southern California professors wrote recently, "and now television is in the process of reinventing man."[1] Television has changed us, whether we realize it or not. Screenwriter Loring Mandel insists that society has been reshaped by television, but, like the spinning of the earth, many are unaware of it because they can't feel it.[2] How can we handle something so subtle, yet so powerful? What are we to do about the visions from picture tubes that now dance in our heads?

As I write this book, I find myself wishing that I possessed some simple, brilliant solution to the dilemma I believe television presents for our society. Should we throw this invasive, seductive technological tyrant out of the house—"nuke" it, as one friend of mine has cheerfully suggested?

Some families have chosen to get rid of their set. Whether or not to own a set is a decision that hinges on a variety of factors, including the kind of environment we live in, the alternative activities we can provide for our children, and agreement between spouses over how to handle television. However, even if we choose not to own a TV set (and its doubtful that many of us will), we will still feel the influence of TV wherever we go. As George Gerbner points out: "Television is for most people the most attractive thing going any time of the day or night. We live in a world where the vast majority will not turn it off. If we don't get the message from the tube, we get it through other people."[3] In some instances, our children may simply end up watching it in the homes of others (removing control one step further from us). Its influence will be imposed at school and in the neighborhood. We can't entirely escape something so pervasive.

So what else can we do about television? Can we change it? Yes and no. Those who use TV could certainly, at times, employ it more positively, or with less prejudice. Those who feel oppressed by its excesses should not merely sit by and let television run roughshod over society like a bulldozer. Yet it is difficult to know what to do. What about current boycotting efforts such as those sponsored by CLEAR-TV? Can efforts aimed at stemming negative trends of morality in television succeed? Should they be supported?

One gray area in the question of boycotting is the way TV advertising time is purchased. Many sponsors buy time through middlemen—advertising agencies—and buys are made by time periods, not by specific programs. Many sponsors are genuinely unaware and not completely in control of what shows they are specifically supporting, if they choose to advertise. However, in spite of the gray areas, I would not discourage any Christian from participating in any responsible effort to influence television. The value of such efforts lies in achieving an equilibrium between the TV industry, sponsors, and viewers. Let me explain.

French theologian Jacques Ellul, in a book called *The Political Illusion*, charges that much of the power of the press and politicians is media created illusion, not reality. Ellul points out that politicians like to perpetuate the myth that the state has the power to solve all problems because this illusion perpetuates their own power. The media unconsciously but willingly collaborate in perpetuating the illusion of power because, through their association with political figures and government officials, they fuel the power of the media—they establish credibility by visibly associating with those perceived to be powerful. This adds to the power and profits of journalism.[4]

Ellul is right. That is precisely how the power game is played out in journalism. Ellul argues that the only defense against power's becoming too concentrated in the two groups is the direct involvement of private individuals in the process. Private individuals must be involved in the process of government, not just to grab power but to keep it from becoming too concentrated in the hands of those who are too easily corrupted by its excesses. Then power is balanced, and, Ellul argues, the political illusion is shattered.[5]

The same perpetuation of power persists between the TV industry and its commercial sponsors, who feed on one another for the purpose of perpetuating each other's existence and accomplishing each other's financial goals. Attempts by individual groups of viewers, such as CLEAR-TV, who band together to influence the process through negotiation and boycott are legitimate and necessary, because they might achieve a much needed balance of power between the broadcasting industry, its sponsors, and concerned viewers. It is because of this very potential that such groups are feared and publicly ridiculed by many in the industry in an attempt to discourage their efforts.

Will boycotts work in the long haul? Frankly, I hope so, but I don't know. It is hard to predict the long-term effectiveness of boycotts because of other emerging pressures within the broadcast industry. At the time of this writing, the entire broadcasting industry is in the midst of tremendous upheaval due to government deregulation and increased competition due to cable, satellite, and other new technologies. New and different economic pressures are emerging that will bring more change—and some of it will not be positive. The direction in which television is now evolving is a complex subject that could fill another book.

Still another problem in influencing TV positively is that the bigger and more diverse the industry becomes, and the more it is controlled by profits, the further it drifts from any concrete value system. Competition spurs the tendency for broadcasters to appeal to humanity's darker side, which is why many reject any kind of programming restraints.

We need to develop less familiarity
with TV itself and more familiarity
with the television process.

Civil libertarians who cry "free speech" fail to recognize that speech on television, either verbally or through imagery, for a myriad of reasons never has been and never will be totally free. Free speech on television is really not the issue in the sense that it is sometimes used in First Amendment broadcasting debates because there are enormous restraints in the very fabric of the TV process. Such a concept of free speech is one more TV illusion used to manipulate those infatuated by individualism. The real issue obscured by such rhetoric is the ability of a relatively small group of unelected people, as well as an institution and a powerful technology with an agenda of its own, to impose mass behavior modification through subliminal technique on millions for the principal reason of making money without restriction.

Whether or not TV ever communicates more positively, I can predict accurately that it will never communicate without some degree of bias, distortion, and "censorship." Viewers must recognize the full extent of the dilemma. Television is not an innocuous medium that can simply be used for good or evil. It is a complex medium with many inherent side effects that are seldom neutral. Television is often both good and evil at the same time, even when it is trying to be nonpartisan.

However, there *is* something that each of us *can* do about television. The answer, in part, is within ourselves. Earlier in this book PBS news anchor Robert MacNeil commented that we know television so well but understand it so little; we are familiar with television but strangers to the televised process. We are well acquainted with TV in terms of use but are frightfully unaware of the true nature of what we ingest. So one important answer to the question of how to handle television is to reverse the priorities expressed in McNeil's statement. We need to develop less familiarity with TV itself and more familiarity with the television process.

The first step is to learn to recognize the full spectrum of biases in television and in so doing begin to "unravel" the television illusion for ourselves. We must become knowledgeable of its inner workings and its weaknesses—and we must take the initiative in doing this.

The Persian Gulf War gave the public a rare, extended glimpse into part of the image factory. In 1991, mass exposure of American audiences to live broadcasts during Operation Desert Storm enabled many to see large quantities of "raw" news for the first time, through live broadcasts of events as they happened and through unedited press briefings. When live broadcasts were later followed by edited and polished network news versions, the inevitable differences between the two became apparent to some viewers. Not only could the audience see differences between the polished and unpolished versions, but watching news as it happened forced viewers into a role of interpreter that is usually reserved for the journalist.

Notes one critic, the phenomenon of raw news thrust viewers into a higher state of mental alertness, forcing them to reach their own conclusions. Suddenly a passive medium was demanding an active response. *New York Times* critic Caryn James notes that the shift was exhausting: "Most viewers had assumed that television was not supposed to be this much work. One of the reassuring illusions about TV was that we could settle back and let Dan and Peter and Tom and their friends tell us what happened."[7]

The immediacy of live satellite coverage did not solve the problems of telereality or pictures lifted out of context, but, to some degree, it transformed viewers into reporters who, in a limited sense, became witnesses to the actual news-gathering process. As a former producer-turned-viewer who watched the Scuds fall on Tel Aviv and the military briefings from Saudi Arabia in my living room, I could feel the role of the news analyst I once was abruptly thrust upon me again.

What viewers saw in the live coverage of Desert Storm was complicated, tentative, unprocessed information something like the way reporters themselves experience it. It was not always a pretty sight, particularly in those live military briefings where reporters hounded military officials for information. News gathering is like making sausage. It's more appetizing if you don't know what goes into it. Much of real life is not quite ready for prime time—too many rough edges. The unsightliness of the process for some was repulsive and disillusioning. As James put it: "Even for a generation that grew up watching Vietnam, television's illusion of authority has never been so thoroughly shattered as it has in recent weeks."[8]

Now that the war is over, it is back to business as usual for both television and its viewers. However, what viewers can do and need to do is to maintain the active role. No matter how uncomfortable many felt during the Gulf War in this new role of analyst, it was more constructive than merely allowing TV to spoon-feed us. It taught us something about unraveling the television illusion.

Much has been said in this book about the final impressions "processed" information leaves in the mind. Viewers need to develop what I call "tele-consciousness"—a conscious awareness of the nature of the camera and editing process, the end result of the shortened format, emphasis on emotion, and cosmetic considerations, to name a few of the factors explored in this book. We need to apply this knowledge when we watch television—and do so discerningly.

The value of some type of debriefing process about the pitfalls of visual imagery can be seen even in extreme situations. Those researchers who measured the effects of erotic violence discussed earlier in this book found that heightening awareness of the illusionary nature of such programs proved to be an effective way of reversing the desensitization brought on by viewing such shows. When researchers talked to their subjects about the violent or erotic portrayals, pointing out the misleading nature and debunking the myths behind the images, they found it had a positive effect. They discovered that teaching their subjects how to view such material reversed the influence it had over those who watched.[8] Although such a discovery is no excuse to indulge in watching such trash, learning *how* to watch can be an effective tool in undermining the effects of media-created illusions.

I wrote this book because I believe that once viewers develop a conscious awareness of the spectrum of biases inherently woven into the television tapestry they can consciously unravel the illusion for themselves. More often than not, the various biases blur into and interact with one another in ways that are not easily distinguishable. I have tried to isolate and label some of these biases individually for the purpose of discussion and clearer understanding.

> *Both kids and adults need to cultivate inner immunity to "mediated" imagery by teaching themselves to doubt its validity.*

Today's grocery consumer has the advantage of glancing at a label of ingredients to determine the individual contents of what he is about to buy for the purpose of bodily consumption. There are few "product labels" in TV to help consumers evaluate what they absorb into the mind. This book was designed to function as a consumer's guide of sorts for TV—a product label to open your eyes to the "contents" of televised imagery so that you can examine television critically for yourself.

Author Neil Postman suggests: "No medium is excessively dangerous if its users understand what its dangers are."[9] We need to question not just what we see but ask ourselves what we don't see. Perhaps we need to paste a sign over our television set that says, "What happened in the world today that was important but lacked a good picture?" The list of answers to that question will be endless. Developing a conscious awareness of what TV can't show and tell us could help us realize how little we have really "seen" in the TV age.

It concerns me that we are a generation passing critical judgment on people, institutions, and life choices based primarily on the mirage that television delivers. Our houses of knowledge are built on the shifting sands of visual illusion, as we make sweeping judgments based on mere fragments of televised information.

A second step in controlling television is to utilize conscious knowledge of television's weaknesses to cultivate mental immunity to its messages. Although children need shielding when possible from TV's most negative messages, we can't isolate ourselves and our children from all that TV imposes. In fact, in trying to do so we may make them more susceptible. Author and seminary professor David Augsburger points out: "Separate a young man from all contact with evil; and when he is suddenly faced with the opportunity, he has little power to refuse it. It is not the sterile safety of perfectly pure surroundings that we need, but inner resistance. Inner immunity to evil."[10] Both kids and adults need to cultivate inner immunity to "mediated" imagery by teaching themselves to doubt its validity.

One way to do this is to learn to argue with the television set. I have a friend named Peter who actually talks back to his TV set. He shouts, argues, and ridicules whatever he sees that he suspects is false or contrary to Christian values. The set may not be listening, but I suspect his kids are. I think he is also listening to himself. Peter's arguments with the tube remind me of an old story about a Jewish prophet who was once approached by a little boy. "Prophet," said the lad, "don't you see? You have been prophesying now for fifteen years, and things are still the same. Why do you keep on?" The prophet answered: "Don't you know little boy, I'm not prophesying to change the world, but to prevent the world from changing me?"[11]

We should argue with the set verbally for the benefit of our children and mentally for the benefit of ourselves. I have started to emulate Peter—I now yell at toy commercials in front of my kids, accusing sponsors of hype and deception and explaining to my children how TV tries to take your money away. Often I take a small portable TV with me into the kitchen or another room where

I work and tune it to what my kids are watching, so that I can monitor and "intervene" at the appropriate times. I shout back at beer commercials now, accusing them of exploiting children and pointing out the dangers of drunkenness and addiction.

Sometimes my children, with eyes as big as saucers, join in and shout the same things with me. I love it. This way my children get an alternative message. Question what you see on TV and discuss it with your children. Teach them that images can lie, that everything they see and hear is not true. I have been told by those familiar with Eastern bloc cultures that some children raised in Communist countries where TV is merely a tool of the state exhibit a deep distrust of it, because their parents have taught them to. Even in the free world, teaching a certain amount of healthy skepticism is desirable.

A third way we can help to unravel the illusion of television is to strengthen the family. Developing family intimacy and a quality home life is vital for neutralizing the effects of television, especially on children. Author and psychiatrist Robert Coles notes: "What children do with television psychologically, depends on the quality of their own lives—the quality of their family life. *A child who is having a rough time of it personally—whose parents, for instance, are mostly absent, or indifferent to him or her, or unstable—will be much more vulnerable to the emotional and moral power of television.*"[12]

In contrast, maintains Coles, "a child whose parents are very much near at hand and who have their own ethical values, their own mental solidity, is not likely to be sucked onto the moral wasteland that one finds while watching certain programs." Coles concludes: *"A stable family, with a vigorous moral life, well and constantly enunciated by parents, will likely provide a persisting immunity to the influence of various shows."*[13] That is why it is critical for parents to understand what TV *prevents* in the family circle and to counteract it. Pollster George Gallup offers the following suggestion: "If more Americans could be persuaded to carve out of their three or four hours of television viewing each day a period of five minutes at bedtime and use this time to ask their child a simple question—'How did things go today?'—and listen, the results in terms of individual families and society as a whole could, I believe, be highly salutary."[14]

Many of television's shortcomings can only be dealt with in our own level of awareness. "Tele-consciousness" can intellectually fortify us against TV's distorted message. We must teach ourselves and our children that much of what TV offers is often a stream of highly manipulated, technological illusions that are sometimes fun to watch but hardly a blueprint for living. What it shows is not a total picture of reality but more often video fragments of a far larger and more complex picture.

Once familiar with the television process, seeing through the illusion should also motivate us to become a little more of a stranger to television.

NOTES

1. Warren Bennis and Ian Mitroff, quoted by Stephen Goode, "The World in a Fun House Mirror," *Insight*, November 27, 1989, p. 46.
2. Loring Mandel, "How I'd Save Television," *Parade*, May 11, 1986, p. 7.
3. George Gerbner, quoted by Neil Postman, *Amusing Ourselves to Death* (New York: Penguin, 1985), p. 140.
4. Jacques Ellul, quoted by Chuck Colson in an interview with James Dobson, "The Use and Abuse of Power," tape CS 118, Focus on the Family radio program, 1982.
5. Ibid.
6. Caryn James, "TV Coverage of War Has Its Own Conflicts," *The Times-Picayune*, February 11, 1991, p. C-8.
7. Ibid.
8. "Media's New Sexual Mood: Sexual Violence," *Media and Values*, Fall 1985, p. 5.
9. Neil Postman, *Amusing Ourselves to Death* (New York: Penguin, 1985), p. 121.
10. David Augsburger, *A Risk Worth Taking* (Chicago: Moody, 1973), p. 39.
11. "Hearing God's Voice and Obeying His Word: A Dialogue with Richard Foster and Henri Nouwen," *Leadership*, Winter 1982, p. 82.
12. "Children and TV: Big Family Role," *Media and Values*, Summer/Fall 1987, p. 29.
13. Ibid.
14. George Gallup, Jr., quoted in "Family Happiness Is Homemade," J. Allan Petersen, ed. (Wheaton, Ill.: Family Concern), February 1988. Bulletin supplement.

25

CHALLENGING THE "UNBEARABLE DISTURBANCE"

Disillusionment with the TV illusion should motivate us to use it less and differently. We should, as Malcolm Muggeridge suggested, escape into reality more often.

Controlling television presents a challenge for the home. The way to begin meeting the challenge is to begin by *evaluating your viewing habits*. Start by taking inventory of your TV life by playing "The Nielsen Game." Conduct a mock survey of your own viewing habits and those of your family for a week by keeping a careful log of how many hours you are actually watching and what you are watching. Log each time the set comes on, even when you think you are just using it as background noise. You may be surprised—and motivated to change—when you actually add up the number of hours you have recorded. I found this to be true after we once became a Nielsen family and had to track our viewing habits for a week. Although I already controlled my television watching to a degree, I was amazed at how quickly the time piles up, even with limited use!

After logging your use for a week, complete the following "Tele-consciousness" exercise:

1. Add up the number of hours you spent with television this past week. (Be honest!) Write the number here:
   _____ hours watched.

2. Look at the list of items below and circle each item that you didn't have time for this week and that you could have done in the time you spent watching TV:
   a. Calling or visiting a friend
   b. Reading or playing with my children
   c. Studying the Bible
   d. Praying or meditating on God's word
   e. Engaging in a hobby or recreational pleasure
   f. Exercising
   g. Doing housecleaning or yard work
   h. Reading a good book
   i. Shopping
   j. Doing volunteer or charity work
   k. _____
      (*You fill in the blank!*)

3. Now ask yourself the following questions:
   a. What am I not doing that I could be doing with the time spent watching?
   b. How could cutting down or eliminating at least some television change my life? How might it reduce my stress level?
   c. List some ways in writing, based on the above list.

4. Next, look at the specific programs you watch most frequently. Think for a moment about the content and messages of these programs. Ask yourself what the messages of the programs are encouraging you to believe about life. Make a list of them.

5. Finally, ask yourself:
   a. What would Jesus have done with His leisure time?
   b. What do you believe God's will for you is in this area of your life?

Chances are you might see some need for change, *so begin to use television differently.* Put limits on how much you watch a day. Try to make it a goal to cut your average viewing time in half. If you are convicted to change but find it too hard to simply turn the set off altogether, try weaning yourself off a few programs at a time. You may find yourself losing your taste for television, if you look at the time it consumes and how your viewing habits influence and control other areas of your life.

Unless you control your own TV habits, you cannot control your child's.

If you find from your personal survey that television is out of control in your home, try cutting back viewing time gradually.

Try to watch programs, not television. Make a rule that the set only goes on for a specific program, and turn the set off after the program ends. Resist the temptation to use TV as a background noise in your home. Instead of always turning to TV for news or entertainment, turn on the radio or visit the library. Try reading a magazine or newspaper. If you think you haven't time, read only the headlines and first paragraph of the most important stories. You'll get as much information as you would through television and will probably retain it better.

Play closer attention to the content of what you watch. At least once, try taking notes during some of your favorite shows regarding the content and ask yourself what messages the show conveys? What attitudes does it teach? What kind of role models are portrayed? How does Christian teaching relate to the message of the program? Write out your answers on paper.

Help your children become "strangers" to TV by becoming more of a stranger to television yourself. You can't control the viewing habits of your children unless you model the behavior yourself. I remember as a child that my own parents always appeared to regard TV as something to do when there was nothing better to do. They never said much about television that I can recall, but most of the time they made other activities a priority, watching only a few select programs now and then. Looking back now I can see that such a casual attitude toward the value of time spent before the screen helped shape my own perception of TV's usefulness. Unless you control your own TV habits, you cannot control your child's.

Limit the amount of time your children view TV, as well as what they watch. If you have preschoolers or young children, be especially aware of the benefits of limiting TV time during the first five to seven years of your child's life. Try to delay much of what television bombards young children with at least until they are old enough to have a frame of reference to evaluate what they see. Give them the opportunity to be children before the televised world of the adult is thrust upon them prematurely. That will mean that you will need to put into practice a modern day version of biblical "fasting"—doing without something to accomplish a greater spiritual purpose. You will need to sacrifice some of your own viewing for their sake. Be aware that there is scientific evidence to suggest that heavy TV viewing:

1. adversely affects the IQ and the ability to read
2. is associated with some types of learning disabilities and hyperactivity
3. raises the aggression and stress levels in children
4. conditions children to mentally process material in a way directly opposite to the school classroom experience
5. suppresses the type of brain wave activity associated with thinking and analysis
6. stifles imagination and creative thinking

The latest research into neuropsychology suggests that TV and other electronic media are changing the actual brain structures of children. Scientists say that what children see and do every day changes their brains both structurally and functionally, particularly in the first seven years of life. Scientists confirm that early language and sensory experience can dramatically alter early brain development. Educational psychologist Jane Healy, the author of *Endangered Minds: Why Our Children Don't Think,* warns that the large doses of TV viewing now common in day-care centers and in some schools and homes are a major contributor to lagging national academic skills. Researchers now have documented evidence that both children and adults exposed to TV suffered a 20 percent decline in average SAT scores over the past twenty-five years. The long-term implications of this are enormous. Warns one researcher, such a decline could spell the end of America as a first-class technological power.[1]

Healy charges that TV and related video games have conditioned today's child to quick gratification and ceaseless, rapidly changing stimulation, damaging his ability to concentrate on sustained mental activities and leaving him in need of constant stimulation. Noteworthy is the fact that textbook publishers now cite this conditioned need for stimulation as a reason behind a growing trend toward occult-oriented textbooks now being offered children.[2]

Researchers urge parents to withhold or discourage TV as much as possible until a child's reading and learning habits are well established. So consider your children's long-term welfare and exert some control. Try sitting down each week and highlighting what your children are allowed to watch in the TV schedule. Then make a list of acceptable programs. (Older children can do this for you.) Post it near the set. Stick to it as closely as possible.

Another helpful device for control suggested by James Dobson and others is the "ticket" method. For example, if you want to limit your child to an hour a day, give him two tickets (one ticket per half hour). Let him choose an hour of programs from the acceptable list and have him surrender a ticket to you for each half hour watched. (This works on the same principle of money and time management and may help instill the same judgment skills in your children.)

Try not to use television excessively as a baby-sitter. "Television," notes one researcher, "has become woven into the fabric of our society as a sacred cow."[3] Some parents who consider TV indispensable as a baby-sitter need to be reminded that parents managed to raise children for thousands of years prior to the invention of TV. Yet many parents today have adopted the mind-set that it is genuinely impossible to get anything done without putting the kids in front of the tube. As the number of two-income families increases, this trend is likely to increase. Ironically, parents who work for more money sometimes are tempted to depend more on TV to "parent." In turn, children who watch more television pressure their parents to buy more, and the parents must work harder for the money to meet those demands. It can become a vicious cycle—so be aware of the pitfalls of the "electronic baby-sitter."

I find that when I hold the line with my kids about turning the set off, an amazing thing happens. They will fuss about being bored and deprived for a while, but then they will proceed to find something to do on their own. Remember, forcing children to cope with boredom is teaching them how to deal with real life. William Eietz of the American Academy of Pediatrics warns of the pitfalls of using the tube as a source of constant stimulation for bored kids: "How can a child become self-sufficient if something is being done for him all the time?" If we raise children to expect thrills every minute, as one minister put it, will today's video kids spend their lives looking for the fast-forward button?[4]

Control television by keeping it from interfering with the family socialization process, especially at critical times of the day. If possible, keep television out of the dining area. Let mealtimes be sacred in terms of interacting together, and make TV off-limits during meals. If possible, consider eliminating television sets in bedrooms—yours and the children's. At least be aware of the threats to socialization and intimacy that television presents in those settings. A set in the bedroom of adults is a tempting alternative to intimacy and communicating in more important ways. One poll of married couples revealed that 72 percent admitted they watch TV every day, but only 30 percent talked with each other every day, and only 11 percent of married couples made sexual activity a priority every day.[5] A set in the child's room gives you less control over viewing habits. Removing it eliminates the tendency for kids to creep off to their rooms and watch where their parents can't see. I keep my set in the family room where it is easier to monitor how much is watched and when.

Try "TV-free time zones" in your home. Teach your children that there are only certain times for television. In our home, for example, television is off-limits to our kids in the morning before school and on Sunday morning before church. After all, how can the average school teacher or Sunday school teacher successfully follow and compete with such stimulation?

Television's influence presents a challenge not only for individual Christians but for the church as an institution. If we are to both hold onto and reach the generation who grew up in front of the set, the church must come to grips with how television has changed this generation.

One way for the church to respond to television's influence is to make developing "teleconsciousness" part of Christian education agenda. Churches can explore this option by using *Television Awareness Training,* a series of materials designed to help the church develop more discerning viewers. It is available from the Media Action Resource Center, 475 Riverside Drive, Suite 1370, New York, N.Y. 10015.

A second way for the church to respond in particular to the challenge of reaching the unchurched baby boomer generation is to cater to the need for visualization through drama.

A recent article in *Newsweek* magazine points out that the roughly two-thirds of baby boomers who dropped out of church in recent years are on their way back. More than one-third have already returned to organized religion[6] and even more may still be searching.

The church must recognize that this new breed of church seeker has been subliminally conditioned to the look and feel of television information and will be unconsciously drawn to church initially by the style of presentation, not by the substance of the teaching. That is not to suggest that there should be no substance in what we present during church, but that we need to adapt our style of presentation to the conditioned expectations of the audience—especially the unchurched—if we are to reach them.

The biggest obstacle to doing this is often those who are thoroughly entrenched in the traditional church culture and are comfortable and entrenched in presenting the "old, old story" in the "old, old way." This mind-set is a major stumbling block to evangelism in the television age. Many evangelical churches cater in style to the already saved who are comfortable with tradition. Do those conditioned to more traditional approaches dare cling to what makes them feel comfortable at the expense of those most in need of being reached—many of whom feel strange and unfamiliar with traditional church formats?

Today's TV-conditioned audiences don't speak in King James English. Phrases such as *born again, evangelical, fellowship,* and *sanctification* mean nothing to, or are misunderstood by, nonbelievers. Long black robes and sixteenth-century hymns, as beautiful as they are to those of us raised with them, can be intimidating to those who grew up outside the church, and they are a turn-off to those disillusioned with traditionalism. They send the visual message to some that the truth of Christianity belongs in a past century.

The church's ability to understand who today's audiences are and how they are conditioned to accept information is essential to capturing their hearts and minds. Says one pastor who is successful in attracting the previously "unchurched" into his congregation, "You have to interest them before you can influence them."[7] If we fail to understand how TV and its electronic cousins have conditioned the interest level of boomers and their way of receiving information, the church's influence will continue in a downward spiral in a TV-oriented culture.

Today's church hunter wants to see as well as hear. He is looking consciously or subconsciously for the same lively, contemporary, *visual* way of packaging the message that modern media use. This is not necessarily bad. "God is not dull," notes theologian R. C. Sproul. "If worship . . . is boring it is not because God is boring. The problem, I think, is with the setting, the style and the content of our worship."[8]

Think for a moment of the sensual impact that Old Testament worship must have had—the visual impact of the furnishings and splendor of Tabernacle and Temple and ritual; the full range of sound provided by harp, lyre, flutes, trumpets, and rhythm instruments. Sproul notes: "Old Testament worship involved all five senses."[9] Trying to incorporate visual elements and greater use of the senses into the church may not be as alien to biblical thinking as some may think. However, it needs to be accomplished now in contemporary ways. Integrating the Old Testament pattern of sensual stimulation in worship with contemporary audiovisual methodology helps bridge the gap to secular culture.

> *The church's mandate in the TV age is to attract people of the "image" and gradually convert them into people of the "Word.*

Television has spawned a generation of viewers, not doers—pews full of spectators. Most so-called baby boomers like to listen to singers, rather than sing themselves, because that is what radio and TV have conditioned them to. They are also conditioned to cosmetic attractiveness, to well-paced formats, and to excellence of presentation. Notes one pastor, "If you are aiming at the unchurched people you have to be able to compete with all their other interests at the same level of professionalism."[10] Today's church must respond to the conditioning effects of television or continue to risk being outdistanced by its biggest competitor.

It can be done. Willow Creek Community Church in South Barrington, Illinois (a suburb of Chicago), now the fastest-growing church in America, and others like it are meeting the TV challenge and dealing effectively with the societal transformation that TV has helped to bring. They realize that newcomers are now spectators. Such churches put a high priority on special music with a contemporary flair in special Sunday morning services designed to appeal to "seekers."

Even more fascinating is that they have tapped into a tool that can compete with and enable to church to subvert the influence of TV. They use drama in the service—dramatic skits geared to TV-influenced baby boomers now seeking a church home. I'm not talking about ancient passion plays with a cast in bathrobes and old bed sheets. I'm talking about contemporary skits that clone TV situation comedies and dramas in the style that their audiences are used to, yet deliver spiritual truth in the message and serve as sermon illustrations. Such visual techniques could put churches on the cutting edge in terms of competing with TV's conditioning influence. Drama can function as a much needed tool for the church. If relevant in content and professionally done in presentation, it can captivate the entertainment mentality of its audience and infuse Christian principles at the same time. The church can learn from "preachers" such as Norman Lear—people today accept information more readily if they are being entertained.

The idea of drama in the church is hardly new—only recycled. Forerunners of modern drama were central to church worship during medieval times. The passion plays and morality plays of that era were the way the medieval church communicated spiritual truth to an illiterate culture. Contemporary drama can be a way for the church to preach subliminally to the "aliterate" television generation.

I believe that the church is standing at a crossroads in communicating the gospel. We are faced with the difficult, but not impossible, task of drawing secular people to the point of faith by first recognizing where their frame of reference is. Bowing to the demands of a TV-conditioned culture and being contemporary in our approach can give a face-lift to the gospel presentation that is a starting point but not the ending. The challenge to the church is to attract those conditioned to the look and feel of popular culture transmitted via the tube, but not merely leave them in the state in which they arrived. Through small group situations and relevant Bible teaching, we must eventually convert these newcomers not just to making a statement of faith but toward a literate understanding of the Word itself. The church's mandate in the TV age is to attract people of the "image" and gradually convert them into people of the "Word."

The idea of drama in the church is more biblical than it might initially appear. It could return the church to Old Testament methodology. Robert Coleman, professor at Trinity Evangelical Divinity School in Deerfield, Illinois, points out that much of our older church leadership is still preoccupied with the Greek mind-set. In their preaching and teaching, they build on abstract ideas and concepts, whereas the younger generation of future church leaders migrates in a different direction. He says:

> If we want to succeed as teachers and preachers, with the wave of television oriented and television saturated people now moving through our colleges and seminaries and into our graduate schools, we will need to become more like the prophets and teachers of the Old Testament, whose ideas are presented through visual images, and symbols. That is the kind of communication we will have to switch to if we want to capture today's generation.[12]

Television now challenges the authority and influence of the church in America. It is time for the church to return the challenge.

Much of the discussion in this book has focused on pinpointing TV's weaknesses and dangers, with little attention devoted to its strengths. That does not mean that I think television serves no positive purpose for our culture. It furnishes fragments of real-life experience for us that we would otherwise miss. It brings us glimpses of the Alaskan tundra and grants us a peek at the underwater sea world of Jacques Cousteau. It delivers the excitement of Olympic glory. It energizes our patriotic feelings by projecting visions of

America celebrating the Fourth of July. Television has been credit-
ed with helping to tear down the Berlin Wall by exposing those
behind it to Western culture and values, blowing through the Iron
Curtain, as Ronald Reagan put it, as though the curtain were made
of lace.[12] Television allowed the world to watch while hundreds of
Germans literally chipped away at the wall in an unforgettably
moving sight and while Russians demanded revolutionary changes.

With its powerful image-delivering abilities, television can
highlight the sights, sounds, and emotional peaks of war, the pain
of famine, the joy of birth, the ugliness of death, and the excitement of the winning touchdown. As wonderful and terrible as all
this is, we must still keep in mind that far from being an unlimted
passport of visual experience, it is only a tiny window on a very
large and complex world. Its images are only fragments of a much
bigger reality that it cannot show. Its images speak powerfully, but
incompletely.

Television will not go away. There is much we cannot change
about it, so we must learn to live with it. It is my hope that this
book will be the beginning of a consciousness-raising process for
many. We can charge networks with the sin of caring only for ratings and profits, but some blame also lies at our doorstep if we
never try to understand and put into perspective what we see. We
need an awareness of how we are controlled by TV so that we can
take steps to control it. Once both functions become a conscious
part of our awareness, we will no longer be as vulnerable to the
television illusion.

After witnessing an early demonstration of television in 1938,
author E. B. White foresaw its revolutionary effects and wrote:

> I believe television is going to be the test of the modern world,
> and that in this new opportunity to see beyond the range of our vi-
> sion we shall discover a new and unbearable disturbance of the mod-
> ern peace or a saving radiance in the sky. We shall stand or fall by
> television—of that I am quite sure.[13]

Some of us who have been insiders to the industry can see that TV is an "unbearable disturbance" more often than a "saving radiance." Salvation is found in truth, not illusion. I believe in the absolute necessity of beginning to look at this technology in a different and more discerning light. Since the Christian is still called to function as salt and light in every generation, his willingness and ability to see TV differently, to decipher its illusions, and to escape its unrealities may be the critical difference in whether the "disturbance" of television shall be unbearable or shall at least be manageable.

NOTES

1. Frederick Case, "Tuning In and Turning Off Brainwashed," *The Seattle Times*, reprinted in *The Times-Picayne*, May 8, 1991, pp. E-1–E-3.
2. Gary Bauer, "Why Can't Kids Think?" *Focus on the Family Citizen*, January 21, 1991, p. 16.
3. Michael Rothenberg, quoted by Case, "Brainwashed," p. E-3.
4. George Conklin, "Find Your Video Values: Questions for the Reflective Viewer," *Media and Values*, Summer/Fall 1987, p. 17.
5. Nina Combs, "Is Your Love Life Going Down the Tube?" *Redbook*, condensed in *The Reader's Digest*, October 1987, p. 147.
6. Kenneth L. Woodward, "A Time to Seek," *Newsweek*, December 17, 1990, p. 51.
7. "Church Planting in Our Own Culture—A Fresh Approach," *International Teams Today*, July 1985, p. 18.
8. R. C. Sproul, "Right Now Counts Forever: The Protestant Over-Reaction," *Table-Talk* 8:3 (June 1984), pp. 3-10.
9. Ibid.
10. "Bringing the Unchurched to Church," *Reformed Theological Seminary Bulletin*, Fall 1987, p. 4.
11. Robert Coleman, quoted by Les Stobbe, in a seminar entitled "Books That Endure and Leave Their Mark," presented at the Mount Hermon Christian Writer's Conference, 1985.
12. Daniel Schorr, "How TV Helped Tear Down the Berlin Wall," *TV Guide*, December 23, 1989, p. 11.
13. E. B. White, quoted by Daniel Schorr, *Clearing the Air* (Boston: Houghton Mifflin, 1977), p. 292.

Moody Press, a ministry of the Moody Bible Institute,
is designed for education, evangelization, and edification.
If we may assist you in knowing more about Christ
and the Christian life, please write us without obligation:
Moody Press, c/o MLM, Chicago, Illinois 60610.